W9-ANN-145

Structural Adjustment
& the African Farmer

FLORIDA STATE
UNIVERSITY LIBRARIES

MAY 1 8 2004

TALLAHASSEE, FLORIDA

Structural Adjustment & the African Farmer

EDITED BY
ALEX DUNCAN
& JOHN HOWELL

With a foreword by
IDRISS JAZAIRY
President of IFAD

OVERSEAS DEVELOPMENT INSTITUTE · LONDON

in association with

JAMES CURREY · LONDON

HEINEMANN · PORTSMOUTH (N.H.)

Overseas Development Institute
Regent's College, Regents Park, London NW1 4NS

James Currey Ltd
54b Thornhill Square, Islington, London N1 1BE

Heinemann Educational Books, Inc.
361 Hanover Street
Portsmouth, NH 03801-3959

*HC
800
.S779
1992*

© Overseas Development Institute 1992
First published 1992

92 93 94 95 96 9 8 7 6 5 4 3 2 1

British Library Cataloguing in Publication Data

Structural Adjustment and the African Farmer
  I. Duncan, Alex   II. Howell, John
  338.1096

  ISBN 0-85255-128-2 (Cloth)
       0-85255-127-4 (Paper)

All rights reserved. No part of this book may be
reproduced in any form or by electronic or
mechanical means, including information storage and
retrieval systems, without permission in writing from
the publisher, except by a reviewer, who may quote
brief passages in a review.

Library of Congress Cataloging-in-Publication Data

Structural adjustment & the African farmer/edited by Alex Duncan
  & John Howell.
      p.   cm.
    Includes index.
    ISBN 0-435-08071-7 (U.S.) — ISBN 0-435-08073-3 (pbk. U.S.)
    1. Structural adjustment (Economic policy) — Africa — Case studies.
  2. Agriculture—Economic aspects—Africa—Case studies.   3. Rural poor—Africa—Case
  studies.   I. Duncan, Alex, 1949-
  II. Howell, John, 1941-   III. Overseas Development Institute (London,
  England)   IV. Title: Structural adjustment and the African farmer.
  HC800.S779   1992
  338.1'096–dc20   92-11274
                                                                CIP

  0-435-08071-7 (Cloth)
  0-435-08073-3 (Paper)

Typeset in 9/11 pt Mallard by Colset Pte Ltd, Singapore
Printed in England by Villiers Publications, London N6

Contents

Contributors

Arne Bigsten Professor of Development Economics, University of Göteborg, Sweden.

Elizabeth Cromwell Research Fellow, Overseas Development Institute, London.

John de Coninck Research Associate, Overseas Development Institute and a development consultant based in Uganda.

Alex Duncan Research Associate, Overseas Development Institute, and Programme Director with the Food Studies Group, International Development Centre, Oxford University.

Adrian Hewitt Deputy Director, Overseas Development Institute, London.

John Howell Director, Overseas Development Institute, London.

Njuguna S. Ndung'u Lecturer in Economics, University of Nairobi, Kenya.

Richard Pearce Research Associate, Overseas Development Institute, and Commodities Division, Food and Agriculture Organisation, Rome.

Kiari Liman Tinguiri Professor of Economics, University of Niamey, Niger.

This book is based upon research originally commissioned from the Overseas Development Institute (ODI) by the African Division of the International Fund for Agricultural Development (IFAD) and presented in 1990 as one of the studies undertaken under IFAD's Special Programme for Sub-Saharan African Countries Affected by Drought and Desertification. This was entitled *The Impact of Economic Recovery Programmes on Smallholder Farmers and the Rural Poor in Sub-Saharan Africa*. As with the original study, the present substantially revised and up-dated book reflects the views of the authors and not necessarily those of IFAD. Nonetheless, ODI wishes to acknowledge the substantial professional support and advice of IFAD's Africa Division Director and staff in the preparation of the original study.

Acronyms

ADMARC	Agricultural Development and Marketing Corporation (Malawi)
AREMA	Avant-Garde de la Révolution Malgache
BDRN	Banque de Développement de la République du Niger
BMT	Bankin ny Tantsaha Mpamokatra (Madagascar)
CA	Centrale d'Approvisionnement (Niger)
CCCE	Caisse Centrale de Co-opération Economique
CNCA	Caisse Nationale de Crédit Agricole (Niger)
COPRONIGER	Commercialization de Produits de Première Nécessité (Niger)
GCMB	Ghana Cocoa Marketing Board (COCOBOD)
GFDC	Ghana Food Distribution Corporation
INRAN	Institut National de Recherche Agricole du Niger
NCPB	National Cereals and Produce Board (Kenya)
NRDP	National Rural Development Programme (Malawi)
OFEDES	Office de l'Exploitation des Eaux du Sous-sol (Niger)
OLANI	Office du Lait du Niger
ONAHA	Office National des Aménagements Hydro-agricoles (Niger)
OPVN	Office des Produits Vivriers du Niger
ORSTOM	Organisation de Recherches Scientifiques d'Outremer
RINI	Riz du Niger
SEDES	Société d'Etudes pour le Développement Economique et Social
SONARA	Société Nigérienne de l'Arachide
UAB	Usine d'Aliments du Bétail (Niger)
UMOA	Union Monétaire Ouest-Africaine
UNCC	Union Nigérienne de Crédit et Coopération

Foreword

IDRISS JAZAIRY
President of IFAD

Over the last decade the countries of Africa have suffered a series of grave setbacks whose cumulative effect has seriously eroded the hopes of more accelerated economic and social development. The causes of what has now been recognized as a structural crisis are extremely varied. External factors, including repeated droughts, the continuing low level of commodity prices in real terms, and the growing burden of debt have played a significant part. Internal factors arising from inappropriate policies, institutional weaknesses and administrative shortcomings also have a major responsibility.

In response to this crisis, more and more countries in the region have undertaken structural adjustment programmes in a determined effort to relaunch the stalled process of development. These programmes, supported by international financial institutions and bilateral donors, have sought to reduce fiscal and payments imbalances through reduction of public sector expenditures and a cutback in the scope of state activities, exchange-rate adjustment, price and import liberalization, institutional reform and a greater reliance on market forces.

The results of these adjustment programmes have, however, been rather mixed. Some of them have helped to stabilize the balance of payments and the domestic fiscal position. There are also some signs, although rather fragile, of a degree of recovery in economic activity. Nonetheless, overall there has been considerable disappointment that, in spite of the considerable sacrifices that African countries have been making, the results have been patchy and slow in coming. Indeed, it is now clear that the process of adjustment is going to be more laborious and protracted than was first envisaged.

In many African countries the rural population constitutes more than two-thirds of the total. The bulk of these depend on smallholder farming and small-scale pastoral activities for their livelihood. Although their productivity is often very low due to the constraints they face, and many of them are below the poverty line, their overall economic contribution is important. In fact, smallholder farmers, particularly women farmers, account for the bulk of food production in Africa. In many countries they also produce a substantial proportion of cash and export crops. It has therefore become evident that structural adjustment programmes in Africa will succeed only if they can mobilize the underutilized capacities and underutilized potential of these small farmers.

The concern here is not primarily a humanitarian one of shielding the poor from the unfavourable consequences of structural adjustment. It is much more an imperative of economic efficiency. The simple fact is that, should adjustment programmes ignore the needs of the majority of the people, they would remain a marginal exercise, unable to bring about stability or sustained development.

This is the central message that emerges out of the African experience of the last few years. IFAD, which is the only international financial institution with a unique mandate to focus on the rural poor, has played a strong advocacy role in bringing about a wider understanding of this reality, and the message is starting to be heard. For example, IFAD has worked with its partners in the Joint Consultative Group on Policy (JCGP) which brings together the major funding organizations of the UN system, to incorporate the needs of the rural poor at the core of adjustment programmes. IFAD has also worked with the World Bank in a joint effort to develop a deeper insight into the issues that affect the impact of adjustment. One important result of this collaboration is the Smallholder Analysis Plan prepared by IFAD which has now been adopted by the World Bank, the African Development Bank and the UNDP within the context of activities of agencies sponsoring Social Dimensions of Adjustment.

The study on which this book is based is part of the continuing efforts that IFAD has made in the context of its Special Programme for Sub-Saharan Africa (SPA) and its collaboration with the World Bank on the Social Dimensions of Adjustment. The study, undertaken by the Overseas Development Institute, presents an assessment of the effects of adjustment programmes on rural households in five representative African countries. It brings out the heterogeneity of the experiences in these five countries and underlines that formulating effective adjustment programmes will have to be location-sensitive and respond to the varying conditions prevailing in each country. The study also underscores the point that the reform process has to be seen as a medium- to long-term endeavour.

But above all, the experience of the five countries shows how much more remains to be done to enable smallholder farmers and other poor rural groups in Africa to participate in the adjustment process. Market failures, inadequate infrastructure, weak public institutions and lack of access to productive services in the rural areas continue to pose severe obstacles. In some cases the retrenchment of public sector activities has even worsened the situation in this regard. The study shows that it cannot be assumed that the withdrawal of state services will automatically be replaced by market-provided services, given the poor transport and weak market institutions in many parts of the continent. In particular, the study highlights that what is required for successful adjustment is not only macroeconomic changes 'to get the prices right', but also the vital need to undertake well-designed, imaginative measures to strengthen the supply response of smallholder farmers and other poor rural groups and give them a real chance to take advantage of the economic opportunities that the reform process will open up. Only then will they be able to produce their way out of poverty and contribute to national food balances and export growth.

This is the challenge. It is not an easy one but the prospects for the future in Africa depend on attacking the real ground-level realities with determination rather than relying only on macroeconomic panaceas.

INTRODUCTION

Assessing the Impact of Structural Adjustment

ALEX DUNCAN
& JOHN HOWELL

Over most of the 1970s and 1980s all five of the African countries examined in this book – Ghana, Kenya, Madagascar, Malawi and Niger – have experienced economic recession. All five countries, in the 1980s, have also undertaken major policy and institutional changes designed to reverse deteriorating economic trends. Such recovery programmes are generally designated 'structural adjustment', a term first used by the World Bank to describe a package of measures intended to reverse economic decline and to stimulate growth.

The impact of these measures on key economic variables – growth, investment and external balances especially – is the subject of several studies (such as World Bank, 1989; Mosley, Harrigan and Toye, 1991; Thomas et al. 1991; and Corbo and Webb, 1991) whose conclusions remain, at least by 1992, mixed and often contradictory. The focus in this book is on reform measures specific to the agricultural sector, and on the impact of wider macroeconomic policy reforms on the sector. In particular, we look at the impact of structural adjustment measures on the largest, and poorest, groups – the smallholder farmers, pastoralists and farm labourers.

A principal concern in all the country chapters is to identify the economic characteristics of these groups. Such households normally produce a number of different commodities and they also consume products and services. They can thus be expected to be affected by structural adjustment programmes in a variety of ways. We are attempting, therefore, to examine the aggregate effect on rural communities of adjustment programmes and not simply the supply response, if any, to policy and institutional reforms. We are also looking for changes in incomes and welfare generally, and not simply changes in output.

A primary problem has been to establish the nature of the links between the economy as a whole, and the way it has responded to structural adjustment, and the specific microeconomy in which smallholder agriculture operates. The most important links are markets, on the one hand, and economic and social infrastructure on the other. Under the term 'markets' we include both product markets, where there have been changes in the relative prices of farm commodities, and factor markets, particularly in labour and capital (but, in some cases, in land also). We also include marketing institutions, particularly those concerned with the supply of production inputs, and with produce evacuation and sale. The term 'economic infrastructure'

1

involves transport, in particular, but also publicly-financed agricultural research and technical services to farmers. The term 'social infrastructure' includes health and education services where these directly impinge upon the economics of the rural households.

In all the five country chapters, the nature of these macro-micro links is central to the analysis. But there are also wider questions. All the chapters examine the different causes of deteriorating economic performance in the agricultural sector and ask how far the various structural adjustment programmes have been able to address these causes. They also consider the extent to which the policy instruments adopted have taken into account the rural communities within each agricultural economy and their potential contribution to economic growth. More specifically, the country authors discuss some of the policy changes and investment opportunities which appear to have the potential for enhancing the incomes and welfare of those poorer groups which are not as yet participating in any economic recovery or which are finding that their own economic status has deteriorated in a period of policy reform.

In this introductory chapter, we provide three sorts of overview. First, there is an account of the general nature of the economic recession in sub-Saharan Africa and of the main characteristics of the structural adjustment programmes put in place in the 1980s. However, just as the nature and depth of the recession have differed between countries, so the adjustment programmes themselves have reflected the different economic circumstances, and the different resource endowments, within the five countries examined in the book. The implications of such diversity for the design of structural adjustment is discussed in the concluding chapter.

Second, we attempt to define what is meant by the terms 'smallholders' and 'rural poor' and describe their main characteristics. This section also examines the mechanisms through which smallholders and rural households generally are linked to the wider economy. This provides a conceptual overview of the country chapters and thus the framework within which evidence has been collected and presented.

In the third overview section the evidence is summarized on how these linkages were operating, prior to structural adjustment, in the five countries under study. The purpose of this is to identify those areas where, on the face of it, structural adjustment is likely to impinge most directly upon the economic prospects of smallholders and where it would be unrealistic to expect any significant effect, in the shorter term at least.

THE CAUSES OF ECONOMIC RECESSION

Most of Africa's post-independence achievements in improving life expectancy, infant mortality, and literacy rates occurred during the period up to the mid-1970s. Since then, progress has generally either slowed or stagnated. The same pattern can be detected in economic performance. There were modest rates of economic growth in most countries up to the mid-1970s, with rapid rates of growth in a few exceptional cases, where minerals production or agricultural exports were buoyant.

For most African countries, including those in this book, the late 1970s and early 1980s mark a watershed. Since that time, Africa as a whole has been in crisis. There has been a persistent growth in concessional food imports reflecting poor agricultural performance, in conjunction with population increase of over 3% in most countries. There has been an expansion in external public debt with debt-servicing difficulties rising sharply. There have been stagnant or falling foreign-exchange earnings. And in some countries there has been evidence of severe, and possibly irreversible, ecological stress.

In all five countries in this book, GDP started to stagnate or decline in the late 1970s or early 1980s. In Kenya, the economy grew during much of the 1970s and accelerated during the mid-1970s coffee boom. In 1979, GDP growth was 5%, but fell sharply the following year and continued to fall back in the 1980s. In Malawi, average economic growth was only 1.7% per year by the end of the 1980s, compared with the average of 7.5% during the decade up to 1974. In Niger, the uranium boom of the late 1970s gave way to stagnation in 1981 and 1982, and a sharp decline subsequently. In Ghana a persistent trend of deteriorating economic performance had been a feature from the early 1970s, continuing up to 1983. Madagascar achieved a modest growth averaging 3% per year up to 1972, but adverse world market conditions contributed to stagnation up to 1979 and actual decline from 1980 to 1986.

There were differences between the countries in the factors exacerbating the crisis. In Niger, ecological deterioration was a dominating factor. In Malawi, the scarcity of farmland had become a major obstacle to increasing per capita incomes and food production. And in Ghana, the condition of the physical infrastructure had come to hinder economic activity. Nonetheless, there were common features to the causes of the economic crisis which affected the five countries.

The roots of the crisis lie both in the international and in the domestic spheres, although the two are closely linked. In particular, the inability, over the previous decades, of the economies to diversify left them poorly placed to adapt to new and adverse external conditions. All the country chapters show the sharp worsening of the international terms of trade in the late 1970s. This was a reflection principally of the end (in about 1978) of the boom in the prices of tropical beverages and (in Niger's case) uranium, and of the rise in oil prices. This deterioration, together with a stagnating or declining volume of exports, resulted in unsustainable balance-of-payments deficits.

The linkage is again demonstrated by the fact that the period of relative prosperity had encouraged at least three of the countries (Kenya, Madagascar and Niger) to undertake increased commitments in public sector expenditure which left them particularly exposed when international conditions worsened. The servicing of international debt also became an increasing burden for all the five countries at this time, exacerbating deficits both on the external account and in the domestic budget. This debt had grown after the end of the export boom, as the first response to the emerging crisis had been to step up borrowing. Governments were thus particularly vulnerable to subsequent rises in real interest rates.

Internal factors also played a major role. A common non-policy factor was the climate. Droughts occurred in Ghana in 1981–3 (together with extensive bush-fires in 1983), in Kenya in the early 1980s and then again in 1984, in the south of Madagascar in 1984/85, in Malawi in 1979/80, and in Niger in 1984. To varying degrees all these economies, with the possible exception of Kenya, lacked the resilience to enable them to overcome these climatic shocks without economic disruption.

Internal policy factors are also important in explaining economic vulnerability, and it is these with which structural adjustment programmes are most concerned (see also Commander, 1989). There are important similarities in the policy regimes in the countries studied, which can be examined along four main dimensions: (i) the foreign trade regime, the exchange rate, and intersectoral terms of trade; (ii) budgetary management; (iii) the role of market forces; and (iv) the extent of public sector involvement in production and trade.

Except for Ghana (where import compression was a major feature), all the countries had widening current account deficits at the beginning of the 1980s, reflecting severe imbalances in external trade. Economic policies contributed to these deficits with attempts, explicitly or implicitly, to protect less productive sectors and to substitute for imports, and to draw resources from agriculture for investment in other sectors or for consumption by other groups. The main elements were the overvaluation of the national currency on foreign-exchange markets, tariffs and quotas on trade that protected favoured domestic sectors, and a variety of internal instruments that shifted intersectoral terms of trade to the disadvantage of agriculture.

Such policies were contrary to the interests of smallholders especially in those countries where they represented a significant proportion of export producers. The exception is Malawi where government policies deliberately favoured export agriculture as the engine of growth. However, estate agriculture in Malawi had been systematically favoured over smallholders, by such means as preferential pricing and, in the past, by exclusive rights to produce crops such as burley tobacco.

A second feature of internal policy weakness was the willingness to allow substantial budget deficits. In all countries, these deficits rose to levels that could only be maintained through measures leading to high rates of domestic inflation. The events leading up to the deficits varied between countries, but a common factor was the pressure to expand the public sector and especially public sector employment. In meeting these demands (often at times of buoyant revenues due to various commodity booms of the late 1970s), expenditures reached levels that could not be easily met when the economies turned down. All countries subsequently implemented some measures to reduce budget deficits. These included cutting expenditures for recurrent costs, which frequently meant problems for the maintenance of capital investments in agriculture. It was difficult to reduce salary expenditure as a proportion of recurrent expenditure, and non-personnel spending was therefore compressed, adversely affecting the operating efficiency of the public sector. In Kenya, for example, salaries accounted for some 70% of public spending on agriculture by 1990.

Finally, it should be noted that all five countries came to independence at a time when the conventional wisdom underlined the shortcomings of market forces in producing efficient or equitable growth and favoured a strong role for government in the economy. The 1960s and 1970s were a period, in all the countries, of growing state interventions to modify the operation of market forces, and of a steady expansion in the activities of state-owned and regulated enterprises. By the early 1980s, however, the net effect on agriculture of government price intervention was recognized (in all the countries except Malawi) as worsening the sector's terms of trade. In addition, the new conventional wisdom was that many public sector trading agencies were operating only by absorbing resources provided by agricultural surpluses, thus contributing to the national budget deficits and inhibiting the development of private sector alternatives to state provision (van der Laan and van Haaren, 1990).

STRUCTURAL ADJUSTMENT

All five of the countries in this book have been engaged, since the early or mid-1980s, in reforming the management of their economies. Some have undertaken a more radical reorientation than others but in all countries there has been a change of emphasis, with official policy statements endorsing a different approach to pricing and market forces, and to the responsibilities of the public sector agencies. Similarly, in all countries there have been substantive changes in policy instruments. Interest rates have been raised, for example, and (Niger apart) all currencies have been devalued. Nonetheless, the nature and extent of 'structural adjustment' varies considerably, and some explanation of our use of the term is needed.

The term includes measures taken as part of both short-term stabilization and longer-term adjustment. Stabilization measures are primarily designed to reduce short-term imbalances between supply and demand which normally manifest themselves in balance-of-payments and budget deficits. The main instruments are designed to achieve reductions in aggregate demand through reducing public sector expenditure, raising taxes and charges, increasing interest rates, and devaluing the currency. Structural adjustment measures are designed to address a wider range of obstacles to growth, many of them limiting the ability of the economy to increase supplies. They are thus longer-term in both implementation and effect. In reality, however, it is difficult to separate 'stabilization' and 'structural adjustment' and there is an overlap in the measures adopted. A single term is generally used throughout this book.

The structural adjustment programmes, in all the five countries, include a core of aims that are broadly similar. These aims are, first, to bring about equilibrium or at least manageable deficits in the fiscal budget and the balance of payments; second, to reallocate domestic resources to the more productive sectors; third, to reduce the role of the state in commercial and productive activities; and fourth, to promote the private sector and the role of market forces.

There are, however, important differences in the priorities of the country programmes. In Kenya and Malawi, for example, diversification into non-traditional exports is a major feature. In Ghana, priority has been given to the rehabilitation of the physical infrastructure. There are also differences in the extent to which distributional aims are explicitly built into the reform programmes. Ghana's second Economy Recovery Programme (ERP) recognized that significant groups had been bypassed by the first ERP and a programme to mitigate the social costs was developed. In Kenya, a major expansion of primary schooling, mainly in the rural areas, was implemented during the period of adjustment. But, in general, the priority given to resumed economic growth has meant that distributional considerations are not in the forefront of many of the reform programmes.

There are similarities between the countries in respect of the range of instruments used to achieve these aims. Common features include a liberalization of foreign trade, with a tendency to replace quantitative restrictions on imports with tariffs and with attempts to provide incentives for exports; monetary restraint, including rises in interest rates; lowering or removal of subsidies; reduced reliance on administered prices; the reform of public enterprises and some divestment of state-owned enterprises. Similarities in the aims are not, however, necessarily reflected by similarities in their implementation, where the actual experience is more differentiated, as the country chapters show.

SMALLHOLDERS AND THE RURAL POOR

Before considering ways of assessing the impact of the economic policy reforms described above, let us first consider the terms 'smallholders' and 'rural poor'. This requires a review of the dominant features of farming systems in the region, and an attempt to define what is usually understood as a smallholder in this context.

While there are exceptions, including areas of irrigated and mechanized production, farming systems in sub-Saharan Africa are generally characterized by technologies which are rainfed and dependent on hand tools. Even in regions where livestock production is common, such as the Sahel, there has been little integration, until recent years, of livestock and crop farming. Where integration has occurred the use of animals as sources of farm energy is rare and is largely a response to the severe droughts which have affected the region over the past fifteen years, causing the sedentarization of many pastoralists. Traditionally, livestock keeping throughout sub-Saharan Africa has been the province of pastoralists, rather than crop farmers for whom it has tended to be an adjunct of the main occupation (i.e. the animals serving as a store of wealth rather than a source of income).

Most farming systems have involved shifting cultivation well suited to the ecology of much of the region, where soils tend to be fragile and acidic, and adequate periods of fallow are needed. With rising population densities, there has been a steady reduction of fallow periods and consequent rapid declines in soil fertility and stability. At the same time the preponderance of mixed cropping, plus erratic rainfall and the fragile nature of many soils, means that agricultural chemicals – even if available – are less readily used than elsewhere. Mixed cropping, rather than pure-stand cultivation, is adopted both as a risk-averting device and as a means of avoiding leaching and erosion (through the use of cover crops). This varies from dryland mixtures involving, for example, millet, sorghum and beans in the Sahel, to mixtures based on root crops and plantains in the more humid parts of equatorial Africa. In the southern and central areas of the continent, where both aridity and humidity are less, maize is the predominant staple and it is normally grown with a variety of pulses in mixed stands.

This broad range of farming systems is concerned exclusively with food production. However, many smallholders are also involved in the production of a wide range of non-food crops (such as tobacco and cotton), the bulk of which are for export. In most countries, however, non-food crop production is dominated either by plantations and large estates, or by farms operating on a scale which would exclude them from the 'poor' smallholder category as defined below. A further caveat is that frequently farming systems are characterized by a gender-specific demarcation of roles which requires women to produce household subsistence needs while men are responsible for land clearing and cash generation, either through the production of crops for sale or through wage labour.

The term 'rural poor' is difficult to define in sub-Saharan Africa. For research purposes, the principal concern is to identify that part of the rural population engaged in agricultural production whose incomes are low relative to the average. In land-scarce agriculture, landholding size often serves as a relevant and easily identifiable proxy for income. Landlessness is emerging as a serious problem for Kenya (Collier and Lal, 1986) and Malawi (Ghai and Radwan, 1983), but in sub-Saharan Africa as a whole, land scarcity is not widespread. The major constraint to production is not access to land but the availability of labour.

As agricultural production methods in sub-Saharan Africa are characterized by little use of either labour-augmenting capital equipment or agricultural chemicals, the quantity of labour available to the household is thus a primary determinant of farm income. Non-family labour frequently comes from sections of the rural population which lack access to land. This access may be denied on the basis of ethnic origin or, alternatively, the composition of the household itself may render it unable to utilize land without the assistance of outside labour. This is particularly common in the case of female-headed households, where the absence of adult male household members necessitates hiring of labour for specific tasks such as land clearing.

The necessity and possibility of hiring outside labour is an important component of rural economies as it provides the opportunity to augment household income through hiring or selling labour. In most cases the employment of outside labour will involve the payment of wages, in cash or kind, in advance of the harvest. The poorer smallholders will have neither the reserves from which to pay wages on a substantial scale, nor access to credit facilities at rates of interest which make such investment worthwhile. In defining the poor smallholder population, therefore, a first criterion will be that relating to the type of labour used in production. Furthermore, although most households may need to hire some labour for specific tasks, poor smallholder households are more disposed to supplement income through selling labour, rather than through labour hire.

A further important dimension of smallholder activity relates to the objectives informing household decision-making. Poorer households do not necessarily attempt to maximize profits from agricultural production. A prior concern is normally the security of household food supplies: risk avoidance dominates decision-making and studies show how the market responses of smallholders will reflect this (Ellis, 1988). It will not always follow, therefore, that an increase or decrease in producer prices will engender a concomitant change in supply. An increase in output prices facilitates the satisfaction of minimum cash needs through a reduced level of sales, and the possibility of an enhanced application of household labour towards the provision of food requirements.

Such a response is possible whether cash sales take the form of food or non-food crops and will be most likely where current marketing institutions, or past market performance, lead the household decision-maker to regard involvement in the cash economy as entailing greater risk than that associated with subsistence production. Apart from the likelihood of a muted short-term price response, a further outcome of farmers' risk-averse behaviour is a reluctance to adopt productivity-raising innovations, even though higher prices would justify investments in farm working capital.

In all five countries the majority of the population – typically 70–90% – are rural, and of these, the great majority are smallholder farmers or pastoralists, and most are poor. It is from these populations that the country chapters selected specific groups for investigation. Pastoralists are a major feature of the rural economy only in the Niger and Kenya country chapters. In these cases, the households are heavily dependent on trade or barter, the fundamental requirement being to exchange livestock for foods and other basic consumption goods.

The emphasis upon lower-income farmers and pastoralists should not disguise the significant role of higher-income smallholders in the economies concerned. In all five countries, smallholders predominate in agriculture, whose share of GDP at between approximately 30% and 45% understates its role as the major productive sector. The sector's contribution to merchandise exports is between around 65% and 85% (except in Niger where uranium is the main export); and in all the countries smallholders play an important, often dominant, role in producing these agricultural exports. It is evident, therefore, that there are some significant groups of smallholders in all five countries who are likely to be strongly responsive to changes in the policy and institutional mechanisms which link them to the wider economy.

LINKS TO THE WIDER ECONOMY

In attempting to isolate the effects of macroeconomic changes on rural households generally it is first necessary to define in more detail the macro-micro links that the country chapters in this book use as a basis for their analysis of policies and institutions. Several aspects of policy changes are best captured by drawing a distinction between tradable and non-tradable commodities, as it is a primary aim of structural adjustment to raise the relative prices of the former and thus bring about a switch in productive resources towards them. The definition of a tradable commodity, for our purposes, is whether it is profitable to export in the prevailing domestic and world market conditions – including subsidy regimes.

This can be a difficult distinction in the case, for example, of crops (such as rice in Madagascar and maize in Kenya) which are grown primarily for domestic consumption but also have export potential. In addition, there may be a substantial, but unmeasured, local border trade in commodities which do not enter the world market, and there may be changes over time in the international tradability of commodities. Nevertheless, the distinction between tradables and non-tradables has value in that it allows us to trace the relative effects of changing economic conditions on these two types of commodity. The impact on different rural households can also be assessed, as its nature will depend, for example, on which households are net producers or net consumers of the commodities in question or whether such households are net suppliers of labour involved in their production.

The tradables/non-tradables distinction alone, and its impact on rural households, is obviously an insufficient basis for assessing the impact of structural adjustment. In this book the distinction is complemented by an assessment (which is necessarily qualitative) of the institutional changes that are occurring as part of economic policy reform. In particular, changes in the structure of input supply and marketing are likely to affect the ability of smallholders to respond to changes in relative prices.

The implications of these policy and institutional changes, taken together, for smallholder agriculture can be examined through three different linking mechanisms: product markets; factor markets; and economic and social infrastructure. With regard to domestic product markets, a shift in relative prices in favour of tradable commodities will benefit those who produce tradables and/or consume non-tradables relative to those who produce non-tradables and/or consume tradables. However, the extent of any benefits or disbenefits will be influenced by the degree of resource flexibility and consequent response to price changes. Additional factors to be taken into account in the product-market analysis include reforms to the tariff structure or the degree of import control and the extent to which imports or local products are intermediate goods.

The resource reallocation induced by recovery programmes will also lead to predictable changes in factor markets. In the labour market the effect on the real wage may vary over time. In the short run, with capital and land markets comparatively immobile, the real product wage is likely to fall in the production of tradables and rise in the production of non-tradables. The effect on the real consumption wage will depend on the proportions of tradables and non-tradables in workers' consumption. If mainly non-tradables are consumed, real wages are likely to rise. In the long run, however, the direction of the real wage change will depend on the relative factor intensities in the two sectors and the extent of unemployment. If the latter is insignificant and production of tradables is relatively labour-intensive, the labour released from the declining non-tradables sector will be insufficient to meet the increased demand for labour in the tradables sector, and hence the real wage could rise.

The capital market, and credit systems generally, are likely to be significantly affected by both policy and institutional changes. The principal variables are changes in the real cost of borrowing and returns on saving. For smallholders in particular, changes in the quantity of funds available and their accessibility are also an important dimension to be studied.

The fiscal contraction required under stabilization and adjustment is likely to reduce the resources available for the provision of economic and social infrastructure. Cuts in economic infrastructure, for example, may counteract the favourable relative price effects enjoyed by producers of tradables, especially in rural areas where access to input and output markets is a factor governing economic returns. Similarly, cuts in health and education spending may reduce the 'social wage' even if the market wage is favourably affected.

Economic services are particularly influenced by the institutional changes which often form part of recovery programmes. In particular, privatization of economic support services can have an impact on market performance and activity, depending on the degree of competition which results in the newly established or expanded private sector and the extent to which the latter is willing and able to respond to new opportunities.

We have described the framework for the analysis of the impact of the wider economy on the smallholder sector. In the final chapter we consider the evidence, in aggregate, of the impact of changes in that 'wider economy' as a result of structural adjustment. At this point, however, we shall describe how, in practice, the linkages generally appear to have worked, in most cases drawing upon the period prior to the adoption of adjustment measures.

Product markets and marketing institutions

Product markets in rural areas are widely used as a means of disposing of farm surpluses, or for purchasing food and other goods, yet there are great differences in their use. In Ghana, for example, a 1986 estimate suggested that 20% of producers marketed the bulk of their produce, while 54% were marginal sellers, marketing only the residual after family needs had been met, and 24% produced solely for family needs. In Niger, it is estimated that only about 20% of total cereal production reaches the market, a proportion that varies greatly from year to year, even more markedly than the variations in production.

Households also differ in the extent to which they rely on markets to meet their own food needs. Low-income rural groups are often net purchasers of food on which they spend a high proportion of their income. In Niger, for instance, the rationale for seasonal labour migration has shifted from its former purpose which was to allow young people to establish herds. Since the country moved into a structural food deficit at the outset of the 1970s, migration has increasingly served as a means to enable households to make up their food shortages. In western Kenya, low-income households, earning around half their income from non-farm sources, are reliant on the market for food purchases. The same patterns are noted in the Malawi country chapter.

As noted earlier, pastoralists present a unique case of reliance on the market. In most cases, they are not able to subsist on the direct production from their herds and flocks, and their own grain production is inadequate and highly unreliable. They therefore sell stock in order to purchase cereals to provide for family food needs.

In each of our five countries, there are parallel formal and informal structures for crop marketing. In Niger and Ghana, virtually all the marketing of domestic food production has always been through the private sector. In Kenya, the National Cereals and Produce Board has played a dominant role, but unofficial private trade has grown and the major proportion of smallholder-produced maize and beans is marketed through intermediaries rather than directly by the Board. In Malawi, the private marketing of maize has long been established, principally in small-scale local sales.

The characteristics of the informal trade vary from country to country, region to region, and, importantly, according to whether the crop is for export or domestic consumption. As far as food crops are concerned, the Niger chapter describes fierce competition among some 25,000 private traders, most of them small-scale, and many of them part-time. There were many fewer large-scale traders, and they were less competitive between themselves than were the smaller operators.

Compared with food crops, the marketing of export crops tends to be highly structured, often restricted to a single publicly-regulated channel which means that producers are more heavily influenced by the efficiency of the marketing organizations responsible. In Ghana, for example, the official prices paid to cocoa farmers were in the past so low, in consequence of both overvalued exchange rates and Cocoa Board inefficiencies, that substantial quantities of the product were diverted to neighbouring countries. In Malawi, the Agricultural Development and Marketing Corporation (ADMARC) has made substantial profits from smallholder tobacco by paying only a small proportion of the auction price realized.

The extent to which smallholders use purchased inputs (such as seed, agrochemicals and fertilizers) varies greatly, but it is on average low, and lowest among the poorest. With the exception of Kenya, and to a lesser extent Malawi (where fertilizer use is well-established in the more intensively cultivated parts of the country), the majority of smallholder farmers in the countries under review do not use chemical fertilizers. In Niger, the official data suggest that only 1.5% of farmers use fertilizer. Such use is virtually confined to the irrigated areas, as rainfed crop production is so variable from year to year that investment in costly inputs is likely to expose the farmers to insupportable losses. In all the countries, most fertilizer is provided through public sector agencies or co-operatives, and poor distribution systems are generally held to be a widespread constraint on its use. In an effort to increase demand, subsidies have been adopted partly in an effort to turn the rural-urban terms of trade to the farmers' favour, yet they are of limited importance while the poorest farmers use very little fertilizer.

Factor markets: labour, capital and land

Rural households use the labour market for two main purposes: to hire in labour on a seasonal or permanent basis to help meet the demands of the production cycle; and to increase family incomes through hiring out the labour of household members. All the country chapters found that rural households made extensive use of the labour market and it is potentially one of the most powerful means by which adjustment policies could affect the well-being of rural groups.

The hiring of labour is widespread, especially on a seasonal basis, even among low-income households. In Ghana, where the major constraint on agricultural production was found to be scarcity of labour, the most recent data (from 1970) suggest that about 60% of rural households use some outside labour, although most cultivation uses family labour. Even among the smallest producers (below 0.8 ha), over one-half used hired labour, and of those described as subsistence producers, one-quarter used hired labour. In Kenya, its use was also widespread, and in Madagascar 32% of 'traditional' producers used hired labour at least once a year.

The country chapters also show that many (sometimes the majority) of rural households hired out family labour, either on a seasonal or more permanent basis. In Kenya in 1981/82, the family farm was found to be the most significant single source of income, but it accounted for less than half of average smallholder family income, and was supplemented by income from the labour market and other enterprises. In Ghana, recent estimates indicate that over one-quarter of those whose main source of income is farming earn the bulk of it from outside their own farm. In Madagascar some 18% of the rural population, often the poorest, hired themselves out. In Malawi this proportion was up to 50%, including seasonal labour, but it was not restricted to the poorest; between 25% and 40% of the incomes of households with over 1.5 ha of land came from wage employment or self-employment in non-agricultural enterprises.

An important feature of the labour market is that it is the market in which the landless and near landless sell what is often their only asset. The Kenya chapter found that non-agricultural income sources are a way out of poverty for land-poor households. The condition of the labour market in terms of the number of workers, and of wages demanded and offered, will thus have a direct effect on their welfare.

The importance of the capital market is less clear. The smallholder production systems that characterize the countries under review demand comparatively little fixed capital. The major exceptions are the minority who use draught animals and small farmers on large-scale irrigation schemes, where the use of purchased inputs is more common and many farmers require borrowed capital to finance it. Many households also have a seasonal requirement to borrow to meet consumption needs prior to harvest.

The extent to which people borrow money is largely unknown in all the countries. The use of formal credit is well enough understood, but it almost certainly represents only a small proportion of the whole. In Madagascar, prior to the adjustment process, only 2% of small farmers were using the formal credit facility. The Kenya country chapter concludes that formal credit for small farmers has not played an important role in recent years. Small farmers in Malawi have better access to formal credit than in most countries, with between 8% and 30% borrowing, depending on the area and the existence of externally funded projects. In Ghana, largely as a result of external aid, the amount of formal credit for agriculture doubled between 1983 and 1987. However, the returns to most small farms outside the cocoa sector remain inadequate to cover the cost of borrowing, and credit supply to the poorer households has not increased.

Several of the country chapters indicate that informal borrowing from traders or moneylenders affects many more people, especially among those households which do not have the collateral the formal system often demands. Little is known about informal rural capital markets, but interest rates are very high compared with those on the formal market. It is not clear, however, whether this is due to the monopoly position of the lender, or whether it reflects real risks and transaction costs.

The land market does not yet play a major role in the rural economy in most African countries, although this may be changing. With rapid population growth, there is an increasing number of landless people, and with the extension of farming into marginal areas, land markets are likely to grow in the future. Land scarcity is already being felt, notably in Kenya and Malawi. In other countries, local scarcities are emerging, for instance in Madagascar in the irrigated paddy land on the plateau, and in Niger in the river valley. In these cases, rental and sale land markets are developing, although there are social and institutional constraints. Rental markets also vary in form; examples include the caretaker farmers in Ghana and visiting tenants on the estates in Malawi.

Economic and social infrastructure

The extent and conditions of the transport system, in particular the road network, play an important role in the economic well-being of the rural population. The most striking case is Ghana, where a fall in public expenditure during the 1970s led to a decline in physical infrastructure which adversely affected markets, raised costs, and lowered the availability of incentive goods. In Madagascar, the country chapter found the poor state of the roads to be one of the main causes of lack of competition in markets. Transport costs also limit the options for landlocked countries such as Malawi where transport costs for exports and imports increased by several fold as a result of the troubles in Mozambique.

In all countries, the high costs of transport have meant that both public and private sectors have had difficulty in providing food and other supplies to consumers in isolated areas and in purchasing surplus production. In these circumstances, the effects of the improvement in pricing structures, and the increased provision of incentive goods and inputs, are unlikely to benefit many rural producers.

In agricultural research and extension, the recent record of support to smallholder farmers in the five countries has been generally unsatisfactory. Even in Kenya, where the services are more developed, the most useful research findings were made available to farmers prior to 1970, for example, on hybrid and composite maize varieties. Research momentum was lost during the 1970s and few useful technical innovations have been made since. In Niger, where the great majority of cereal producers use indigenous varieties of millet and sorghum, the role of extension has been modest, outside the irrigated areas where rice varieties have been developed in conjunction with the international institutes. In Ghana, the research and extension services declined during the 1970s, and have had little direct impact on the large majority of farmers. In Madagascar, similarly, the lack of appropriate technical recommendations for smallholders has limited the effect of extension services.

Education and health services are also limited in their economic impact on most rural households. However, the availability of education services, in particular, is highly variable, both between and within countries, and its quality is difficult to assess. Kenya is perhaps best served; the introduction of structural adjustment coincided with a rapid expansion of primary education, although secondary education still favours the urban areas. In Niger, by contrast, the proportion attending primary schools is about 20% and declining. In Malawi, primary enrolment varies from 72% in the north to 25% in the south. In Ghana, the lowest point for both education and health services was reached in 1983 as a result of the long-term fall in government revenues. Public health spending in all the countries appears to be more heavily biased in favour of urban areas than is the case with education, and it is normal for rural households to purchase most of their medical supplies on the private market.

Conclusion

Several lessons may be drawn from this review of the links between small farmers and the rural poor and the wider economy. First, the general condition of the economy is of considerable importance to the majority of rural people, particularly affecting the extent to which they can secure income-earning opportunities off the farm to supplement agricultural earnings.

Second, product markets and, in some countries, public marketing institutions have a strong influence on rural people both as producers and consumers. The macroeconomic or sectoral adjustments that affect the conditions of access to these markets are likely to have major consequences for smallholders and the rural poor. The high costs of public marketing institutions have made them a principal focus for the adjustment process, although this is also one of the most difficult areas in which to undertake reform.

Third, rural transport systems exercise a powerful influence over most aspects of rural life, affecting the scope for efficient administration, the development of the private sector, the availability of incentive goods, and non-agricultural employment.

Finally, smallholder farmers and the rural poor have been poorly served by agricultural services, even before the economic crises of the early 1980s. Currently, most smallholders use neither fertilizer nor formal credit, and have not benefited from recent findings of agricultural research. Thus, budgetary reductions in agricultural services seem unlikely seriously to affect the rural poor in the short term. However, given the large percentage of agricultural production by smallholders, renewed and sustained agricultural growth appears to require an enhanced level of services through either the private or the public sector. On the face of it, price incentives and improvements in physical infrastructure are unlikely to be sufficient in themselves to produce increased output.

References

Collier, P. and Lal, D. (1986) *Labour and Poverty in Kenya 1900–1980*. Oxford University Press, Oxford.

Commander, S. (ed.) (1989) *Structural Adjustment and Agriculture: Theory and Practice*. James Currey, London.

Corbo, V., and Webb, S.B. (1991) 'Adjustment lending and the restoration of sustainable growth', *Journal of International Development*, 3(2), April.

Ellis, F. (1988) *Peasant Economics: Farm Households and Agrarian Development*. Cambridge University Press, Cambridge.

Ghai, D. and Radwan, S. (eds) (1983) *Agrarian Policies and Rural Poverty in Africa*. International Labour Office, Geneva.

van der Laan, H.L. and van Haaren, W.T.M. (1990) *African Marketing Boards under Structural Adjustment*. African Studies Centre, Leiden.

Mosley, P., Harrigan, J., and Toye, J. (1991) *Aid and Power: The World Bank and Policy-Based Lending* (2 Vols.). Routledge, London.

Thomas, Vinod, Chhibber, Ajay, Dailami, Mansoor and de Melo, Jaime (1991) *Restructuring Economies in Distress: Policy Reform and the World Bank*. World Bank, Washington DC.

World Bank (1989) *Adjustment Lending: An Evaluation of Ten Years of Experience*. World Bank, Washington DC.

1

GHANA

RICHARD PEARCE

I. BACKGROUND

In 1983 the Ghanaian Government was faced with an economic crisis of considerable severity precipitated by a variety of internal and external factors. Internal causes included both droughts and domestic policy mismanagement, the combination of which resulted in a rapid decline in agricultural performance. This was exacerbated by persistent, and often sharp, deteriorations in the international terms of trade, and by the escalation of world interest rates.

In some respects the origins of the crisis can be traced back to the character, and the nature of implementation, of policies adopted immediately following independence in 1957. Heavily influenced by the development theories then in fashion, which high-lighted the inadequacies of domestic markets, private capital formation and inter-national trading systems, these policies promulgated the substitution of private economic activity by state intervention and advocated import-substituting industrial-ization behind high tariff walls and reliance on short-to medium-term foreign borrowing.

Such an 'industrialization first' strategy is not without its virtues or antecedents but, in the Ghanaian case, as in many others, it involved an unrelenting squeeze of the agricultural sector which, in turn, slowly eroded the foundations of the strategy. More than any other factor, the taxation of the cocoa sector, which was the major source of foreign-exchange revenue in the mid-1960s, initiated and sustained a deteriorating economic cycle, culminating, in the early 1980s, in a major economic crisis. Cocoa pro-duction fell drastically, and with it real export earnings. This reduced the tax base, which in turn placed constraints on government expenditure. As a consequence, infrastructural maintenance was neglected, which reduced export earnings still more as cocoa deliveries were further inhibited. Large government deficits were also main-tained to support a highly inefficient network of parastatals, in particular the Cocoa Marketing Board. These deficits proved extremely inflationary and, in the context of a fixed exchange-rate regime, led to a massively overvalued currency. This in turn continued the erosion of incentives facing cocoa farmers.

Table 1.1 demonstrates the pervasive economic decline from the early 1970s onwards. Per capita GDP declined throughout the period as did domestic savings and investment, the latter from 12% to 4% of GDP between 1975 and 1983. The fall in export earnings was caused, however, not only by the shrinking of the cocoa sub-

Table 1.1.   *Key indicators of the pre-adjustment period*

	1970	1975	1980	1983
Real GDP/capita (1975 = 100)	114	100	92	73
Balance of payments				
(Current accounts US$m.)	−81	−51	−55	−230
Debt servicing (% of exports)	5.4	5.0	7.7	20.9
Govt. expenditures as % of GDP	–	27	18	8
Dev. exp. as % of total	–	31	18	8
Govt. deficits as % of GDP	–	16	11	3
Cocoa production ('000 tons)	413	396	258	159
Real cocoa prod. price (1972 = 100)	106	90	45	34
Official exchange rate (cedis per $)	1.02	1.15	2.75	3.45
Ratio of parallel/official rates	1.6	1.7	5.8	22.2
Monetary growth (% p.a. in M2)	10	39	34	38
Rate of inflation (% p.a.)	9	30	50	122
Real minimum wage (1977 = 100)	183	225	44	42

Source: Loxley, 1988.

sector but also by a general decline in the production of exportables. For example, output of gold, diamonds and minerals fell by 55% in the period 1975–83, and of timber and timber products by 57%. However, imports also fell steadily over this period, because of foreign-exchange shortages and rationing, thus keeping balance-of-payments deficits to almost manageable levels. The continuation of rapid inflation and a stagnant economy had a disastrous impact on real wage levels, and most employees were forced to survive by means of activities outside of, and frequently in addition to, formal employment. The resulting parallel economy reached such proportions that many official statistics relating to economic activity may be profoundly misleading.

Although food self-sufficiency had been falling throughout this period, the food-producing sub-sector fared less badly than that producing export crops. But in the years 1981–3 Ghana experienced the worst droughts for many decades, culminating in 1983 in widespread bush fires which left it bereft of food supplies. In addition, several external factors combined with domestic mismanagement and misfortune to produce a crisis without precedent. These external factors included the oil price hikes which exacerbated the decline in Ghana's international terms of trade, caused primarily by falling world cocoa prices, and the forced repatriation in 1983 of more than one million Ghanaians from Nigeria, which imposed enormous burdens on already overstretched food resources and social services. In addition, as a result of the international community's loss of confidence in the viability of the Ghanaian economy, there was a significant decline in foreign assistance.

Consequently, Phase 1 of the Economic Recovery Programme (1984–6) was launched by the Provisional National Defence Council government in April 1983 in collaboration with the International Monetary Fund and the World Bank. IMF support included three standby arrangements totalling SDR 540m., while the World Bank extended a Reconstruction Import Credit of US$40m. and an Export Rehabilitation Credit of $93m. The African Development Bank and bilateral donors also provided substantial assistance over the period of the first programme. Commitments in official development assistance totalled over $1.4bn, although disbursement was not always as rapid as expected.

The programme was conceived and launched before the worst excesses of the 1983 drought had taken effect; consequently it was not until 1984 that the main policy changes were introduced. A second phase was initiated (ERP II) covering the period 1987–9, with a more sectoral focus.

II.   THE ECONOMIC RECOVERY PROGRAMME

The first phase of the ERP was aimed at establishing a new macro policy framework for the period 1984–6, many of the reforms being the conditions set for IMF and World Bank finance. The principal objectives were concerned with monetary and fiscal reform to reduce the level of inflation; rationalization of the exchange rate to stimulate exports; and a realignment of prices in order to redirect resources towards the more productive sectors of the economy, particularly towards the cocoa sub-sector. In addition, rehabilitation of the ruined productive and social infrastructures was high on the list of priorities.

The objectives of the second phase were principally to sustain the progress made in the first. They also reflected, in rhetoric at least, a growing concern for the less fortunate majority of the Ghanaian people who did not appear to be benefitting from the reforms of Phase 1. Thus an additional aim was to mobilize resources to improve the living standards of the 'underprivileged, deprived and vulnerable'.

Policy instruments

The central instrument of the reform programmes was the fairly rapid depreciation in the external value of the cedi. Following an initial devaluation in 1983, there was a series of adjustments until, in September 1986, a two-tier system was introduced, under which proceeds from, inter alia, cocoa exports and payments for oil and the majority of government borrowing passed through window one, while other transactions were carried out via a second window where foreign exchange was provided through a weekly auction. The system was unified in February 1987 and a Dutch auction introduced. Further liberalization occurred in September 1987 with approximately 40% of consumer goods imported under special licences being brought into the auction. Incentives to exporters were simultaneously introduced. For example, exporters of non-traditional exports were allowed to retain a proportion of foreign-exchange earnings for their own use. This incentive was subsequently extended to cocoa producers.

Prior to the reform programme, government development expenditure had declined, while the fiscal deficit had increased substantially. An explicit part of the macroeconomic reforms was the facilitation of a fiscal expansion, in order to rejuvenate the physical and social infrastructures, while reducing and ultimately reversing the budget deficit. Exchange-rate reform went some way towards improving the fiscal position since it raised the revenue from export duties. Other tax reforms included increasing petrol duties, and other commodity taxes. Health and education charges were also raised. The move towards putting the government budget on a sounder footing was also helped by the removal of price controls on many items, and substantial increases in the prices of public services, such as water, electricity and telecommunications, reduced the potential levels of government subsidy.

At the same time the progressivity of the tax system was weakened in order to improve the incentive structure of earnings, and to retain highly skilled personnel within the civil service. There was also a decrease in the rate of tax levied on non-labour incomes, and reductions in the cocoa export tax. In general, attempts were made to broaden the tax base.

As well as reducing the budget deficit, the programme was concerned to change the structure of government expenditure in order to increase the proportion of development spending. The fiscal balance was to be further improved by reductions in existing spending obligations, in particular by means of improved management of public institutions. A major part of the reform programme has been a policy of retrenchment in the public sector. Reflecting the concerns of adjustment programmes in general, this policy has sought to reduce the role of the public sector as an employer, partly in order to improve the efficiency of the grossly overstaffed parastatals, and partly to reduce the burden on the budget. The extent to which public sector retrenchment has been mirrored in private sector expansion is difficult to estimate, but increases in the minimum wage, made unavoidable by the inflationary impact of devaluation, have apparently led to a reluctance to retain workers in the private sector. Offsetting these developments there has been some degree of employment creation through, for example, public sector investment in road maintenance and rehabilitation.

In the monetary sector efforts were made to set ceilings on expansion in response to government or private sector deficits. Some attempt was also made to allow interest rates, which had been persistently negative in real terms, to reflect the market value of borrowing and thus encourage the domestic rate of saving.

Macroeconomic performance

At first glance, the resurgence in the economy since 1983 has been extremely encouraging. There has been a substantial recovery in real GDP levels, and given a population growth rate of around 2.5% per annum, per capita GDP has also grown continuously since the introduction of the reform programme, largely because of the resurgence of export earnings, as shown in Table 1.2.

The extent to which the recovery is due to the adjustment measures taken, or to a variety of fortuitous circumstances, is difficult to ascertain. Certainly the depreciation in the exchange rate, coupled with other measures to increase incentives to cocoa producers, will have played a part, but the impact of the climate is probably more pervasive than any other factor, and the excellent harvest of 1984, followed by relatively clement climatic conditions, has undoubtedly been a major factor in the economic recovery.

Nevertheless, it is clear that, without the macroeconomic changes and the increased availability of foreign exchange which accompanied them, the recovery would not have been as dramatic, not least because the physical infrastructure had deteriorated to such an extent that only a massive injection of foreign capital could have brought about an improvement. There is already an apparent slowdown in economic growth, however, and cocoa production is not continuing to expand at the expected rate. Moreover, the short-to medium-term outlook for cocoa prices on world markets is not good, and the negative trend in the international terms of trade is likely to become more pronounced.[1] Non-traditional exports are not, as yet, growing fast enough to ameliorate the situation caused by declining cocoa prices.

Part of the conditionality attached to the IMF and World Bank loans was increased control of public spending, in particular a reduction in the level of deficit financing

---

[1] For information on the decline in the world price of cocoa, see Appendix Table 1.1.

Table 1.2. *Some macroeconomic indicators*

	1979	1980	1981	1982	1983	1984	1985	1986	1987	1988	1989
% Growth in GDP	-3.4	0.4	-2.5	-6.7	-4.5	8.7	5.1	5.2	4.8		
% of GDP:											
Exports	11.2	8.5	4.7	3.4	6.1	8.0	8.9	19.2	20.6		
Imports	11.2	9.2	5.3	3.0	9.2	10.7	10.7	22.4	23.7		
Govt. Exp.	16.6	18.0	12.2	11.3	8.0	9.9	12.3	13.8	13.7		
Fiscal Def.	5.8	10.4	5.9	5.9	2.5	1.5	1.5	-0.6	1.2		
Exch. Rate											
Cedis/US$	2.75	2.75	2.75	2.75	3.45	33.34	60.00	90.00	153.7	202.4	270.0
Parallel/Off. Ratio	5.7	5.8	9.5	22.4	22.2	4.0	2.7	2.0	1.8		
MS Growth (%)	11.8	30.1	63.0	21.2	53.6	42.9	63.2	48.7	42.1	44.9	
Rate of Interest (%)[a]	12.0	12.0	18.0	8.0	11.0	14.5	16.5	18.5	23.5	26.0	
Inflation (%)	54	50	117	22	123	40	10	25	40	31	
Foreign Borrowing[b]	103	120	127	158	152	303	287	390	413		
Minimum Real Wage[c]	4.0	3.6	3.7	3.0	2.5	2.6	5.1	5.4	5.1		

Sources: Quarterly Digest of Statistics – various issues; Supplemented by material from the Bank of Ghana; minimum wages from IFAD (1988); 1988 & 1989 figures from IMF, *International Financial Statistics*, April 1990.

Notes: (a) The rate of interest given is that for savings deposits   (b) US$m.   (c) cedis per day which had proved so inflationary. Table 1.2 demonstrates some success in this, although the extent to which the resulting economic stringencies are justified is a matter of some controversy. Certainly the decline in the social infrastructure, discussed later, seems a heavy price to pay.

Monetary restraint was part of the mechanism for introducing fiscal reform, and certainly inflation has been brought down to manageable levels, although this may owe as much to the fall in real food prices following the excellent harvest of 1984 as to government policy. Official data do not show the level of monetary growth as an instrumental factor in the considerable reduction in the rate of price increase which occurred between 1984 and 1985. Current indications are that domestic inflation may be rising again to unmanageable proportions. Interest rates too, after reaching positive levels in 1985, were liberalized in 1987, and are again negative in real terms. The level of government borrowing from the central bank, in the past a source of inflationary activity, has been substantially reduced, however, in spite of the growth in government activity. This can, of course, be partly explained by the increase in government borrowing from abroad.

The growing current account deficit is not surprising, since it had previously been kept in check by rationing foreign exchange rather than incurring foreign debt. Since the domestic economy was being starved of imported inputs, this was a major factor leading to the economic decline, and the temporary financing of deficits through borrowing is a first step in economic recovery. Such a programme assumes, however, that the funds and resources generated will lead to sufficient export growth to furnish the interest and debt repayments, as well as facilitating a continuing expansion in imports. In this respect the trend in the earning capacity of exports, as given by the external terms of trade, does not suggest an optimistic scenario. On the other hand, it should be noted that much of the debt (IMF standby credits excepted) is long-term and highly concessionary, and unlikely, therefore, to generate immediate problems of debt service.

The overall picture is one of progress towards meeting many of the initial objectives of the reform programme, but the likelihood of positive trends continuing will depend on the ability of policy-makers to overcome a variety of constraints which appear to be emerging. The real rate of economic growth has begun to fall, with declining levels of profitability as a result of infrastructural bottlenecks and rising input costs. The latter have been induced by exchange-rate depreciation and reduction in subsidies, and exacerbated by the liquidity squeeze.

III.   IMPLICATIONS FOR THE AGRICULTURAL SECTOR

The pre-adjustment period

In addition to a grossly overvalued exchange rate, the agricultural sector, prior to the adjustment programme, was subject to a range of interventions affecting the production of both food and commercial crops. Rationing the limited quantity of foreign exchange meant that imports of inputs, for example fertilizer and other agrochemicals, tools, equipment and machinery, were less than adequate to meet demand at prevailing prices. In the export sector, implicit taxes and low earnings acted as disincentives and effectively undermined export production.

The consequences were disastrous. From 1970 onwards there was a steady decline in the production of all food crops except cassava, leading to increasing imports of the staple cereals with a negative effect on the already low prices of domestically produced crops, and a further decline in production. This further expanded the scope and magnitude of the food trade. Moreover, cocoa production and exports suffered a cataclysmic fall. By 1983 exports had fallen from 469,863 tons in 1971/2 to 158,953 tons in 1983/4 with no corresponding growth in other exports. Buoyant parallel markets developed in Côte d'Ivoire and Togo, and it is unofficially estimated that these took up to 35% of production.

Sector-level reforms

The macroeconomic changes outlined above had profound implications for agriculture, in particular the currency devaluation through its effect on the producer price of cocoa. In addition, specifically agricultural reforms covered the three main policy areas of trade liberalization, domestic price liberalization, and institutional reform. The first phase addressed the cocoa sub-sector, the second extended the reforms to other key agricultural activities.

External

Trade liberalization   entails the removal of import subsidies and the elimination or reduction of tariffs to levels optimal for domestic production. Import prices were liberalized but selected items remained subject to tariffs or enjoyed various levels of subsidy. The prices of imported rice, maize, sugar and textiles remained controlled, though their importation became less restricted. Subsidies were maintained on fertilizers and other chemicals, but tools and equipment continued to be admitted free of duty. It was planned, however, to eliminate all subsidies on imports by the end of 1990.

The prices of major agricultural exports remained statutorily determined. Because of the importance of cocoa in total foreign-exchange earnings (60%), it was planned to pay the producer 55–60% of the border price by 1990, with the balance distributed between government taxation and a marketing margin of 15%. Thus between 1983 and 1987 the producer price rose from 20,000 cedis to 150,000 cedis per ton (see Appendix Table 1.1).

Domestic

Liberalization of domestic agricultural markets did not turn out to be an important achievement in practice as the food-crop market was already effectively a free one. The policy reform rather sought to promote the production of strategic staples and industrial crops through price guarantees. Minimum prices, which were already in existence prior to adjustment, were raised to provide an incentive framework for allocating more resources to preferred activities. Five crops were supported by minimum prices: maize, rice, oil palm, cotton and tobacco. Price guarantees were effective for the last three, which are industrial crops sold in controlled markets, and were generally effective for rice which is purchased by the Ghana Rice Company, a subsidiary of the Ghana Food Distribution Corporation (GFDC). However, domestic rice production is only an insignificant part of consumption, with demand being primarily met through imports.

Intervention was ineffective for maize in spite of the statutory role played by the GFDC, since in practice the latter purchased less than 5% of production. Thus, maize prices, like those for other major foodstuffs, e.g. cassava, plantain, yams, cocoyams, millets and sorghum, were already market-determined. Nevertheless, an important element in the liberalization process has been freeing the GFDC from the obligation to purchase and distribute the main food staples, and to maintain adequate stocks of cereals to ensure national food security.

Institutional reforms. The most significant reorganization was to bring all cocoa-related activities under the umbrella of the Ghana Cocoa Marketing Board (GCMB), which became the COCOBOD, a statutory public corporation, reorganized into 4 operating divisions (or pre-harvest sectors) and 4 wholly-owned subsidiaries (or post-harvest sectors). Its head office provided support services.

A cutback in personnel was initiated in November 1985 to be completed by 1988/9. This was intended to reduce the labour strength from approximately 92,000 in 1983 to a target of 32,000 and so reduce COCOBOD's marketing margins of about 37% (reportedly the highest in the world) to the world average level of about 15%, while at the same time attaining a high level of institutional efficiency. In addition, COCOBOD divested itself of 52 of its 92 cocoa and coffee plantations, and freed itself from the implementation of its feeder roads programme.

As with cocoa, the basic elements of the non-cocoa reforms involved both restructuring and divestiture, together with steps to strengthen the delivery of certain services. These included the privatization of input supplies and their removal from the extension services. Departments under the Ministry of Agriculture were reorganized into more specialized units, the Economic Research and Planning Service (ERPS) was restructured into the Policy Planning, Monitoring and Evaluation Department (PPMED), and a new Extension Services Department (ESD) was created out of the Extension Services Unit of the Crop Services Division. In addition, all 18 State-Owned Enterprises (SOEs) previously under MOA supervision were earmarked for reform, with the major establishments becoming joint ventures. The GFDC was also to be reorganized and the Irrigation Development Authority (IDA) strengthened.

The impact of the reforms

Product markets. The impact of policy changes within the agricultural sector will be principally felt, in the short run at least, in the markets for its products. This is particularly true of stabilization measures such as exchange-rate devaluation and import deregulation, both of which influence product market activity more quickly than other proposed measures, which impact more on the market environment rather than on prices directly.

Of primary interest to the present study are the markets of the main agricultural commodities produced by smallholders: maize, rice, sorghum and millet among the cereal staples, starchy crops such as cassava, yam, cocoyam and plantain, and cocoa as the main, non-food commodity and principal export earner.[2] Cocoa is mainly exported in unprocessed form as cocoa beans, so that no internal market for it exists.

[2] These commodities can be categorized as exportables (cocoa), importables (maize, rice) and non-tradables (the starchy crops).

Similarly, no external market of any consequence exists for the starchy staples. There is a world market for millet and sorghum but Ghana plays little part in it, though there may be some illegal cross-border trade with traders from Burkina-Faso.

This study therefore undertook a full analysis only for maize and rice. To avoid what can be the misleading results of taking national market averages, import prices were calculated as they applied to three main cities: Accra, Kumasi and Tamale, situated respectively on the coast, in the middle of the country and in the north. These were contrasted with the relevant domestic price in each area. Border-price calculations were also made, using both official and parallel rates of exchange, the latter as a proxy for a free-market equilibrium exchange rate. The results can be expressed as net protection co-efficients (see Table 1.3), and used to highlight the impact of tariffs and other trade restrictions.

Table 1.3.   *Net protection co-efficients for maize and rice**

Year	1979	1980	1981	1982	1983	1984	1985	1986	1987	1988
Maize										
Accra (a)	4.64	9.45	16.65	20.56	66.65	4.52	2.82	3.38	3.64	
(b)	0.82	1.63	1.75	0.92	3.00	1.18	0.95	1.70	2.09	
Kumasi (a)	2.39	4.48	5.94	7.13	14.72	2.56	1.61	1.96	2.22	
(b)		0.63	1.23	1.31	0.74	2.28	0.89	0.70	1.17	1.46
Tamale (a)	1.34	2.42	2.92	3.48	6.58	1.87	1.18	1.45	1.70	
(b)		0.45	0.87	0.92	0.55	1.63	0.64	0.48	0.78	0.97
Rice										
Accra (a)	2.87	4.59	7.55	22.10	58.94	7.22	3.56	3.13	2.82	
(b)	0.51	0.79	0.79	0.99	2.65	1.78	1.33	1.58	1.62	
Kumasi (a)	3.04	4.86	8.01	23.44	62.50	7.66	3.77	3.32	3.00	
(b)		0.54	0.84	0.84	1.04	2.81	1.89	1.41	1.68	1.72
Tamale (a)	2.53	4.04	6.83	19.44	51.83	6.35	3.13	2.75	2.48	
(b)		0.45	0.70	0.70	0.87	2.33	1.57	1.17	1.39	1.43

Sources: The world prices and freight charges used in the calculations are given by source in Appendix Tables 1.2 and 1.3, as are the sources of price data and the methods used to estimate transport costs.

Notes: (*) = a co-efficient of greater than 1.0 implies the commodity should have importable status at existing exchange rates; (a) = world price equivalent at official exchange rates; (b) = world price equivalent at parallel exchange rates.

The impact of the adjustment measures is most clearly demonstrated by reference to relative real price trends. Some relevant indices are presented in Table 1.4. Deflated by the rural consumer price index, the calculations show real prices for cereals increasing over the early part of the period, reflecting the growing seriousness of the droughts (which reached a peak in 1983), and falling back thereafter. With the exception of 1983 and the recovery in cassava prices, real prices of starchy crops have been persistently below the levels of 1979, and the other main subsistence crops, groundnuts and cowpeas, reveal a similar pattern. Until recently, however, food crops have fared considerably better than cocoa, with their producers being the most obvious beneficiaries of devaluation.

Some idea of the impact of exchange-rate liberalization and trade deregulation can

Table 1.4.   *Real price trends (1979 = 100)*

Year	1980	1981	1982	1983	1984	1985	1986	1987
Index
Staples	92	72	84	150	94	77	97	104
Cereals	148	119	141	268	147	105	108	126
Starchy Crops	42	61	73	124	80	68	90	93
Cocoa	62	89	73	59	57	99	123	158
Importables	137	117	143	257	145	118	112	138
Non-Tradables	89	72	83	146	93	72	95	101

Source: As for Table 1.3.

Table 1.5.   *Price ratio indices (1979 = 100)*

Year	1980	1981	1982	1983	1984	1985	1986	1987
Index
PM/PX	221	132	196	436	254	119	91	87
PM/PN	154	163	172	176	156	164	118	137
PX/PN	70	124	88	40	61	138	130	156
PM*/PX*	151	193	195	167	141	130	114	121
PM*/PN	87	52	31	11	168	188	141	163
PX*/PN	58	27	16	7	76	145	125	136
PM/PM*	79	140	137	91	79	144	196	261
PX*/PX	128	71	73	110	128	70	51	38

Source: As for Table 1.3.

be gained from the indices presented in Table 1.5. The general trend which emerges shows that since 1983 there has been a shift in relative prices favouring exportables relative to importables and marginally towards non-tradables relative to importables. The latter is inconsistent with the premise that exchange-rate devaluation would benefit tradables at the expense of non-tradables. The former may be partly due to the fact that a rise in the price of an imported good will be reflected in the price of a domestically produced substitute only to the extent that the two goods are perfect substitutes. In the case of maize this is certainly not the case, imported yellow varieties being generally regarded as inferior (for direct human consumption) to local white maize. The market is also distorted by the fact that a substantial proportion of rice imports are in the form of concessional shipments through the World Food Programme.

A further influence is the impact of both import and export taxes. As outlined below, tariffs on imported cereals have been reduced since 1983 (and have recently been reduced still further). In addition, reductions in export taxes and the first moves towards streamlining the activities of the Cocoa Marketing Board have meant that producers have received an increasing share of the price of exported cocoa (see Appendix Table 1.1). Whereas the importable to non-tradable ratio moved persistently in favour of the latter prior to 1983, the trend has subsequently been reversed. The first trend reflects the increasing scarcity of maize and rice in the drought years, relative to the availability of the more drought-resistant non-tradable staples. This climatic influence appears to compensate fully for any impact of the increasing overvaluation of the exchange rate, while the reversal of trend in the post-adjustment period appears to reflect the recovery of maize and rice harvests. The PX/PN ratio most clearly demonstrates the devaluation effect, the trends directly reflecting those of the degree of exchange-rate distortion.

A comparison of PM/PX and PM*/PX* is revealing. PM*/PX* represents a ratio of border prices as opposed to that of prices actually received by producers. In making a comparison the exchange-rate effect is entirely absent. At equilibrium, given perfect markets, the two would be equal. The difference between them, therefore, is a reflection of the differential impact of changes in tariffs and other trade restrictions. This is more clearly demonstrated by the ratios PM/PM* and PX*/PX. These describe directly the degree of price distortion caused by trade impediments.[3] It can be seen that tariff restrictions have been much more effectively reduced in the case of exportables than importables, where the impact of restrictions appears to be growing. Tariffs on both rice and maize were imposed at the rate of 35% between 1979 and 1983, before being reduced to 25%, with a further reduction to 20% in 1988. Such import taxes are not the only form of trade restriction, however, imports being subject to periodic restrictions and quotas depending on the availability of local supplies. Thus no apparent trend is observable. The PX*/PX index demonstrates the increasing proportion of the world price being received by producers (Appendix Table 1.1).

Factor markets.   The rural *labour market* is differentiated into a large informal sector and a small formal sector. Casual labourers are not necessarily unemployed but may be owners of small farms or workers in the formal wage sector. Agricultural production is based essentially on the combination of family and hired casual labour, and even very small farmers require some hired labour. Wages in the informal sector are significantly higher than those in the formal sector, commonly by a factor of more than two. The highly restricted opportunities for formal employment (which is preferred by most agricultural workers) would seem to enhance the supply and availability of labour to the informal sector. At the same time, scarcity of labour and rising labour costs are almost universal characteristics of agricultural production.

In contrast to the immediate pre-adjustment period, the minimum wage increased between 1983 and 1988 almost nine-fold in nominal terms, from 21 to 180 cedis per day, while in real terms it more than doubled (see Table 1.6). The average agricultural daily wage in the informal sector was 90 cedis in 1983 (about 4.3 times the formal wage), and rose to between 300 and 350 cedis per day in 1988 (i.e. by a factor of 3.3). Given the relationship between formal and informal wage rates, it is likely that the policy, since 1983, of periodic adjustment in minimum rates has helped to maintain higher informal sector wages than would otherwise have been the case.

The policy of cutbacks in public sector employment, which mostly affected unskilled labour, should have increased supply to the informal sector in the short term. Indeed, specific encouragement, albeit largely rhetorical, was given to the redundant labour from COCOBOD and other sectors of the public services to take up farming. The available evidence suggests that a majority of those made redundant actually ended up in the informal service sector, and that the small number of workers remaining in the rural sector (largely from COCOBOD) started farms of their own, thereby marginally increasing the demand for labour rather than adding to its supply.

In the cocoa sub-sector, at least, producer price increases have generated an

---

[3] Note that the figures are indices and do not represent actual measurements. In the case of exportables (cocoa), the ratio has been reserved in the calculation to make it consistent with others in the table, since the impact of an export tax on producers is as a negative tariff.

Table 1.6. *Trends in nominal and real rages*

	1981	1982	1983	1984	1985	1986	1987	1988
				(cedis per day)				
Min. wage (a)	12	12	21	32	70	90	120	180
Agricultural								
wage (b)	30	60	90	100	120	150	250	350
Real min. wage								
(1979 prices)	3.7	3.0	2.5	2.6	5.1	5.4	5.1	n/a
Ratio a/b	2.5	5.0	4.3	3.1	1.7	1.6	2.1	1.9

Source: IFAD (1988) supplemented by material provided by Ministry of Agriculture.

increased demand for labour. The extent to which these developments have been translated directly into higher wages, however, is clouded by interregional migration of both farmers and agricultural labourers. Since the mid-1970s, there has been a steady migration of labour from the traditional cocoa-producing regions of Ashanti and the Eastern Region (as well as from the Central and Volta Regions), into the Western Region, as a result of the availability of virgin cocoa land in the latter, and the relative shortage of land in the former.

This movement has become intensified with the support provided to the cocoa sector in the form of free seedlings. In addition, regional labour scarcities have been exacerbated through the rapid development of modern palm oil and small private plantations in the Eastern and Central Regions. In some areas, however, such as the Northern and Upper Regions where production is largely subsistence-orientated, adjustment policies have had little impact on labour markets.

A tentative conclusion concerning the impact of the ERP on labour markets, therefore, is that the capacity has been created, through higher producer prices for certain crops, for increased absorption of labour into the farming sector, and that this has expanded the base for general employment. This effect is being realized more in some regions than in others. At the same time, both formal and informal sector wages have been pushed up. Whereas the changes may tend to benefit those whose primary source of income is from the sale of household labour, they have not necessarily had any positive impact on those households whose livelihood is primarily derived from the production of non-traded food crops. In fact, the possibility exists that these households have been squeezed between increasing labour costs, on the one hand, and relatively stagnant or declining output prices on the other.

Specific developments in the *capital market*, consequent upon adjustment programmes, relate to the increased supply of foreign capital through loans and grants; changes in the supply of domestic capital; and higher interest rates. Foreign borrowing has facilitated support to both the private and public sectors. At least 16 public sector programmes aimed at smallholders have been provided with adequate levels of funding. This has eased the pressure on the domestic budget, and enhanced programme performance.

The second area of impact concerns the volume of domestic capital being channelled into the agricultural sector. While most commercial banks lend to the sector, it is the Agricultural Development Bank, the Ghana Commercial Bank and the Rural Banks which carry the main burden of financing agricultural investment. Between 1983 and 1987 total credits to the agricultural sector rose from 2 to 10 billion cedis, an increase, in real terms, of almost 100% (see Table 1.7).

Efforts have been made to redress the situation of negative rates prevailing prior

Table 1.7.   *Formal sector agricultural credit*

	1979	1980	1981	1982	1983	1984	1985	1986	1987
					(million cedis)				
Tot. credit	308	412	670	1109	2004	3773	5208	7476	10713
@ 1979 prices	308	275	206	279	226	305	382	440	451
Int. Rate % (nominal)		13.0	13.0	22.0	9.0	12.5	16.0	18.5	22.5	(a)
Int. Rate % (real)		−41	−37	−95	−13	−111	−24	+8	−2.5	−14
% of ADB appl. financed							36	42	26	19

Note: (a) Following deregulation in September 1987, interest rates have been in the range 22.5% to 30%. Real rates have been calculated using an average of these.

Source: Bank of Ghana.

to the reforms. This process was helped by the dramatic fall in the rate of inflation to as low as 10.4% in 1985. Subsequently, however, real interest rates have again become negative. Even so, the current rates of 22.5% to 30% are proving too high for some domestic borrowers, most notably small farmers, whose access to formal sector capital is, in any case, extremely limited. The evidence suggests that, while increasing numbers of applicants are requesting loans, the numbers actually financed are falling.

The adjustment programme contained no reforms affecting the distribution or utilization of land with any direct impact on *land markets*. Although information is limited, landlessness is not, at present, a major problem in Ghana even though there are areas where the demand for land for agricultural purposes is beginning to outstrip available supply.

With regard to *input supply*, fertilizer imports have fallen since 1984, reflecting both a drop in demand following the price increases resulting from the exchange-rate adjustment, and the inadequacy of the resources allocated for their import. In fact, the on-going privatization of fertilizer importation and distribution could have serious consequences for rural small-scale producers. Private importers and transporters may not find the business lucrative enough to make the necessary investments in transportation and distribution networks, especially given the decline in fertilizer sales. In contrast, the availability of farm tools, spraying equipment, and insecticides, as well as the distribution of consumer goods, has improved since the implementation of the reform programme.

IV.   CHARACTERISTICS OF THE RURAL POPULATION

This study has been based on the premise that the impact of adjustment on rural groups is felt through changes in key factors linking the rural economy with the wider economy. These factors are, principally, markets for farmers' output and the prices they receive, labour and capital markets, and other agricultural services. Yet different rural groups will vary considerably in the extent to which they use or rely on these markets and services. This section identifies some of the numerically significant low-income rural groups, categorizing them by, for instance, their degree of market orientation or their reliance on wage employment.

It is commonly accepted in Ghana that poverty spreads upwards from the south. The 'north', consisting of the Northern, Upper East and Upper West Regions, can be differentiated from the rest of the country by ecological characteristics, which can broadly be divided into the northern savannah, with relatively low rainfall and one rainy season per year, and the southern forest zones, where the rainfall is higher and generally more reliable, and there are two rainy seasons. The savannah areas support significantly fewer people per square mile, with the exception of the Upper East Region where, for largely historical reasons, population density is not only relatively high, but also predominantly rural, factors which, given the poor rainfall and lack of irrigation potential, combine to make this the poorest region of the country. In general, the north comprises 40% of the total land area, supports 20% of the population and produces 14% of the nation's food.

In the rural areas, agriculture is the predominant occupation. While 69% of the economically active population reside in rural districts, 83% of these have agriculture as their major activity and, outside Greater Accra, there is little regional variation in these respects. Although detailed information is lacking, it is widely accepted that the dominant constraint to agricultural production is the availability of labour (IFAD, 1988). While population growth and the encroachment of plantations, irrigation schemes and other development projects may lead to localized land shortages, for the country as a whole, with only 12% of the land area cultivated, land availability would not appear to be an inhibiting factor. Labour shortages have in the past been exacerbated by migration, and even after the return of migrants from Nigeria, it is doubtful if the rural labour supply has grown sufficiently to meet demand. Partial confirmation of this is evidenced by the fact that rural wages are generally substantially greater than the minimum wage.

In these circumstances the most effective indicator of relative poverty in rural areas is the distribution of land. While holding sizes have shown a downward trend since 1970, the distribution remains skewed. The 1984 agricultural census revealed a gini coefficient of 0.64, which can be broken down into coefficients of 0.52 and 0.67 for the north and south respectively, suggesting greater income inequality in the south. In fact, these figures probably overestimate the degree of inequality nationally and the north-south difference, since the 1984 figures exaggerate the number of smallholders in the south compared with the current situation. Nevertheless, data on the size distribution of farms do reveal that agriculture is dominated by small-scale production.

A survey carried out in 1986 by the Ministry of Agriculture (Giri and Oku, 1988) recorded over two-thirds of holdings (68.6%) as being under 2 acres, although the degree of regional variation is significant. Average holding size appears to be much higher in the drier northern areas, with only 31.1% of holdings under 2 acres, compared with 79.7% in the rest of the country. This difference is not a reflection of average income, however, since the potential productivity is substantially lower in the north.

It is not only the vagaries of climate which affect the riskiness and level of agricultural income. For those producers who, for whatever reason, market a substantial part of their output, variations in product market conditions can also be of crucial significance. The 1986 survey recorded 19.6% of farmers as marketing the bulk of their produce, 54% as being marginal sellers, whose main production orientation is providing the household's consumption needs, and the remainder as producing solely for subsistence. In reality, the proportions within the latter two categories will vary from year to year with the bounty of the harvest, since the typical marginal seller is marketing an unplanned surplus, that is, a surplus over and above household sub-sistence requirements. It is unlikely, however, that any household has zero cash requirements. Those categorized as pure subsistence producers, therefore, as well as many of the marginal sellers, supplement their income, to a greater or lesser extent, through some off-farm activity, frequently the sale of household labour.

An additional feature is the incidence of tenancy, although the cultivation of tenanted land is almost exclusively a phenomenon of the south. In total about 14% of plots are cultivated under some form of tenancy, but this figure rises to 19% for the southern regions, and to almost 30% in the Central and Eastern Regions. Approx-imately one-third of tenancies are in the form of cash rents, while some form of sharecropping accounts for over 50%. If share tenants are excluded from the analysis, the proportion of plots under tenancy falls to 6.6%. Share tenancies are of two forms, ebunu and ebusa. The former, which mainly involves food-crop production, provides for the division of produce on an equal-shares basis. The latter, common on cocoa farms, distributes the output or its equivalent value in the proportions of one-third each to landlord and tenant, and a further third to the landlord as remuneration for non-labour expenses.

There is a lack of current data on the numbers whose primary source of livelihood is agricultural labour. The 1970 census showed that, while the bulk of farm labour is provided by the holder's household, over 60% of all households employed some outside labour, and even at the lowest recorded farm size level (0-2 acres) over half hired labour. This proportion increases with the degree of market orientation, but even amongst those supposedly producing solely for subsistence, one-quarter resort to the hiring of labour. This labour-use pattern arises because certain farm tasks such as land clearing and weeding require either a substantial labour input over a short period of time, or a specific type of labour which may not be readily available from within the household.

According to the census, there were 501,100 agricultural labourers in 1970, or 28% of those gaining their principal livelihood from the sector. Many, if not most, of these are also likely to have small holdings of their own; 57% were classified as temporary workers, that is primarily those supplementing their own-holding income by selling their labour to other farmers during periods of peak demand. Permanent workers would include those employed on plantations and state farms, and also the 'caretaker' farmers or sharecroppers; it is likely that many of these also supplement their income through the produce of their own subsistence plots. One can assume, therefore, that the majority of these agricultural labourers were farming mini-holdings, but that through either ethnic origin (i.e. they were 'stranger' farmers), household composition (e.g. an unsuitable labour profile for on-farm production), or land shortage (in a small number of districts), they were unable to acquire sufficient land to meet their income requirements through direct production.

Between 1970 and 1984 the rural population increased by one third, and it is unlikely that the area under crop production increased proportionately. Moreover, rural-urban migration has continued, albeit at a slow pace. Migrants, particularly single migrants, are frequently the most able-bodied members of the household. Thus the quality of the rural labour supply may have declined. Under these circumstances it would seem reasonable to assume that the 1970 figures provide a minimum indica-tion for current estimates, and that the proportion of producer/workers is most pro-bably higher than 28%.

The place of women in the rural economy merits special emphasis. Of those working in agriculture it is interesting to note that the proportion of females is equal to, or greater than, that of males in most regions, excepting Greater Accra and the Northern and Upper East Regions. In fact, the proportion of female-headed households in rural areas is 30%. Again there is a marked contrast between north and south. Whereas in most southern regions the figure is close to 35%, in the north it is closer to 10%. The reasons for this dichotomy are both economic and cultural.

Traditionally women's contribution to agricultural production was gender-sequential or task-specific. With the advent of commercial farming, particularly cocoa farming in the south, production of food crops became increasingly their sole responsibility, and was frequently seen as a separate, and gender-specific, activity. In the north, where the opportunities for cash-crop farming were more limited, women's role remained confined to particular tasks rather than crops.

With economic growth and the emergence of non-agricultural opportunities, plus the increasing cash requirements of households, migration began to influence the age and gender of those engaged in agriculture. One result, in the southern areas, has been the rise in the number of households headed by women, following the men's temporary or permanent migration. In the north, however, where cultural traditions are more influenced by Islam, where inheritance patterns are patrilineal as opposed to matrilineal, and where extended family relationships are stronger, migration of male household heads usually results in another male member assuming responsibility.

Smallholders and the rural poor

The definitional characteristics of both smallholders and the rural poor vary considerably, even in the Ghanaian context. A typical rule of thumb often used by the Ministry of Agriculture is to assume that all holdings under ten acres in size are 'smallholdings'. But this is far too broad a category, encompassing almost the entire agricultural population. The IFAD study of 1988 used a maximum holding size criterion of six acres in the north and four acres in the south. While this coincided with the categories used by the agricultural census of 1984, it is still somewhat broad. In the present study an attempt was made to provide these rules of thumb with a more rigorous foundation, as outlined below.

Ghanaian agriculture is dominated by the peasant sector, plantations and state farms being responsible for only a small proportion of aggregate production, although for particular crops these proportions may be very significant. Apart from these, there are relatively few large-scale, capital-intensive farms. The great majority and the relatively poorest, therefore, tend to be those operating very small holdings, using traditional technologies, and operating under difficult environmental conditions with regard to both soil quality and climate. The bulk of these producers, perhaps inevitably, tend to have a low market orientation.

A further distinguishing characteristic is the regional specialization resulting from localized climatic and soil conditions. In general, the country can be divided into a number of broad ecological zones ranging from the coastal savannah in the southern coastal region, through the forest zone covering most of central and southern Ghana, to the northern savannah. The types of soils, and more importantly, the rainfall pattern lead to a very different range of outputs. For example, the drier, shallow soil of the northern savannah necessitates a staple diet based on millet, sorghum and beans, while the variable soils and bi-modal rainfall pattern in the southern zones lead, in some areas, to cash cropping, particularly production of cocoa, and staple food production dominated by maize and cassava.

The obvious first criterion in the selection procedure was that of household income,

Table 1.8. *Basic needs income by region*

Region	W.	C	G.A.	E	V	A	B.A.	N	U.W	U.E.
Crop Y/acre (000 Cedis)	17.6	16.9	18.2	36.1	37.1	30.5	50.5	52.2	20.5	11.7
Household size adj.	0.82	0.72	0.85	1.00	0.92	0.93	0.99	1.76	1.66	1.10
Acres for 75% of bni	3.8	3.5	3.8	2.2	2.0	2.5	1.6	2.8	6.5	7.6
Acres for 25% of bni	1.3	1.4	1.3	0.8	0.7	0.8	0.5	0.9	2.2	2.5

Source: Computed from IFAD, 1988.

Notes: bni = basic needs income

Regions: W = Western; C = Central; G.A. = Greater Accra; E = Eastern; V = Volta; A = Ashanti; B.A. = Brong Ahafo; N = Northern; U.E. = Upper East; U.W. = Upper West. Northern Region was taken as being halfway between the two main ecological types.

and whether agricultural production was the major or a secondary source of income. Income data are extremely sparse, and where available, notoriously unreliable. Holding size is therefore taken as a proxy. Calculations were based on estimates of smallholder income derived from imputed cropping patterns and prevailing prices, and compared with a standard basic needs income, adapted from ILO estimates (see Tabatabai, 1986). Using the 1986 survey data, it was estimated that 51% of the rural population (a total of 3.8 million people) had incomes below the minimum standard. In addition, the calculations suggest that, given the low population density in the northern regions compared with the more populous southern areas, poverty is more widespread in the north in terms of the proportion of the population classified as poor, but that the absolute numbers are greater in the south, and the largest numbers of the poor are found in the richest region (Ashanti). Poverty is not, therefore, a regional phenomenon.

The crop income per acre was estimated for 1986 on a regional basis. The basic needs income estimate for that year was then used to calculate the holding size necessary to achieve 75% of this income from crop production, these estimates then being adjusted to take account of regional variations in household size, to give the required holding size for each region, and averaged in an appropriate manner given the ecological variations of the country. Table 1.8 shows the main results of the calculations, based on a basic needs income of 108,000 cedis per annum, and assuming that in each household at least one member was engaged in non-farm activity or that remittances from non-household members contributed to household income.

The second selection criterion stemmed from the clear distinction to be made, in terms of market responses and therefore the impact of, and responses to, adjustment measures, between those farmers geared significantly towards market production and those whose principal orientation is towards subsistence. It must also be noted that many of those with the smallest holdings have substantial cash needs and, in some areas, are confronted by a land constraint such that they are forced through circumstance to sell the bulk of their labour on the casual labour market. These producer/labourers constitute a separate category, being substantially integrated into market activity, but in this case through factor, rather than product, markets. In reality, the great majority of farm-worker households, whether employed on a permanent or casual basis, derive a part of their subsistence needs from their own miniholdings. The maximum holding size for this category assumes that no more than 25% of income is derived from crop production.

On the basis of these two criteria three principal groups were identified: (i) smallscale producers and (ii) producer/workers, both of them substantially integrated, for whatever reason, into market activity, plus a third group consisting of small-scale producers who consume the bulk of their produce. Market-orientated producers can broadly be divided between those who produce for the market through disposition, i.e. food producers (e.g. pure stand producers of rice and maize), and those whose market activity is inevitable because of the nature of the cropping pattern (e.g. producers of crops destined for export or industrial use). The other two groups can be usefully subdivided on the basis of the local ecology, which is largely reflected in the cropping pattern. The holding size necessary to achieve a given level of income will be considerably larger for farmers operating in dryland conditions. Livestock production, in general limited because of tsetse fly infestation, is also a more prominent feature in this ecology.

Thus the categories to emerge from this procedure, and to be considered in more detail below, were as follows:

(i) Market-orientated producers
    (a) Export/industrial   holding size 0–3 acres
    (b) Food   holding size 0–3 acres

(ii) Subsistence-orientated producers
    (a) Dryland farming   holding size 2–6 acres
    (b) Mixed cropping   holding size 1–3 acres

(iii) Producer/labourers
    (a) Dryland areas   holding size 0–2 acres
    (b) Mixed cropping areas   holding size 0–1 acres

Market-orientated producers

Export/industrial crop producers.   The principal non-food crops produced in Ghana include cocoa, coffee, oil palm, coconuts, rubber, shea nuts, cotton, tobacco and sugar. In addition, pineapples, various vegetables, and yams are exported in small quantities, and the government plans for their expansion as part of its drive to diversify export earnings away from reliance on cocoa.

Of the non-food crops only cocoa beans, oil palm nuts, and coconuts feature in smallholder cropping patterns. Most of the oil palm is processed for household use, and thus would not be regarded as a cash crop. Production of coconuts is concentrated in coastal areas of the Western Region, and producers are unlikely to figure significantly among the smaller farmers. Cotton, tobacco and sugar are mainly grown by large-scale farmers or estates, while shea nuts, though possessing potential for northern smallholders, are, at present, gathered rather than farmed. Of the food crops exported, yams and vegetables are primarily grown for domestic consumption, and producers of these are best analysed in the category of food-crop producers. The bulk of pineapple production, particularly that part destined for export, is produced by growers operating on a scale which places them outside the smallholder category.[4]

The relevant group, therefore, consists almost exclusively of small-scale cocoa producers. As noted earlier, cocoa is by far the most important non-food crop and, in terms of value, second only to cassava overall. The cocoa sub-sector employs 24% of the labour force and accounts for over a third of the cultivated land (IFAD, 1988). Traditionally grown in the Ashanti, Eastern, Central and Volta Regions, production has declined (particularly in the latter two) in recent years, while there has been some partially compensating expansion in the Western Region (see Appendix Table 1.1).

Cocoa has traditionally been one of the main sources of wealth in rural Ghana. The number of cocoa holdings has been estimated at 265,000, although breakdown in terms of holding size is unknown. It is accepted, however, that many holdings are substantial. The IFAD report of 1988 suggested that cocoa is not a smallholder crop; the reasoning is based on the premise that the average size of cocoa holding is approximately 4.5 acres, and that this puts producers well outside the smallholder category. However, cocoa holdings of up to 200 acres have been recorded, suggesting that many holdings may be well below this average. Other sources also refer to cocoa smallholders as a recognizable category (e.g. Seini et al., 1989), and discussions with officials of the Cocoa Marketing Board confirmed their significance.

---

[4] Information is obtained from IFAD, 1988 and from discusions with members of the Ministry of Agriculture and the Export Promotion Council.

Apart from those smallholders with title to their own land, there is also a large number of cocoa sharecroppers. It is estimated that there are 500,000 cocoa producers (IFAD, 1988), of whom approximately half are sharecroppers. Many owners of cocoa holdings lease them out to a number of tenants under the *ebusa* system. If these are combined with the small-scale owner-operators mentioned above, it is likely that the smallholders make up around half of all cocoa producers.

Most anecdotal and other evidence suggests that these farmers possess small subsistence plots as well as the cocoa holding. Small-scale cocoa production is characterized by limited use of chemical inputs, and the main mechanical aids used are mistblowers and machetes. It is likely that the sharecroppers, at least, employ a certain minimum of off-farm inputs, since their use is often stipulated in the contract and paid for by the landowner (accounted for by the third share). The bulk of household income is likely to be from the sale of cocoa beans. In delineating the acreage range for the group as a whole, it is assumed that all household cash needs will be met by cocoa sales, and that the sale of household labour does not feature prominently in income profiles; thus all cocoa producers occupying 3 acres or less are included.

Food-crop producers.   Farmers falling within this category will be marketing at least 50% of their output. This implies an orientation towards market production, rather than the intermittent sale of seasonal surpluses. It is assumed, therefore, that, like the cocoa producers, their cash needs are fully met from the sale of produce rather than labour, hence the acreage range of 0–3 acres. The principal crops grown specifically for sale range from paddy in the north and west to maize in much of southern Ghana. Given that the overall number of farmers using fertilizers, other chemical inputs and improved seeds is low, the number of smallholders doing so is even lower. Nevertheless it can be assumed that amongst food-crop farmers pure-stand producers are the most likely to use purchased inputs. Thus, although production technology remains labour-intensive, it can be classified as improved rather than traditional.

It can be reasonably assumed that the numbers in this group will be small, and that most of them will be located in the southern regions. Some indication of their overall significance can be gained through comparison of the proportion estimated to market more than 50% of their produce, and the proportion having holdings below 3 acres. According to the 1986 survey, 19.6% of holders are market-orientated. Of these 14% live in the three northern regions. Only 8.8% of northern farmers can be described as market-orientated, as against 23.6% in the south. At the same time, almost 40% of holders have holdings greater than 3 acres; for southern areas the figure is over 31%. It is reasonable to assume, therefore, that the great majority of those marketing the bulk of their output fall outside the smallholder category.

Given the information currently available, it is impossible to estimate, with any precision, the likely numerical significance of this group. It is reasonable to assume, however, that where cultivation is in pure stands, there is a far higher probability of producers being market-orientated. Since 37% of maize is planted in pure stand, almost entirely in the south, and paddy is rarely grown in mixtures, there is a high probability that there will be small numbers of maize and paddy producers meeting the characteristics of this category.

Subsistence-orientated producers

Dryland farming.   Smallholders in this category, as indicated above, depend for their primary subsistence needs on production of dryland mixtures, mainly composed of millet, sorghum and beans. Maize may also be included in areas with relatively more rain. While it would be misleading to locate these farmers purely on the basis of administrative region, the ecology of the country ensures that they will mostly reside in the Upper regions and the northern part of the Northern Region.

It is difficult to estimate the numerical significance of this group from the 1986 survey, since holdings over 5 acres were undifferentiated. An idea of the minimum number can be gained, however, by taking the numbers of those with holdings of between 3 and 5 acres; i.e. 35% of holders in the Upper regions and 43% in the Northern Region. If the assumption is made that all these smallholders in the Upper regions and half of those in the Northern Region are, through ecological necessity, dryland farmers, then 30% of all households (98,300) in the three regions fall within the category.

Livestock are far more common in the northern part of Ghana than in the rest of the country. From the survey information it can be deduced that approximately 60% of dryland farmers can be expected to own cattle. The information is not specific to size-class, however, and it can be assumed that the proportion of smallholders with livestock is lower than the average. Nevertheless it is likely that for many in this group cattle will feature as a source of income, of traction and of organic fertilizer. In other respects, however, the prevailing technological pattern is likely to be labour-intensive and traditional, with little or no use of improved seeds or other purchased inputs.

Mixed farming.   The most pervasive agricultural system in the southern regions is of shifting cultivation and the growing of maize and cassava, together with other crops such as cocoyam and plantain, in mixed stands. The crops are sown randomly rather than in lines in order to minimize risk and maximize the capacity for differing plant growth patterns to reinforce each other. Mixed cropping makes the use of fertilizers and other chemical inputs difficult if not inefficient, and the use of mechanical aids, other than for ground clearing and soil preparation, impossible. In addition, the advantages of improved varieties and planting material under such regimes are minimal if not negative. Such farming systems are land-intensive, ecologically sound and consistent with societies where consumption patterns require relatively low levels of surplus agricultural production and where the bulk of farm produce is consumed by the household.

The majority of Ghanaian farmers fit the above description, and the proportion of smallholders doing so is very high indeed. According to the 1986 survey over 76% of farmers in the southern area (assuming this includes all the farmers of the southern regions plus half of those in the Northern Region) are producing either totally or primarily for household consumption. At the same time, 66% of holdings (over 767,000) in this area are less than 3 acres in area, and it can be assumed, as with the market-orientated food producers, that most of these fall into the category of subsistence-orientated producers. Unfortunately there is no information with regard to the proportion of these holdings falling in the range selected as appropriate for households able to provide the bulk of their income from on-farm production, since there is no breakdown of holding size below 3 acres. It is reasonable to suggest, nevertheless, that this will form the numerically most important of the categories.

Producer/workers

For households involved in subsistence-orientated production and using traditional labour techniques, such as those in the previous two categories, the problems of achieving an expansion of agricultural surplus in response to an increase in consumption needs can be immense if there is insufficient land or household labour available. Intensification of production in these circumstances, without a change in the farming system, may be impossible, and many households, which are unable to expand their scale of production because of lack of resources, are forced into a cycle of poverty and indebtedness.

The majority of producer/workers or part-time farmers fall into this category, operating very small subsistence holdings and obtaining the greater part of the household income from the sale of labour, either temporary or permanent, on relatively large farms and plantations. A proportion may temporarily hire themselves out in order to provide cash income for some specific purchase, for example for a capital input into some other enterprise. In addition, they may be households with strong cash needs, for example, to finance the education of children.

The distinction between temporary and permanent labour may be quite significant. As noted earlier, both are subject to minimum wage legislation, but actual wages are usually well above the legal minimum owing to high demand. Wages for casual labour are often higher than for permanent labour, although the latter frequently benefit from security of income and medical and other social services. Despite the labour shortage, the demand for casual labour is seasonal and insecure. The main demand is for labour for physically difficult work such as land clearing, and comes particularly from households headed by the old or by women.

It is difficult to give an accurate estimate of the numbers involved, although 35% of households in the dryland farming area fall into a holding size category (less than 3 acres) judged inadequate to provide more than a minor part of household income from farming. According to the 1970 census the scope for agricultural labour was greater in the south than in the north, thus it is reasonable to assume that at least that proportion of southern households fall into this category (i.e. with holdings of under 1 acre). Estimating on this basis, approximately 500,000 households would fall into this category of part-time farmers.

Summary.   To recapitulate, six different rural groups have been identified for the study:

A	Market-orientated cocoa producers	2 acres
B	Market-orientated food-crop producers	2.5 acres
C	Subsistence-orientated producers of dryland farming type	4 acres
D	Subsistence-orientated producers of mixed farming type	2 acres
E	Producer/workers from dryland farming areas	1 acre
F	Producer/workers from mixed farming areas	0.5 acres

In the following section the impact of the reforms on these groups is evaluated.

V.   THE IMPACT OF THE REFORMS ON HOUSEHOLD INCOMES

In the absence of direct evidence concerning household income for the groups concerned, the approach taken was to hypothesize the production activity of typical group members and deduce, given knowledge of prices, likely trends in net barter and income terms of trade for each group, with a view to ascertaining how these changed during the pre-and post-adjustment periods.

In the case of the cocoa producers, it was assumed that 75% of their holding was devoted to cocoa production and 25% to a mixture of food crops, the proportions of which would be described by the cropping pattern of the south subsistence mixed farmers. The cropping pattern for the market-orientated food producers was derived by calculating the proportion of each crop under pure-stand cultivation using data from the 1986 sample survey (Giri and Oku, 1988), weighted by the number of smallholder holdings in each region and the estimated average for the country as a whole. Obviously, no individual smallholder's activity would correspond to the cropping pattern thus derived, but it was hoped that the result would reflect the broad characteristics faced by all such producers. Those crops which featured only marginally were eliminated from the final division of area. ·

For the subsistence-orientated producers, cropping patterns were calculated based on southern and northern characteristics, with the area under mixed cropping in each region taken as a starting point (Giri and Oku, 1988). For the dryland farmers the weights used were for the two Upper regions, plus half the population weight of the Northern Region. Similarly for the mixed farmers the weights were derived for each southern region plus half the Northern. This corresponds to the earlier view that regional borders do not correspond with ecological differences, and that different parts of the Northern Region might fall into either category. For the producer/labourer groups, it was assumed that cropping patterns would be as for the subsistence farmers.

Holding size was taken as the median of the range given in the previous section for each group, with the qualification that for market-orientated producers holding size would be unlikely to fall within the mini-holding range typically characterizing the producer/worker category. Thus for cocoa producers the operative range was taken as being between 1 and 3 acres, with a median of 2 acres, assuming that holdings of 1 acre or less are likely to be used purely for subsistence. In the case of market-orientated food producers, an operative range of between 2 and 5 acres was chosen, with a median of 2 acres, since it was considered likely that holdings below 2 acres would fall into the subsistence category.

Yields for each crop were taken from IFAD (1988). It was not possible to make any allowance for year-to-year variations in yield. Thus output per holding was calculated using single-year yield estimates. In calculating the value of output per holding it was assumed that producers received only a given proportion of the wholesale price. These proportions were estimated from data provided by the Ministry of Agriculture, 1988. Thus it was assumed that producers received 100% of the wholesale price in the case of cocoa, 80% in the case of maize and dryland crops, 75% for paddy and 70% for starchy crops. As far as possible wholesale prices pertinent to the region where the bulk of the crop is produced were used in the calculations.

In calculating the net barter terms of trade, current year value weights were used and the result deflated by an expenditure deflator. It was assumed that the expenditure patterns of the market-oriented farmers and producer/workers would be dominated by food purchases, since these groups were well integrated into market activity. Taking as a starting point the maxim that a minimum of 20% of essential expenditures are for non-food requirements, together with the previous assumption that these groups are 75% market-orientated, it was assumed that 75% of 80% of expenditures would be for food purchases, i.e. 60%. A similar set of assumptions were used to hypothesize the expenditure patterns of the subsistence farmers, namely 20% food and 80% non-food. Food and non-food price indices were then derived from government data (Quarterly Digest of Statistics, 1988) and the two weighted deflators calculated.

In calculating income terms of trade, the principal issue requiring some explanation concerns the income estimates for the producer/labourer category. Given that in southern areas the use of both casual and permanent labour is apparently much more widespread than in the north, it was assumed that the estimate of average earnings represented the wage income for the southern workers, and an average of the latter and the minimum wage was a close approximation of wage income for the northern workers, i.e. reflecting a lower labour demand. It was also assumed that workers found work for an average of 5 months per year. This estimate is based purely on anecdotal evidence and may well be an overestimate, but it should be remembered that the category included a minority of permanent labourers. Table 1.9 outlines the trend in net barter and income terms of trade pertaining to the various groups.

Table 1.9. *Net barter and income terms of trade*

Year	1980	1981	1982	1983	1984	1985	1986	1987
				(1979	= 100)			
Barter								
Group								
A	60	86	65	61	56	106	130	175
B	94	82	92	132	109	88	94	117
C	135	137	156	210	123	97	83	109
D	91	76	90	139	95	71	75	90
Income								
Group								
A	79	96	84	106	79	98	124	187
B	07	97	101	157	110	90	105	141
C	128	116	132	203	113	79	78	100
D	107	102	111	201	103	72	90	143
E	107	93	86	89	96	111	118	147
F	109	83	81	91	102	105	120	172

Source: Computed from Giri and Oku (1988), IFAD (1988), *Quarterly Digest of Statistics* (1988).
Note: No indices for barter have been presented for groups E and F, since these would be the same as for groups C and D respectively.

In some respects the barter indices should be treated with caution, since they do not reflect the powerful influence of changing weather conditions on quantities produced. In other respects, however, the implications of the table are straightforward and as might be expected following the analysis of commodity price trends in section II. Cocoa smallholders suffered declining terms of trade throughout the preadjustment period, a trend which has been reversed subsequently. For food producers the impact of the drought is apparent, although for the subsistence-orientated farmers for whom a higher proportion of expenditure is on non-food items, the post-adjustment period has proved substantially less advantageous than the years prior to the reform programmes. These figures reinforce the widely held view that terms of trade moved relatively in favour of food producers prior to adjustment, and that the process has been reversed as a consequence of the reform programme. It is worth emphasizing, however, that amongst food producers it is subsistence-orientated farmers who appear to be most disadvantaged and that these groups are likely to be amongst the poorest of the rural population.

This view is reinforced by reference to the income terms of trade. The figures are misleading to the extent that, using constant product weights, the impact of the drought on farmers' income is not correctly represented. For example, the positive income trend between 1981 and 1983 is certainly incorrect. The table is interesting, however, for the differences between groups which it demonstrates. It reinforces the view that, in the short term at least, it is food producers, particularly of non-traded staples, who are most likely to have been disadvantaged by the adjustment process, while producers of traded goods, particularly exportables, have seen their potential incomes increase relative to 1979. Interestingly, the wage-earning categories of part-time farmers, presumably because of the scarcity of labour in many rural areas coupled with the impact of an increasing minimum wage, fare better than the subsistence-orientated smallholders.

The principal ways in which the economic reform programme might, in the short run, be expected to impact on rates of return are through changes in the exchange rate, and in tariffs and other impediments to trade. The impact of these on the groups considered here can be discussed as follows. Given that at equilibrium the domestic prices (Pi) facing any hypothetical producer will be equal to world prices, the difference between the two represents the degree of distortion. Over time this difference will change, inter alia, in response to the exchange rate and the tariff structure.

Given $Pi = Pi^*(1 + t)$

where Pi = the domestic price set or weighted average price by producer i, Pi^* = the weighted average using world prices for the tradable commodities and t = equivalent rate of tariff,

then $Pi/Pi^* = (1 + t)$

Changes in the ratio will reflect the impact of changes in the tariff structure affecting the various groups.

Table 1.10. Pi/Pi^* measurements

Year	1979	1980	1981	1982	1983	1984	1985	1986	1987
Group
A	0.34	0.46	1.74	2.12	0.84	0.27	0.77	0.36	0.36
B	1.04	0.98	1.10	1.09	1.11	1.07	1.08	1.06	1.10
C	0.98	1.00	1.01	1.02	0.99	1.00	1.03	1.00	1.01
D	0.99	1.03	1.04	1.03	1.04	0.99	1.01	1.03	1.01

Source: As for Table 1.9.

In the case of taxes on exportables in the form of export taxes or restrictions, this would result in a ratio of < 1, while for importables positive tariffs would lead to ratios of > 1. The calculations suggest that the influence of the reform programme on tariff structures has been generally very slight, as borne out by the discussions in previous sections of this study. The anomalies which occur for cocoa producers in 1981 and 1982 are due to domestic prices failing to reflect sudden and substantial falls in world prices during these two years.

The influence of currency depreciation on rate of return can be described by the ratio Pi^*/Pi^{**}, where Pi^* is as above and Pi^{**} refers to price calculations using, where appropriate, shadow exchange rates (for information on shadow rates see Table 1.2). The results are given in Table 1.11.

Table 1.11.   *Pi*/Pi** measurements*

Year	1979	1980	1981	1982	1983	1984	1985	1986	1987
Group
A	0.15	0.14	0.09	0.04	0.04	0.21	0.16	0.48	0.54
B	0.87	0.99	0.91	0.90	0.99	0.98	0.93	0.93	0.98
C	0.91	0.98	1.00	1.00	0.99	0.98	0.93	0.96	0.98
D	0.93	0.99	0.98	0.93	0.98	0.97	0.97	0.98	0.99

Source: As for Table 1.9.

As would be expected, the influence of exchange-rate depreciation is close to zero for the subsistence farmers whose producing patterns are largely dominated by non-tradables. Even for food-crop producers there appears to be little influence, reflecting the way in which the hypothetical producer was constructed. In reality, the influence is likely to be greater for maize or rice producers than for those marketing yam or cassava. Nevertheless the data suggest that the reform programme has had significant implications only for producers of exportables, a conclusion reflected elsewhere in this study.

The above analysis would facilitate stronger conclusions if detailed information had been available regarding expenditure patterns and costs of production. Nevertheless, using the expenditure deflators as a proxy, a tentative conclusion to be drawn is that, with the exception of the cocoa producers, the potentially positive implications of the first phase of the ERP have, to a large extent, by-passed the categories considered in this study. Given the influence of the adjustment measures on consumer expenditure and therefore inter-sectoral terms of trade, it is likely that for the largest category at least, i.e. the subsistence farmers, the implications have so far been marginal and, for some amongst them, even negative.

The above calculations give an indication of the impact of the reforms on the income side of household accounts. With regard to expenditures, information which would facilitate evaluation of the impact of the reform programme on the relevant *consumption profiles* is largely unavailable. Some general statements can be made, however, which point assessment, on balance, towards a negative conclusion. In the first place it should be noted that devaluation of the cedi, and the consequent increased availability of foreign exchange, coupled with the elimination of the many restrictions governing the import of consumer goods, greatly increased the supply of consumer goods to the rural areas. This, if anecdotal evidence is to be believed, has acted as a positive incentive to rural producers, as well as promoting the diversity of consumption patterns.

Availability, however, does not necessarily imply accessibility, and the obverse of devaluation is the increased prices of imported consumer goods, such that they become increasingly outside the purchasing range of the rural poor. The ratio of food to non-food prices, as demonstrated in Table 1.12, is witness to this reduction in purchasing power.

Since the start of the ERP prices of non-food items have risen substantially more than food prices. It might be argued that the food/non-food ratio is a product of the increased demand manifest for consumer semi-durables consequent upon rising rural incomes, but it is questionable to what extent these have risen. A major influence on the trend is likely to have been the weather, but since the reversal in trend is also closely correlated with the exchange-rate policy introduced as part of the adjustment

Table 1.12.   *Food and non-food price indices*

Year	1980	1981	1982	1983	1984	1985	1986	1987
					(1979 = 100)			
Food	166	339	455	1,073	1,191	1,102	1,326	1,634
Non-food	157	336	375	833	1,426	1,732	2,113	2,670
Food/non-f. ratio	106	101	121	129	84	64	63	61

Source: Adapted from IFAD (1988).

process, it seems reasonable to conclude that the ERP has also contributed to a decline in smallholder purchasing power.

To the extent that these conjectural remarks reflect the real situation, it could be assumed that the relevant consumption profiles have become more orientated towards food consumption than before. Given the scarcity of consumer items prior to adjustment, however, it is likely that there has been little change in the consumption patterns of the poorer sections of the population, particularly of the rural poor.

At the same time, if consumption patterns have changed little, and for some of our categories incomes have either stagnated or declined, it is safe to assume that, given certain requisite items of non-food consumption, these households now consume less of them. A qualification to this conclusion is that households previously consuming 'non-essential' social goods, such as education and medical care, may now find such commodities beyond their reach.

VI.   CONCLUSIONS

The principal conclusion to be made concerning the impact of the economic reform programmes in Ghana is that, while some short-term goals have been achieved, the longer-term objective of extending the benefits to all Ghanaian citizens may prove far more intractable. In particular, although some of the categories considered in this study have undoubtedly benefitted from the economic recovery programmes, others have not. Indeed, they have probably become worse-off. Whether they would have prospered in the absence of the reforms, however, is a different matter, since the economy was, in any case, on the point of collapse.

The macroeconomy

The reform programmes are most advanced where they have tackled macroeconomic issues, and it is here that most apparent success can be observed. Real GDP has risen consistently, and the exchange rate has been brought very close to what is likely to be an equilibrium level. In fact, the massive devaluation has been achieved while inflation has been controlled. This in itself is quite an achievement, although helped by the fact that imported goods prior to adjustment were not only in short supply, but, when available, were frequently sold internally at prices reflecting the parallel rate of exchange. To some extent, however, this space may have been used up, and the inflationary impact of future currency depreciation may prove more difficult to contain.

Reform of fiscal policy has also proved relatively successful. While some success has been recorded in revitalizing the incentive structures as described by income differentials, and in restructuring the tax system, the fiscal deficit has fallen significantly as a proportion of GDP. Serious efforts have also been made to improve the structure of government expenditure. Domestic credit expansion has been kept within reasonable limits as, concurrently, has government domestic borrowing. At the same time, foreign borrowing has increased substantially. Against such a backdrop, the relatively sluggish growth in export expansion, especially given that this is a priority of the programme, is a cause for concern.

As regards employment, the retrenchment in the public sector was no doubt necessary and will continue. Overall it is likely that unemployment has risen in spite of an increase in demand for agricultural labour. Against this, real wages have risen, partly as a result of adjustments in the minimum wage, and partly owing to growth in demand. It is likely, however, that the latter is localized and specific primarily to cocoa-producing areas.

Sectoral issues

More pertinent to the interests of the study is the extent to which the macroeconomic changes have impacted at the sectoral and household levels. The analysis of product markets at the sectoral level was hindered in some respects by lack of data, for example by the absence of border-trade information. In some cases a degree of inaccuracy can result when the assumption is made that exchanges involving imported commodities are made at official market rates rather than at parallel rates. Nevertheless, the results are broadly what might be expected. Real price ratios have moved in favour of tradables relative to non-tradables, and in favour of exportables relative to importables, the latter reflecting the quantitative restrictions placed on imports.

With regard to sector-specific actions, the most notable achievements are those in the cocoa sector, where producer incentives have improved and the declining trend in output has been reversed. Whether incentives have improved sufficiently to foster the desired upturn in output, which in the long run depends on an increase in replanting, is not at present clear. The current tailing-off in the rate of increase, while partly owing to climatic factors, also suggests that incentives must improve further if they are to restore the confidence of cocoa farmers. With regard to non-cocoa export crops, it would appear that any initiatives have so far been few and far between, and consequently have had little or no appreciable impact.

There are considerable short-run gains to be had from revitalizing the cocoa sector. This can be viewed as a short-term strategy to provide the necessary resources through which more sustainable growth can be achieved. To this end price incentives have been increased dramatically (following the massive devaluation), and the results in terms of marketed production are moderately encouraging. Further reorganization of cocoa marketing may result in the possibility of further incentives, if the savings made are passed on to producers in the form of higher prices. The strategy of export-led growth can only work in Ghana, however, if the short-term room for manoeuvre provided by the regeneration of the cocoa sector is used to promote alternative foreign-exchange earning activities. The future for cocoa on international markets appears less than encouraging, and it is likely that any substantial increase in Ghana's cocoa production will serve more to drive down world prices than to raise foreign-exchange earnings. The implications of the past failure to diversify the sources of export earnings, therefore, and the apparent current lack of success in this respect are particularly disturbing. Diversification must be the medium-term strategy if the current surge in economic growth is to be maintained. In this respect, the rapidly increasing debt-service ratio adds greater poignancy.

Monetary policy pursued since 1983, involving a gradual reduction in the element of subsidy in rates of interest, has probably served to place formal credit sources even further beyond the access of small farmers, as witnessed by the increasing disparity between potential demand and actual supply of credit. Information concerning informal credit arrangements is notoriously difficult to acquire, but it is possible that an increasing number of smallholders have been forced to resort to the relatively costly informal sector. This trend coincides with rising costs of inputs consequent upon devaluation and partial removal of subsidies. Thus, outside the cocoa sector, there has been no improvement in incentives for technical innovation, even though there has been an increase in the availability of many inputs.

The intended privatization of fertilizer distribution, to coincide with the removal of remaining subsidies, is a subject of some controversy. While existing distribution practices leave much to be desired, it is questionable whether the incentives currently exist for the private sector to supply the many remote areas of the country, where distribution is costly and demand currently weak. These incentives may decrease even more following the elimination of the subsidy and a further fall in demand.

The impact on smallholders and the rural poor

While real prices have risen for cocoa producers, and the terms of trade between tradables and non-tradables have moved in favour of the former following the macroeconomic reforms, any stimulus to the rural economy resulting from higher incomes of those producing tradables would appear to be currently too weak to ameliorate the situation facing the bulk of rural households, who do not produce export crops nor have access to invigorated labour markets. It is not that the majority of these households merely remain untouched by the adjustment process; for many, particularly those generally classified as subsistence-orientated, there appears to be a growing discrepancy between the cost of essential purchases and household purchasing power.

In terms of the groups demarcated in this study, those smallholders with access to cocoa-producing land appear to have benefitted from the shifts in relative price patterns brought about by the recovery programme. Moreover, the increase in demand for labour in cocoa-producing areas, and the knock-on effect this has had on labour supply and therefore wage levels in non-cocoa-producing areas, has benefitted those part-time farmers from the producer/worker category. However, while the improved inter-sectoral terms of trade faced by cocoa producers have had some impact on employment prospects for rural labour, the nature of this impact is to some extent reduced by the shortage of land in the traditional cocoa-growing areas, and blurred by migration to the Western Region. Outside these areas, the effect has been slight, although a general labour shortage persists. The availability of land in most districts, however, coupled with the low per acre returns achieved by the majority of smallholders, particularly food-crop producers, means that the demand for labour is limited by its high opportunity cost, and remains a constraint both to expansion of farm activity and to improved employment opportunities.

Estimates of gainers and losers are based on hypothetical estimates of net-barter and income terms of trade. Although attempts were made to take account of likely cost increases these have not been based on actual farm costs. While the subsistence-orientated farmers appear to have been disadvantaged by the relative price changes, with the partial exception of those producing cassava, the study's findings may in fact underestimate the degree to which they have been squeezed by relative price shifts.

Given the necessity of hiring labour even on the smallest farms, their position may, in fact, have deteriorated further than the study indicates, if account is taken of the higher wage levels.

The findings indicate that generation of higher smallholder incomes, both in the non-cocoa-growing districts of the south, and in the north, would further stimulate demand for labour, leading to multiplier effects benefitting producer/workers. There would be a coincidence of interest if this were to coincide with the essential macroeconomic pre-requisite of export diversification through promotion of alternative export crops, and through agricultural import substitution. Despite the lack of information regarding smallholder activity, access to credit and input supplies, and prices actually received and paid for essential purchases, it is clear that these groups still need to be integrated more closely into the growth process. The adjustment effort will ultimately fail in its objectives if this is not achieved, i.e. if smallholders currently orientated towards subsistence production as well as part-time farmers do not benefit from, and therefore contribute to, the regeneration of economic activity.

References

Giri, R. and Oku, S. (1988) *Final Report on the Annual Sample Survey of Agriculture, Ghana, 1986*, Ministry of Agriculture, PPME, and UNDP/FOA Improvement of Agricultural Statistics Project GHA/84/003, Accra, November.

IFAD (1988) *Report of the Special Programming Mission to Ghana*, Vol. 1: main report, Vol. 2: annexes. Rome, April.

Loxley, J. (1988) *Ghana: Economic Crisis and the Long Road to Recovery*. North-South Institute, Ottawa.

Republic of Ghana *Quarterly Digest of Statistics (QDS)*, Various issues.

Republic of Ghana Ministry of Agriculture (1988) *Report of the Pilot Studies on Marketing Costs and Margins*. Department of Policy Planning, Monitoring and Evaluation, MOA March. (An FAO sponsored project).

Seini, W., Howell, J. and Commander, S. (1989) 'Case-study of Ghana' in Simon Commander (ed.). *Structural Adjustment and Agriculture: Theory and Practice*. James Currey, London.

Tabatabai, H. (1986) *Economic Decline, Access to Food and Structural Adjustment in Ghana*. World Employment Programme Research, Working Paper WEP 10-6/WP80, ILO, Geneva, July.

Appendix Table 1.1. *The cocoa sector*

	1980	1981	1982	1983	1984	1985	1986	1987
Prod. price (cedis/tn)	4,000	12,000	12,000	20,000	30,000	56,600	85,500	150,000
Real PP[a] (cedis/tn)	2,485	3,550	2,906	2,347	2,285	3,961	4,931	6,332
World price (cedis/tn)	7,142	5,698	4,780	7,293	79,859	135,000	185,760	292,824
Prod. price (US$/tn)[b]	1,455	4,364	4,364	5,797	900	943	950	1,020
Prod. price (US/tn)[c]	252	458	195	261	222	354	480	586
World price (US$/tn)[d]	3,285	2,597	2,072	1,738	2,114	2,391	2,250	2,064
Export unit price ($/tn)[b]	3,359	2,111	1,605	1,520	2,351	2,189	2,407	2,278
Exports[b] (000 tons)	211	190	239	159	150	172	195	198
Ratio (b)/(d)	0.44	1.68	2.11	3.34	0.43	0.39	0.42	0.49
Ratio (c)/(d)	0.08	0.08	0.18	0.09	0.15	0.11	0.15	0.20

Production by Region

	258	225	179	158	175	219	228	173
Total (000 tons)								
				Percentage				
Western	17.5	19.4	19.9	25.3	30.0	29.6	33.4	30.4
Ashanti	35.5	31.5	31.0	29.6	25.7	24.9	25.0	27.9
Brong Ahafo	18.5	22.1	19.7	18.7	16.5	16.7	14.3	15.9
Eastern	18.1	16.4	17.5	16.1	16.3	15.8	14.7	15.5
Central	9.9	9.8	9.9	8.7	10.9	12.6	11.8	9.3
Volta	0.6	0.8	2.1	1.6	0.6	0.5	0.8	1.0

Notes: (a) Real producer prices expressed in constant 1979 prices; (b) US$ at official exchange rates; (c) US$ at parallel exchange rates; (d) London spot market prices.

Sources: Bank of Ghana, *QDS*; IFAD (1988); FAO, *Commodity Review and Outlook* (various issues) for world prices and Cocoa Services Division for production data.

Appendix Table 1.2.   *World and border prices*

	1979	1980	1981	1982	1983	1984	1985	1986	1987
MAIZE									
World ($/tn)	116	126	131	110	146	124	111	87	79
Freight costs ($/tn)	17	31	36	30	20	21	21	21	18
Border prices									
Accra	366	433	460	384	573	5,120	7,151	9,634	4,588
Kumasi	609	784	1,108	951	2,220	7,765	10,769	14,278	20,528
Tamale	870	1,161	1,804	1,560	3,989	10,608	14,655	19,266	26,908
PADDY									
World price ($/tn)	334	434	483	294	277	252	217	210	230
Freight costs ($/tn)	28	45	54	46	30	30	30	30	25
Border prices (cedis/tn)									
Accra	994	1,317	1,477	936	1,057	9,402	14,820	21,600	37,555
Kumasi	1,156	1,560	1,909	1,314	2,191	11,211	17,300	24,759	41,605
Tamale	1,330	1,821	2,373	1,720	3,409	13,154	19,916	28,152	45,955
COCOA									
World price ($/tn)	3,285	2,597	2,072	1,738	2,114	2,391	2,250	2,064	1,992
Freight costs ($/tn)	26	47	54	44	30	31	32	31	28
Border price (cedis/tn)	8,962	7,013	5,550	4,659	7,190	78,682	133,080	182,970	288,904

Sources: World prices are taken from UNCTAD, *Monthly Commodity Price Bulletin* (various issues). Freight charges are estimated using information derived from FAO, *Food Outlook* (various issues) and are approximate, being adjusted accordingly.

Appendix Table 1.3. *Domestic prices for maize and rice*

	1979	1980	1981	1982	1983	1984	1985	1986	1987
MAIZE									
Local transport costs (cedis/tn)									
From Accra									
Kumasi	243	351	648	567	1,647	2,646	3,618	4,644	5,940
Tamale	504	728	1,344	1,176	3,416	5,488	7,504	9,632	12,320
Bolgat	729	1,053	1,944	1,701	4,941	7,938	10,854	13,932	17,820
To Accra	340	491	907	794	2,306	3,704	5,065	6,502	8,316
Adjusted wholesale prices (cedis/tn)									
Accra	1,700	4,092	7,569	7,895	38,190	23,144	20,175	32,588	53,168
Kumasi	1,459	3,513	6,576	6,779	32,790	19,871	18,322	27,980	45,649
Tamale	1,168	2,810	5,261	5,423	26,232	15,897	13,858	22,384	36,519
PADDY									
Local transport costs (cedis/tn)									
From Accra									
Kumasi	162	243	432	378	1,134	1,809	2,457	3,159	4,050
Tamale	336	448	840	728	2,184	3,472	4,760	6,160	7,840
To Accra	336	448	840	728	2,184	3,472	4,760	6,160	7,840
Adjusted wholesale prices (cedis/tn)									
Accra	2,854	6,043	11,154	20,689	62,301	67,918	52,705	67,564	106,028
Kumasi	3,026	6,407	11,826	21,936	66,054	72,010	55,880	71,633	112,415
Tamale	2,511	5,315	9,810	18,197	54,794	59,735	46,355	59,424	93,253

Sources: Local transport costs are derived from single-year estimates presented in MOA/FAO March 1988, calculated for other years using the CPI transport and communications index (QDS, 1988). Wholesale prices for each city are derived from average national prices. Provincial data are available for the year 1987, and the proportions of the national average for that year used to adjust the data for the remaining year. All price data were supplied by the MOA.

2

KENYA

ARNE BIGSTEN
& NJUGUNA S. NDUNG'U

I. ECONOMIC OVERVIEW

The period up to 1978

Kenya gained independence in 1963, but already in the 1950s the peasants had been allowed to grow cash crops, the White Highlands had been opened up, and extension services had been organized. This commercialization of smallholder agriculture led to a rapid increase of production.

After Independence agricultural growth expanded even more rapidly. Most of the remaining restrictions on smallholder agriculture were lifted. Substantial amounts of previously European lands were transferred to African farmers, and large resources were devoted to land registration and adjudication. High-yielding cereals were introduced and there was a push to increase the shares of high-value crops also in smallholder production. Fiscal and monetary policies were on the whole cautious during the 1960s. Government revenues were growing rapidly, and the expenditure programme, which focused particularly on education, stayed within the limits of the resources available and was generally well run. The 1960s may thus be characterized as a period of successful economic development with a GDP growth rate of over 6% per annum, fiscal balance, low inflation, and a stable exchange rate.

Kenya first experienced balance-of-payments problems in 1971 owing to falling terms of trade and expansionary budgets. Import controls, credit restrictions, some price controls and a more restrictive budgetary policy were instituted, resulting in a large drop in private investment. The credit constraints were later lifted, but price and import controls were largely retained. In 1973 oil prices quadrupled and there was a 30% increase in other import prices. At the same time export volumes fell. Credits from the International Monetary Fund and the World Bank as well as bilateral aid financed part of the large external deficit.

Rapid inflation set in 1974. GDP growth was down to 2.8% in 1975, the lowest since Independence, and imports and investments fell drastically. In Sessional Paper No. 4 of 1975 the government's strategy for coping with the crisis was spelled out. To improve the external balance the currency was devalued by 14%, an export subsidy of 10% was instituted, and the import controls were tightened. There was now a recognition of the need to use fiscal policy actively in the stabilization effort. However, by 1976 the coffee boom eased the pressure, and the degree of restraint was

Table 2.1. Shares of GDP

	C	I	G	X	M	F	Tr	Tx	S	S-I	G-Tx	X-M + F + Tr
1979	63.6	12.3	30.1	26.4	32.4	-2.8	1.6	28.2	7.0	-5.3	1.9	-7.2
1980	61.1	16.5	33.8	28.7	40.0	-3.2	2.1	27.6	10.2	-6.3	6.2	-12.5
1981	60.8	15.9	31.7	26.3	34.7	-3.2	1.4	29.6	7.9	-8.0	2.1	-10.1
1982	62.2	12.4	29.3	25.9	29.8	-3.3	1.1	29.3	5.5	-6.9	0.0	-6.9
1983	60.1	13.1	27.3	26.1	26.6	-3.3	2.0	29.7	8.9	-4.1	-2.4	-1.8
1984	60.0	13.7	27.4	26.7	28.1	-3.5	2.4	25.3	13.3	-0.3	-2.1	-2.5
1985	63.1	12.0	26.0	25.9	27.0	-3.7	3.2	25.9	10.5	-1.5	0.1	-1.6
1986	59.1	13.4	27.3	26.0	25.9	-3.6	2.9	25.7	14.4	0.9	1.6	-0.6
1987	61.0	15.2	28.8	21.2	26.2	-3.8	2.7	25.8	12.0	-3.2	3.0	-6.2
1988	60.6	15.0	29.5	21.8	26.9	-4.1	4.0	27.4	12.1	-3.0	2.2	-5.1
1989	60.1	15.2	29.5	23.4	29.2	-4.3	4.6	28.7	10.6	-4.6	0.8	-5.4

C Consumer expenditure
I Gross private domestic investment
G Total government spending
X Exports of goods and services
M Imports of goods
GDP Gross domestic product at market price
F Net factor incomes from abroad

Tr Net transfers from abroad
Tx Total revenue
S Private savings
(S-I) Net flow of private savings into the financial market
(G-Tx) Government demand for financing
(X-M + F + Tr) Foreign sector's demand for funds to finance deficit

Source: Government of Kenya, Statistical Abstracts, Economic Surveys.

small. With a 16% improvement in the terms of trade (due to the commodity boom), ideas for restructuring the economy were abandoned. It was decided that the increased prices for coffee and tea were to be passed on to the peasants, who received the full world price apart from deductions for marketing and processing. After a certain period government revenues as well as public expenditure increased.

Real GDP growth in the three years 1976–8 was on average 6.8%. Income growth shifted towards the agricultural sector, but the industrial sector also grew dramatically – by over 14% a year. This was partly owing to the easing of import controls which brought in needed inputs, to the more expansionary fiscal and monetary policy, and to a building boom. Considerable import-substituting investment was undertaken.

During 1978 it became clear that the boom was over and that policy changes were needed. The liquidity ratio was increased from 15 to 20%, interest rates were raised, and a cash ratio was imposed. These measures failed, however, to stop the banks, whose funds were very liquid, from lending to the private sector, and investment reached record levels, growing by 21% in 1977 and 18% in 1978. The familiar policy of tightening import controls was pursued instead, but it was not sufficient to halt the decline in foreign reserves.

The period from 1979

Between 1978 and 1980 coffee prices fell to normal levels, while there was a second oil price shock in 1979. Moreover, large quantities of food had to be imported because of a drought. The year 1979 was thus a difficult one, but until the oil price hike the economy was still growing, with a GDP growth rate of 5%. With the oil price increases, however, the deficit surged to 12% of GDP. The government had not previously been heavily dependent on external loans and grants to finance its budget, but in the period 1978–81 this increased from 10 to 15%. Table 2.1 shows a fiscal deficit in 1979 of 1.9% of GDP. This implies that the total revenue was not sufficient to finance government expenditures on consumption and investment. Thus all budgetary transfers (unrequited transfers and interest payments) had to be financed plus the fiscal deficit. According to our estimate the deficit including transfers was 5.2% (see Table 2.2).

Once again the government chose to postpone adjustments, and relied on foreign borrowing. The first tranche of a standby from the International Monetary Fund had already been drawn at the beginning of 1979. After the oil price increase the government managed to obtain a World Bank loan, balance-of-payments support from some bilateral donors and a large commercial Eurodollar loan. A programme was agreed with the IMF in August 1979, which included measures to improve tax revenues, real reductions in government spending, a 15% ceiling on the expansion of bank credit to the private sector, a policy of wage restraint (implying reductions in real wages), careful control of public debt, and an import deposit scheme.

However, the course of events soon took another direction. The policy package agreed with the IMF was not adhered to. In mid-1980 the government was refused its IMF credit. Simultaneously, it made a major effort to raise revenue and to restrain credit. The 10% sales tax was increased to 15% on most goods and to 25–30% on luxuries.

Although the balance-of-payments situation was critical, growth remained above 4% in 1980. Agricultural output fell, but industry and public services continued to

Table 2.2. *Public sector deficit components, 1979–89*

Year	Fiscal surplus	Unrequited transfers	Domestic interest	Foreign interest	Total transfers	Total deficit	Deficit % of GDP
1979	−43.94	29.4	27.8	17.5	74.7	118.6	5.2
1980	−163.30	41.1	31.5	26.5	99.1	262.4	10.0
1981	−64.32	51.2	52.1	41.2	144.5	208.8	6.9
1982	+0.12	46.0	78.2	54.0	178.2	178.1	5.3
1983	+90.90	58.0	98.6	64.4	221.0	130.1	3.4
1984	−93.46	48.6	115.4	69.4	233.3	326.8	7.7
1985	−4.19	57.4	148.4	82.4	288.4	292.6	6.1
1986	−90.57	53.4	186.2	93.7	333.3	423.9	7.3
1987	−199.83	59.4	255.0	105.9	420.3	620.1	9.5
1988	−165.03	61.8	278.2	138.7	478.7	643.7	8.6
1989	−72.08	62.4[a]	320.2	164.3	546.7	618.8	7.3

Note: (a) Estimated.
Sources: GOK, *Statistical Abstracts, Economic Surveys.*

expand at a fairly high rate. Money supply accelerated again, and inflation was about 12% (see Table 2.3).

The overall budget deficit reached its peak in 1980 as shown in Table 2.2, partly due to falling government revenues, but even more to the large increase in expenditure during the coffee boom. This proved hard to reverse, largely owing to the fact that the public sector workforce had increased. It has turned out to be difficult to reduce current expenditures, particularly on salaries, and easier to abandon or postpone capital projects.

The large fiscal deficits of the early 1980s led to an acceleration in domestic money creation and inflation. Although the economy was still growing, the basis for this growth was being eroded because of the huge external and internal deficits. The serious consequences of public debt on the growth of government interest payments are shown in Table 2.2.

To pave the way for a structural adjustment loan the government put forward Sessional Paper No. 4 of 1980 on *Economic Policies and Prospects* and the 1980/81 budget made a start in the implementation of its proposals. Import controls were liberalized and interest rates increased. It was difficult, however, to carry out the proposed incomes policy and the government was reluctant to introduce new tax measures. It was also extremely difficult to contain government spending. A new credit was negotiated with the IMF in October 1980 with laxer policy conditions except on one point: it was agreed that import policy was to be changed from quantitative restrictions to tariffs. However, government expenditures increased faster than budgeted, partly due to a 30% increase in civil service salaries and the food shortage, but even more to poor budgetary control, primarily caused by the erosion of budgetary procedures during the coffee boom.

The improvements in the external balance in 1981–3 were brought about by domestic measures, while the external effects continued negative until 1982. It was increases in investment and government expenditures that brought the trade balance under pressure in 1980. There was a drastic cutback in imports from 1980 to 1983.

In spite of the large deficits on the current account in 1979 and 1980 the government refused to devalue. However, the precariousness of the food situation continued in

Table 2.3   *Growth of money supply and the inflation rate (% changes), 1979–89*

Year	Monetary Base	Broad Money	Inflation
1979	21.3	16.1	8.4
1980	10.3	−1.1	12.8
1981	7.2	13.3	12.3
1982	22.9	16.1	22.3
1983	−2.2	4.9	14.5
1984	9.7	12.9	9.1
1985	20.2	6.7	10.7
1986	37.9	32.5	5.7
1987	13.6	11.2	7.1
1988	8.3	7.9	10.7
1989	15.1	12.9	10.5

Definitions:

Monetary Base – Public holdings of currency plus bank holdings of deposits at the Central Bank.

Broad Money – Currency in circulation plus all deposits except those of the Central Government and Non-Resident Banks.

Inflation Rate – Average price increases in Nairobi.

Source: GOK, *Economic Surveys*.

1981, and more food imports were necessary. Exports stagnated, and even with a drastic reduction the current account deficit was still large in 1981. In the second half of the year the reserves were more or less depleted and had to be restored by borrowing from the Eurocurrency market. Belatedly, the government conceded a measure of liberalization under pressure from both the IMF and the World Bank and devalued the currency.

The IMF and the World Bank became the most important sources of foreign exchange. In contrast to many other African countries, Kenya managed to develop a reasonably good relationship with the IMF, but that with the World Bank was at times strained. The negotiation of the two Structural Adjustment Loans (1980 and 1982), containing among other things conditions relating to trade policy, was difficult, and the second SAL of 1982 was interrupted when the conditions could not be met. In January 1982 a third standby agreement with tougher conditions was reached with the IMF. Again there were restrictions on government borrowing and a reduction of the budget deficit from 10.6 to 5% of GDP. Commitments for medium-term trade liberalization were also agreed and devaluation was made a precondition. But the agreement was soon suspended; by the middle of 1982 bank credit to the government had broken through the agreed ceiling.

In the 1982 Report and Recommendations of a Working Party on Government Expenditure there was extensive discussion of public sector inefficiencies, particularly the problems of the parastatal organizations and the Treasury's inability to exercise adequate financial control in this area. This was the first explicit recognition by the government that something drastic had to be done about the imbalance in the economy. The 1982–3 budget announced that 20% of the items on the quota-based import schedule would be removed, but this was never implemented because of the growing foreign-exchange crisis. The individual scrutiny of import licences was reintroduced in mid-1982.

The abortive *coup* of August 1982 led to a considerable capital flight, and in turn sizeable policy changes. Three weeks after the attempted *coup* President Moi spelled out the government strategy (GOK, 1982). This included reintroduction of the export compensation scheme, reduced government investment in development projects and enterprises, support for private industry and the development of agriculture, and a curtailment of expenditure to reduce the budget deficit. There was a strong commitment to get the macroeconomy under control.

The current account deficit was now beginning to come down. New reductions in both private investment and government expenditures contributed to this improvement, while private consumption grew again. Private savings fell drastically between 1980 and 1982 and inflation soared to over 22%. The long-term capital inflow was reduced considerably.

The political disturbances made it difficult to fulfil the conditions of the 1982 agreement and in 1983 a new IMF standby agreement of SDR 179.5m. was signed, conditional on a further devaluation, increases in agricultural prices, reductions in bank lending and reforms in credit policy. This was the first programme for several years actually to be implemented; with regard to the budget deficit the government performed better than targeted.

The exchange rate regime was changed back from a fixed rate against the dollar to a more flexible rate pegged to the SDR; in practice the policy has been one of a crawling peg. Interest rates were raised to a positive level in real terms. Since 1982 Kenya has tried to keep real interest rates positive, but nominal rates continued to be rigid and attempts were made to control the banks through liquidity ratios, and 'nonbanks' through other asset requirements.

The budget deficit was gradually brought under control. By 1982–3 there was a fiscal surplus. Credit to the central government was the driving force behind money supply growth up to 1982; money supply growth was reduced and inflation fell to 14.5% in 1983. Capital formation had declined and investments were squeezed out of the government budget during the crisis. The ratio of development to recurrent expenditure fell from 44% in 1979/80 to 21% in 1982–3.

By 1983, the current account balance was again under some control, but only through drastic cuts in imports. This had inevitable effects on growth potential; GDP growth fell to under 2%, and per capita incomes in real terms fell. Agricultural production continued to grow, while manufacturing stagnated. Public sector growth had also slowed down. By 1983 the government had thus managed to get both the budget and the basic trade deficit under reasonable control, but debt-service charges were now much larger. Growth prospects were therefore bleaker than before. Capital formation ceased to fall, but in both 1982 and 1983 its share of GDP was lower than at any time since 1975.

In 1984 Kenya was hit by the worst drought since the 1930s. Agricultural production fell by as much as 3.9% and this in turn depressed growth in the rest of the economy; GDP growth fell to a mere 0.8%. The government distributed imported food to the affected areas to avoid famine. It chose not to reduce the foreign-exchange allocation to manufacturing, which managed to maintain relatively satisfactory growth. Later in the year there was a mini-boom in tea, which brought in much-needed foreign exchange.

The following February a new standby agreement was signed with the IMF for SDR 85.2m., to alleviate the consequences of the drought. Among its conditions were restraint on expenditure, stronger price incentives, export orientation, import liberalization, and the retention of a competitive exchange rate.

The after-effects of the drought took the form of a substantial drop in coffee output in 1985. There was also a fall in livestock production due to the decline in herds the previous year. By mid-1985, however, the country was getting through the worst of the crisis and the government began to consider long-term issues. Sessional Paper No. 1 of 1986 (on *Economic Management for Renewed Growth*) set out its goals and the structural reforms and guidelines for achieving them. The Paper contains extensive discussion of fiscal and monetary policies, the rural-urban balance, food security and agriculture, trade and industry. By this time finance to support stabilization and adjustment had been negotiated with the IMF, the World Bank and the United States Economic Fund. The government now felt that the short-run problems were under a measure of control and that some progress had been made in reorienting the economy. It argued that it was time to look further ahead, and noted that the most urgent problem was to renew economic growth.

The extensive foreign borrowing to sustain imports and growth in the late 1970s and early 1980s and the expensive IMF loans meant a rise in the debt-service ratio from 5% in the mid-1970s to over 30%. Nevertheless Kenya has incurred no arrears on its current payments and has not been forced to renegotiate its external debt in the Paris Club. In the budgeting process debt service has first claim on revenues.

In spite of the proclaimed change in exchange-rate policy, the effective rate of the shilling did not depreciate initially. Instead it was allowed to appreciate by 4-5% a year during 1983 and 1984. In 1985, however, the effective rate was gradually adjusted downwards again, and since then there has been a real depreciation of some 5% a year with the black market rate only marginally above the official rate.

From 1982 the declared aim was import liberalization, but it was not until 1985 that any real progress was made. Kenya has a system of different tariff schedules for different commodities. In June 1985 a number of items were shifted to less restrictive schedules, and in 1986, though there were no further shifts, there was still some liberalization because the schedules were administered less tightly.

Between 1980 and 1985 the share of government expenditure in GDP fell from 34 to 26%. Debt-service charges rose markedly and personnel expenditures increased. Outlays on salaries as a share of recurrent expenditures increased from 47% in 1979/80 to 60% in 1984-5. This has had serious consequences for efficiency in the public sector. There was a reduction in fixed capital formation, transfers to parastatals and non-wage operating and maintenance expenditures. It has been difficult to find efficient ways of cutting the development budget. Small funds are now spread thinly over a large number of projects, and delays are frequent. Efforts are being made to rationalize the parastatals, and to divest some investments to the private sector and improve the performance of the rest. Progress in this process is slow, however. The share of government expenditure in GDP has crept up to about 30% again.

A drought in Brazil in 1985 caused coffee prices to rise by about 40% between 1985 and 1986. Together with falling oil prices this led to an improvement in the balance of payments and a rise in economic growth to 5.5% in 1986. The accumulation of reserves enabled the repayment of part of the outstanding IMF debt. The boom was short-lived, however, and did not have the dramatic consequences of the 1970s.

In 1986 there was a record maize harvest, followed, however, by a new decline in 1987 because of poor rainfall in some parts of the country. For example, maize production fell by 25% and wheat by as much as 34%. Real coffee and tea prices also fell, leading to a serious foreign-exchange situation. Import schedules were again restricted. In 1988 the system was reorganized and liberalized to a certain extent.

The overall budget deficit increased in 1986, to some extent due to specific factors, namely the cost of holding the All Africa Games in Nairobi and the bumper harvest. The National Cereals and Produce Board was obliged to buy the surplus at the guaranteed price, which required the allocation of large funds. The government also decided to allow the private sector to buy 20% of the crops marketed outside the regions where they were grown. This was to be undertaken mainly by co-operatives, but they were also short of money. Nevertheless, there have been significant movements of food around the country in recent years.

Inflation, which went up to 22.3% in 1982, had fallen to 5% by 1986, a surprisingly good result bearing in mind that the currency had been allowed to depreciate. Private savings again increased to a respectable level. During 1986 there was a crisis of confidence in the financial sector, which meant that it sold government debt, a proportion of which was thus monetized. This, together with the coffee price increases, led to a rapid increase in money supply. During the second coffee boom few new fiscal initiatives were taken, but there was a built-in stabilizer in the progressive coffee tax.

In 1988 and 1989 the rains were good and the availability of inputs improved. Changes in marketing arrangements increased efficiency somewhat, with payment delays reduced to some extent, although some parastatals are still highly inefficient. The prices of coffee and tea increased slightly in 1988 from the very low 1987 levels, but in 1989 they fell again. For the fifth consecutive year there was a GDP growth rate of about 5% in 1989, which is quite impressive given the collapse of coffee prices. Imports expanded quite rapidly with liberalization, which meant that both agriculture and industry could expand at a relatively high rate. The level of investment was quite high during the last three years of the decade, although a substantial part of it was financed by foreign savings.

The overall budget deficit, according to official estimates, came down in 1987/8 to 4.1% of GDP, from 6.6% in 1986/7. Since then it has fluctuated between 4 and 5%. The external balance has weakened somewhat due to slow export expansion, lower coffee prices, rapid growth of imports, and higher oil prices. Given the heavy debt-service burden, the foreign-exchange constraint seriously affects growth. It may be noted, however, that Kenya has managed over the last few years to improve the terms of payment of its foreign debt significantly, which has contained the growth in debt service. The average interest rate on government loans and government guaranteed loans is now as low as 2.9%, while the grace period is longer than it used to be. There was a standby and Structural Adjustment Facility (SAF) arrangement with the IMF covering 1988–90.

Experiences with Structural Adjustment Loans

The Kenyan authorities have implemented successive stabilization and structural adjustment programmes. IMF conditionality has been directed towards curtailing the budget deficit, restraining public borrowing from the banking system, and re-establishing the external balance. To achieve this the IMF has tried to secure a range of fiscal and monetary reforms, among them higher interest rates, trade liberalization, wage restraint, a realistic exchange rate, increased taxation and reductions in both development and recurrent expenditures.

While the IMF has emphasized general measures, the World Bank has focused on more specific forms of conditionality, for example incentives for infant industries, export promotion schemes, agricultural pricing and marketing arrangements, land and population policies, supervision of agricultural schemes, forward budgeting in the public sector, and the curtailment of investments in parastatals and public companies.[1]

By the mid-1980s the World Bank found the results of the structural adjustment programmes disappointing. The reasons identified were that only the Ministry of Finance was really committed to the programmes, that they were too complex to be viable, that external shocks made them difficult to sustain and that there was too little consultation with the private sector. The Bank therefore decided to disaggregate further structural adjustment lending into a series of sector operations, more sharply focused on key sectoral issues and intended to facilitate inter-ministry co-ordination and commitment. The first of these sectoral adjustment credits was the Agricultural Sector Operation, which had some success, and was followed by a second agreement.

Project implementation has faced great problems in Kenya because of limited absorptive capacity. Net disbursement from the World Bank fell from US$125m. in 1982 to minus $36m. in 1986, but it has since increased again. The Bank has scaled down some investment projects to conform with the government's capabilities. There is now an emphasis on better donor co-ordination and more effective use of technical assistance and pilot projects in designing investment projects.

The first Agricultural Structural Adjustment Operation of 1986 amounted to SDR52.8m., and the first payment was approved in March 1987. The money has been used to finance imports of fertilizers, pesticides, petroleum, agricultural machinery, spare parts, and transportation equipment. The programme had five components:

Agricultural inputs supply: The aim was to increase the use of fertilizers by smallholders through improving the mechanisms for its allocation and distribution. A new pricing formula based on world market prices was adopted. User charges for livestock services were also increased.

Producer incentives and marketing: Here the objective was to maintain attractive producer prices for domestic products, to increase price flexibility, to speed up payments to farmers, to reduce consumer subsidies, and to begin to deregulate agricultural markets.

Budget rationalization: More of the government budget was to be allocated to agriculture and this was to be done in a more rational way.

Parastatals: The objective was to reduce the share of parastatals in public expenditure by divesting some enterprises, restructuring others and strengthening management. The major changes to grain marketing have, however, occurred with the support of the European Community through the Cereals Sector Reform Programme.

Agricultural credit: The aim here was to rehabilitate and restructure the Agricultural Finance Corporation which is involved in providing credit to farmers. Over the years it has gone mainly to large-scale farmers, and the programme was intended to extend credit facilities to smallholders.

In general it seems that Kenya, like many other countries undertaking adjustment, has found it easier to implement price-related than institutional reforms. In Kenya it may be argued that prices of crops, credit and foreign exchange are now reasonably realistic, but the institutional reforms are still progressing slowly. There has been modest progress in the reform of parastatals.

[1] Hecox (1986) provides a useful summary of the various structural reforms requested by the major donors.

The relationship between the government and the World Bank is still good, although the Bank is worried about the slippage in economic policy-making. A major problem is the lack of fiscal control. The Bank eventually wants to shift to traditional lending, but so far the balance-of-payments situation has turned out to be worse than expected, and this has made it difficult. Export promotion should therefore be a top government priority in the future. One of the major problems arises from the fact that industrialists have been overprotected so far and find it difficult to meet competition. The newly-established Export Processing Zones may lead to some inflow of investments from, say, Hong Kong by investors wanting to escape export quotas. The value added in these operations will not be large, however, which means that it is imperative to continue the drive to increase exports within the normal system.

With regard to the Industrial Adjustment Loan, the World Bank is of the view that the Kenyans have nearly achieved their goals. Imports have been liberalized and attempts have been made to improve the investment climate. With regard to the financial sector operation, which is combined with substantial technical assistance, the government has more than lived up to its commitments. New legislation is being enacted regarding banks, the capital market, and the supervision of the system by the Central Bank. Alternatives to credit ceilings to regulate the credit market are being considered. Technical assistance is also being given to the development finance institutions.

In parallel with the policy changes, the rural sector has also been affected by some institutional reforms. The District Focus for Rural Development and the Informal Sector Development Programme have become essential elements in the government strategy regarding rural-urban balance. Various measures are being undertaken to support smallscale suppliers and contractors as well as efforts to develop technical training in the rural areas. A municipal surcharge is being introduced to strengthen the local tax base.

To sum up, important policy changes have taken place during the 1980s. The fixed exchange-rate regime has given way to a flexible system with frequent adjustments. Low interest rates have been replaced by rates above the rate of inflation. The budget deficit was brought under some control by 1983 through measures which increased revenue and through expenditure controls, but since then has increased again. There have also been institutional changes including parastatal reforms and a shift of emphasis in planning towards the district level. The consequences for smallholders of the various shocks and policies will be considered below.

II.   IMPACT OF POLICY CHANGES ON THE AGRICULTURAL SECTOR

Basically there are three different categories of poor people in the rural areas: smallholders, pastoralists and the landless. None of these groups is homogeneous. The dominant group is the smallholder category, and this is far from uniform even in specific agro-climatic zones. Smallholders differ by holding size, the extent to which they have non-farm incomes, and their degree of market orientation. Pastoralists are found in the semi-arid or arid zones. The landless can be found in all areas. This category contains both very poor day labourers and wealthy businessmen plus government employees. Collier and Lal (1980) estimated that landless households constituted 11% of rural households, but that only 7% could be considered poor.

Fiscal changes which may affect smallholders include reductions in the provision of public services as well as a deterioration in their quality, largely owing to a lack of money to cover running expenses. The importance of this may be difficult to measure. Reductions and changes in the orientation of public investments may also affect smallholders. In the attempt to restore budgetary balance various taxes have been raised, the incidence of which is not easily determined. Nevertheless, it is likely that increases in indirect taxes on consumer goods will have a considerable impact on the poor. In general, changes in monetary policy affect smallholders via increased real interest rates, and more specifically if there are changes in the availability of agricultural credit. And everybody is affected by inflation, resulting from a number of influences such as fiscal and monetary policy and exogenous shocks.

With regard to trade policy, the major change affecting smallholders has been the variations in the exchange rate. Since the majority of exports are produced by the agricultural sector, depreciations tend to benefit the sector as a whole. Import contraction as a result of the foreign-exchange shortage has, of course, also affected smallholders. A liberalization of import controls should bring down domestic prices of imports and import substitutes which will benefit them.

A crucial issue for smallholders is the prices they receive for their products. It should be noted here, however, that efficient marketing organization is also essential. For example, delays in payment are a serious problem for many smallholders.

Furthermore, it should be pointed out that smallholders in Kenya are involved in a whole range of off-farm activities, which means that they also suffer when the rest of the economy faces a downturn.

In this section we shall investigate what the impact of policy changes has been on the well-being of smallholders. Since we do not have a full-scale model, it is difficult to separate the effects of different policy changes. We have to content ourselves with an analysis of changes in the major variables, and a tentative discussion linking these to changes in policies. We look first at relative price changes for the different economic sectors. We then examine the changes in the prices of agricultural products, inputs, and goods that the rural population buys, and what this implies for rural terms of trade. Thirdly, we consider whether adjustment programmes have meant any major changes in the provision of economic and social services and whether adjustment has meant cuts in human capital-enhancing expenditures. Finally, we discuss the effects on capital accumulation and, thus, the longer-term prospects.

Sectoral changes in relative prices

In analyses of adjustment one often wants to determine the impact on the real exchange rate, which may be defined as the relative price between tradables and non-tradables. This is common in Dutch Disease models, where exportables and importables are grouped together into a composite category – tradables. However, in an economy like that of Kenya, where there are considerable trade interventions, this is not an appropriate strategy. Here one needs to distinguish between importables and exportables, since the domestic relative price of the two tradables is not constant.

For a conceptual framework, we shall use the three-sector model outlined in Collier (1988).[2] It is assumed in the model that there is sufficient wage and price flexibility to maintain full employment. The analysis is of a comparative static nature, and not much can be said about disequilibria or dynamic changes. This is illustrated in the relative price space in Figure 2.1. On the vertical axis we measure the ratio of the domestic prices of exportables (Px) to those of importables (Pm). Trade liberalization

---

[2] This is an extension of a model by Dornbusch (1974).

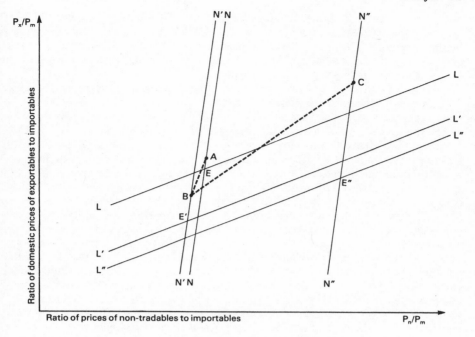

Figure 2.1.   Price ratios of exportables and non-tradables to importables

would lead to an increase in this ratio, while higher tariffs or stricter quotas would lead to a fall in the relative price of exportables. On the horizontal axis we measure the price of non-tradables (Pn) relative to the domestic price of importables (Pm). Implicit in these two relative price ratios is a third relative price, namely that of exportables to non-tradables. There are thus three relative prices in the model, two of which are independent. The NN line is the locus of equilibrium points in the non-tradables market, given real income, money balances, and the capital stock in the sector. It has a positive slope which is greater than a ray from origo (see Collier, 1988, pp. 2–3). To the right of NN the non-tradables market is in excess supply, while it is in excess demand to the left. The LL curve is the locus of equilibrium points in the monetary market, given real income, asset demand and money supply. Below LL the money market is in excess demand, since the price level is too high. One can see this by comparing a point on the LL curve with a point vertically below it. Since P_x is fixed, both P_m and P_n must be higher below LL than on it. Thus in aggregate the prices are higher. Above the LL curve the money market is in excess supply. The intersection of the two lines at E represents the full equilibrium of the model.[3]

The domestic price of exportables is determined by world market prices, the exchange rate and export subsidies or taxes. The domestic importables price is determined by the world market price, import controls and tariffs. The relative price P_x/P_m is thus determined by international terms of trade and trade restrictions. The

[3] We assume that LL and NN hold even if other markets are in disequilibrium, that is, NN is taken to represent market clearing values even when the money market is out of equilibrium.

non-tradables price is determined by domestic demand, which is a function of fiscal and monetary policies, and supply. The real relative price P_n/P_m is thus determined by the exchange rate and domestic macroeconomic policy. Disequilibria in an economy like that of Kenya may be caused by, for example, terms-of-trade shifts or by fiscal and monetary expansion.

We now need to classify commodities in the above-mentioned categories. This is difficult, since this is not a breakdown found in the national accounts. Nevertheless, we derive proxies which come as close as possible. The definitions are given in Table 2.4, where the respective price series and relative prices are shown.

Can we now tell the Kenyan story with the help of these ratios? First of all, we distinguish primarily between two distinct phases, 1979–82 and 1983–8. (In 1989 there was again a new situation, but this is only briefly touched upon in the discussion.) The first period is characterized by a fall in the price of exportables relative to importables, caused by an exogenous fall in the external terms of trade because of increasing import prices and more restrictive quotas during this period. The fall in real income caused by the terms-of-trade loss also negatively affects demand for non-tradables, whose relative prices also fall.

The changes are illustrated in Figure 2.1. We start in the late 1970s at A with a situation characterized by excess supply of money, that is, an external deficit. The full equilibrium at this point would be E. Kenya then experiences a severe terms-of-trade deterioration, due mainly to higher import prices, which reduces real income. This shifts NN to N'N'. At the same time there is an expansionary fiscal and monetary policy, shifting LL to L'L'. Because of the exogenous price changes on imports and a more restrictive trade policy, both P_x/P_m and P_n/P_m fall. We move from A to B, which is below the radius from origo to A since P_x/P_n declines. At B we are still not in equilibrium (would require E'), but have a current account deficit.

However, we did not start from an equilibrium situation and a considerable part of the price changes in the early 1980s was an overhang from the coffee boom. The coffee boom led to price decreases for both non-tradables and import substitutes, reflecting the investments it induced. Runs with a CGE-model (Bevan et al., 1990) show that the boom was responsible for the increase in capital goods prices and the long-run decrease in the prices of non-tradables and importables.

Economic policies were expansive also after 1983, and this tends to shift the money market equilibrium further downwards (to L"L"). The increase of real money balances leads to increased demand for non-tradables, which means that the non-tradables equilibrium locus shifts from N'N' to N"N". We thus get a situation with excess demand for non-tradables, which leads to an increase in their relative price. At the same time there is trade liberalization, which means that there is a considerable increase in P_x/P_m. We thus move north-eastwards to C in 1988. The figure illustrates a situation with equilibrium in the non-tradables market, but an excess supply in the money market and thus a balance of payments deficit. There is still need for policy changes in the trade or fiscal and monetary fields to restore a viable long-term equilibrium (E" in the figure).

Finally, in 1989 Kenya faced falling terms of trade owing to falls in the coffee price, which means that the economy shifted southwest in the figure again (not shown). The relative price shift in favour of agricultural exportables that had been achieved since 1982 was undone in one year. Unless the external terms of trade improve again, demands on the adjustment policy will be even harder.

Table 2.4 Price indices

Year	P_{xt}	P_{mt}	TOT	P_{ms}	P_{mm}	P_n	$P_a = P_x$	P_x/P_{ms}	P_n/P_{ms}	P_x/P_n
1979	100	100	100	100	100	100	100	100	100	100
1980	120.4	131.1	91.8	112.1	120.0	109.9	107.5	95.9	98.0	97.8
1981	132.8	166.6	79.7	124.3	153.8	121.5	116.4	93.6	97.7	95.8
1982	145.9	191.5	76.2	138.3	184.8	135.1	127.5	92.2	97.7	94.7
1983	175.1	245.1	71.4	145.0	253.1	157.3	138.5	95.5	108.5	88.0
1984	210.4	250.8	83.9	157.2	258.8	173.5	151.2	96.2	110.4	87.1
1985	207.3	296.8	69.8	168.9	323.2	192.0	168.5	99.8	113.7	87.8
1986	221.9	281.5	78.8	177.3	304.8	218.0	181.3	102.3	123.0	83.2
1987	183.9	285.3	64.5	190.3	339.9	235.5	219.3	115.2	123.8	93.1
1988	211.6	314.1	67.4	207.5	399.0	261.3	239.4	115.4	125.9	91.6
1989	227.7	379.2	68.5	269.7	484.0	298.6	252.9	93.8	110.7	84.7

Prices: P_{xt} – total exports
P_{mt} – total imports
TOT – international terms of trade
P_{ms} – domestic manufacturing taken here to be the proxy for import substitutes
P_{mm} – manufacturing imports
P_n – non-tradables
P_a – agriculture, here considered the proxy for exportables, is a very imperfect one since some products in the sector are obviously import-substitutes.

Notes: Import and export prices are for products, while the remaining ones are GDP deflators and thus for value added. Non-tradables include building and construction, wholesale and retail trade, restaurants and hotels, transport, storage and communication. In the following section we shall use another price deflator for agriculture, which gives slightly different results.

Sources: GOK, Statistical Abstracts, Economic Surveys.

Changes in smallholder incomes

What did these changes imply for the smallholders, who are our main concern here? During phase 1, up to 1982, farmers as a group tended to lose from the fall in the relative price of exportables, which are mainly agricultural. Subsequently, during phase 2, they gained from the reverse of the trend for exportables. This was due to the depreciation of the Kenya shilling; the relaxation of trade controls also contributed to the reduction of rents in the import-substituting sector. To determine the impact of the increase in the relative price of non-tradables relative to importables is not easy. Finally, in phase 3, that is 1989, the fortunes of the smallholders were reversed again, but it is to be hoped that this is just a temporary setback.

What, then, can we say about the effects on agricultural production of these relative price changes? If we compare the relative development of agriculture (see Table 2.5) we find that no significant quantity effect can be observed from the favourable relative price shift in the second period. This is not surprising, since production is also dependent on a range of other factors, notably the weather and changes in the institutional set-up. For example, in 1984 Kenya was hit by the worst drought since the 1930s. Nevertheless, since then agricultural production has expanded reasonably fast.

An analysis of the effects of adjustment on different socio-economic groups also needs to consider how factor markets are affected. One may theoretically illustrate the effects of shocks and adjustment on factor incomes with the help of the simple Figure 2.2, which shows isocost curves for the three commodities, exportables (XX), importables (MM), and non-tradables (NN). We assume that exportables is the most labour-intensive commodity, while importables is the least labour-intensive.

The initial equilibrium is at E_0, where the three isocost curves intersect. The effect of a terms-of-trade shock, because of higher import prices, is illustrated by a shift of the MM curve to $M'M'$. Higher wage-rental combinations are possible in the importable sector. The new equilibrium will be at E_1 when P_n has also risen shifting NN to E_1. At this new equilibrium wages have fallen relative to capital rentals. It is the resource reallocation out of exportables into importables and non-tradables which leads to lower wages. The negative terms-of-trade shock thus hurts households selling labour. If we assume that capital is sector-specific and cannot be reallocated, then the effect on wages will be ambiguous (at least in the short run). Capital owners in the

Table 2.5 *Population and sectoral production indices at constant prices*

Year	Population	GDP	Agric.	Manuf.	Non-tradables
1979	100	100	100	100	100
1980	103.9	103.3	98.7	105.2	105.1
1981	107.9	110.1	104.7	109.5	114.0
1982	112.2	112.7	109.5	112.0	109.0
1983	116.5	116.2	114.2	117.0	109.5
1984	121.1	117.3	109.9	122.1	111.3
1985	125.8	123.1	113.9	127.6	117.0
1986	130.7	129.8	119.5	135.0	124.5
1987	135.8	136.0	124.1	142.7	131.5
1988	141.1	143.0	129.5	151.3	139.2
1989	146.6	150.2	134.6	160.2	143.8

Sources: GOK, *Statistical Abstracts, Economic Surveys*.

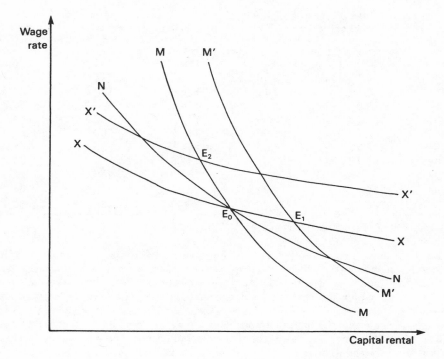

Figure 2.2. Isocost curves for exportables (XX), importables (MM) and non-tradables (NN)

exportables sector will definitely lose, while those in the two other sectors will gain.

In phase 1 (as well as 3), we would thus expect wage-earners to lose. In the short run capital owners in the exportables sector lose, but gain in the long run if capital can be reallocated. If the specific factor is land, which is the case in smallholder agriculture, it is not possible to reallocate even in the long run. Smallholders will therefore lose both as wage-earners and land-owners.

With a policy of adjustment with devaluation, we would instead have a shift of the XX curve to, say, X'X', which would lead to a shift of the equilibrium point to E_2. In this case we would have higher wages and lower capital rentals.

If we also assume capital (or land) to be sector-specific we see that owners of specific factors in the exportables sector will gain, while the effect on wages will be ambiguous. Smallholders will thus in this case tend to gain as wage-earners (at least in the long run) and as land-owners.

We have seen that in phase 2 policy changes mean that relative prices of exportables were increasing and should thus tend to be more beneficial to smallholders. However, along the transition path there may be unemployment, with negative welfare consequences. The reduction of non-tradables production may imply reduced government services, which also may affect welfare negatively.

We now need to see if the actual changes in Kenya correspond to those outlined in the theoretical model. We have seen that from 1982 to 1988 relative price changes tended to benefit agriculture, and that production was growing relatively fast after 1984. Table 2.6 shows how the prices directly relevant to smallholders have changed since 1979.

Table 2.6   *Indices of agricultural prices*

Year	Agr. output	Purch. inputs	Rural cons.	Prices paid	Agr. TOT
1979	100	100	100	100	100
1980	108.1	110.8	112.3	112.0	96.7
1981	118.4	123.1	130.6	128.8	91.6
1982	129.6	146.3	158.0	155.2	83.7
1983	147.2	152.4	179.8	172.4	85.3
1984	168.4	183.0	211.7	204.0	84.2
1985	177.3	176.5	244.5	226.4	78.7
1986	194.7	180.2	252.6	233.2	83.2
1987	191.9	189.5	265.0	245.7	77.8
1988	215.4	212.7	282.1	263.8	81.3
1989	225.2	229.2	290.6	280.4	80.1

Sources: GOK, *Economic Surveys.*

We first show the general price index for agricultural produce. According to this prices increased somewhat more rapidly than according to the GDP deflator. One may assume that the index used here is the more accurate one. We also observe a break in 1982, after which producer prices increased more rapidly than the costs of purchased inputs. In an analysis of welfare effects one should also consider the price changes of the goods the household purchases for consumption. One must thus take the pattern of consumption into account; a household consuming a big share of importables and non-tradables tends to lose when their relative prices go up.

When we take into account the prices paid by smallholders on the consumer goods they buy the picture worsens. Using an aggregate of input and consumer goods prices we see that the terms of trade of agriculture declined quite rapidly up to 1982. They then fluctuated until 1989. These data corroborate the picture drawn above with a first phase up to 1982, when the relative prices for farmers deteriorated significantly, and a second phase up to 1988, when the situation changed for the better.

The output price index in Table 2.6 shows the development of average agricultural prices, but different smallholders produce different product mixes. Nevertheless, the prices of major cash crops such as coffee, pyrethrum, and cotton have increased at a slower rate than the price of maize, and this relative price shift within agriculture would tend to benefit the poorer farmers or those in the less fertile regions (see Bigsten, 1980).

What, then, can we say about the development of smallholder agriculture since 1979? Using GDP estimates we see from Table 2.5 that aggregate agricultural production grew by over 35% between 1979 and 1989. The smallholder share in marketed production did not, however, increase over the same period. It is, therefore, unlikely that smallholder production grew by more than 35% between 1979 and 1988. Since the population, over the same period, grew by 47%, smallholder per capita production should have declined by about 10% in real terms. We have also seen that the agricultural terms of trade probably declined over the same period, so in terms of purchasing power the decline was even larger than 10%. It should be noted, however, that the price changes have been more beneficial to smallholders since 1982 than they were before then.

With regard to the development of different kinds of producers, it seems as if over the period in question it was the cash-crop producers who experienced the slowest development in prices. Since these are mostly the better-off it is possible that the poorest farmers suffered less income decline than the better-off smallholders.

However, Kenyan smallholder families do not live only on income from their own farms (Bigsten, 1985). They also also have a range of other income-generating activities. It is, therefore, vital for them that the rest of the economy flourishes. The level of wage employment has increased substantially between 1979 and 1989, while real wages have fallen. Agricultural employment in the modern sector, which is of particular importance to smallholder families, actually fell up to 1983. Since then it has increased again to a level above that in 1979.

Changes in the public sector

The development of public services is shown in Table 2.7. In total, service production increased over the period by about 61%, that is, faster than the growth of population. There has been a very rapid increase in the provision of educational services. Health services have expanded approximately on a level with population growth, while the provision of agricultural services has stagnated. On the whole, it still seems that the government has chosen to maintain and expand human capital-enhancing expenditures.

However, the situation may not be as good as these figures suggest. Throughout the 1980s employment in the public sector has been maintained and even increased, thus a decreasing share of the budget has gone to working capital. This has meant decreasing service efficiency in many institutions. For example, the health institutions have been plagued by shortages of drugs, particularly in the rural areas.

Table 2.7.   *Indices of growth of production of education, health, agricultural, and total government services, 1979–89, at constant prices*

Year	Population	Education	Health	Agr.s.	Total
1979	100	100	100	100	100
1980	103.9	109.4	106.4	98.8	105.6
1981	107.9	113.2	109.7	110.1	111.2
1982	112.2	116.8	116.8	116.1	115.4
1983	116.5	120.2	122.6	123.0	120.3
1984	121.1	127.1	124.2	123.6	123.5
1985	125.8	137.7	127.3	123.2	129.8
1986	130.7	151.9	133.5	103.3	133.7
1987	135.8	162.5	141.1	100.4	141.7
1988	141.1	172.8	139.2	109.8	151.6
1989	146.6	194.2	142.5	119.0	160.7

Sources: GOK, *Statistical Abstracts, Economic Surveys.*

Service provision has been kept up, but from 1981 the rate of investment in the public sector fell. In the course of two years, its share in GDP fell from 5 to 2.5%. In the last few years, however, public investment has picked up again. Of the services considered here, education has fared best, while both health and agricultural service investments are still far below the 1979 level. The share of recurrent revenue in GDP has fallen considerably over the period in question. Changes in the structure of revenue are modest, so there is no reason to suppose that there have been significant negative incidence shifts towards the smallholders.

Table 2.8.   *Capital formation by sector*

Year	Agric.	Manuf.	Private Non-tradables	Total
1979	100	100	100	100
1980	100.4	80.0	106.2	111.0
1981	104.0	79.7	95.3	116.6
1982	83.1	48.7	75.0	91.8
1983	71.1	58.8	72.2	79.2
1984	65.6	50.3	83.8	75.0
1985	82.5	47.8	76.7	85.1
1986	87.3	61.5	94.4	95.2
1987	95.5	65.7	102.3	100.9
1988	97.5	82.5	89.1	108.6
1989	77.4	79.6	73.7	110.3

Sources: GOK, *Statistical Abstract*, 1985, 1987; *Economic Survey*, 1989, 1990.

Changes in capital formation

Finally, we must mention briefly what has happened to investment in the major sectors we are concerned with in our macro framework. The development of investment at fixed prices is shown in Table 2.8.

We note that investment in all three sectors has fallen in real terms. Agricultural investments, for example, were 23% lower in 1989 than in 1979, although it should be remembered that in 1979 Kenya was in the midst of an investment boom owing to the effects of the coffee boom. Nevertheless, the decline in investment will tend to slow down future growth.

III.   SMALLHOLDERS AND THE RURAL POOR

The smallholder population

About 82% of the total population of Kenya live in the rural areas, and almost 70% are to be found on small holdings. As noted earlier, a significant part of the rural population not defined as smallholders are pastoralists, but, unfortunately, very few systematic data exist concerning them.

There is a female dominance among the smallholder population, reflecting, among other things the extensive migration of male household members (see, for example, Bigsten 1988). The Integrated Rural Surveys of 1974–79 also show that about half of the smallholder population is less than 15 years old, while about 6% is over 60. This gives a high dependency ratio, with serious implications both for family welfare and for the national economy.

The average household size for smallholders is about 7 persons (IRS 1), with the Coast province having the largest size (8 persons). Smallholders in Central province are best provided with educational facilities, while the situation is worst in the Coast province. Differences in younger cohorts are much less, but the human capital distribution among provinces is still uneven.

The distribution of heads of household by main occupation in 1978/9 (see Appendix Table 2.1) shows that 71% were occupied in agriculture, while the rest were employed in a range of activities. In this respect, Central province was the most developed and best diversified, with only 56% employed in agriculture. The table also reveals that a large fraction of rural households own no land at all, and that Central, Nyanza, and Western provinces are the most land-scarce regions. Differences in land quality need, of course, to be taken into account, but in the densely populated regions there is hardly any new land to be brought into production and increased output must come mainly from increased productivity.

Apart from land, the major asset of smallholders is livestock (see Appendix Table 2.1). It is particularly in the Rift Valley that we find households with large herds, as would be expected. In the densely populated Central and Western provinces smallholders cannot keep large herds of livestock. However, grade cows are much more common in the more developed regions, and this means that the distribution in terms of values is different from that given in the table.

Structure of incomes and activities

Appendix Table 2.2 shows the absolute incomes in 1976 of the respective types of households. Income from self-employment dominates, but wages are a very important source of income for smallholders in most parts of rural Kenya. Estimates of the labour usage pattern (in the 1970s) show that about 15% of the male labour force work outside agriculture, as compared with only 3% of women. The demand for agricultural labour fluctuates seasonally particularly in the smallholder areas, and this determines its price. At weeding or harvesting peaks smallholders have to pay a considerably higher wage than the annual average. In the coffee and tea zones there is a more or less uniform wage.

Appendix Table 2.3 shows how incomes vary with the type of employment of the head of household. On average 80% of household heads have no other work than on their own holding, about 10% have another rural job, while about 9% are engaged in government and urban employment. Families with a head in the wage labour market are generally better-off. On the whole, own-farm income makes up about 57% of total family income, but this varies a lot between regions. In the Coast province only 25% comes from the farm, while the proportion is as high as 71% in Nyanza. These diverse patterns are important determinants of how changes in various sectors of the economy are transmitted into income changes among smallholder families.

More up-to-date information from the Rural Household Budget Survey of 1981/2 (see Table 2.9) shows that own-farm income constitutes the most important source of income, but that it represents less than half the total income for the rural population. The data are not, of course, restricted to smallholders. It is also noteworthy that savings are positive in all districts and that they are quite high. This may to some extent represent an underestimation of expenditures, but it should also reflect a real savings potential in the rural areas which can be and is used for investment. The average share of farm income in total income was 48%. The high figure for Kajiado (83%) should be treated with some caution, however.

We now look in greater detail at the data for 1982 pertaining to Central and Nyanza provinces, the two most important smallholder regions in Kenya containing about half the smallholder population. Bevan et al. (1989) showed that, in general, when the holding size is small, more land is used for crops and less for grazing, and a certain area is always set aside for subsistence crops. It was concluded that the land-use

Table 2.9. Income and expenditure levels (Kshs/month)

District	Farm Enterpr.	Non-Farm Enterpr.	Salary and Wages	Other Sources	Total Inc.	Total expend. cons.	Savings
Lamu	249	118	226	71	663	245	418
Kwale	312	145	422	59	937	627	310
Taita Taveta	371	141	134	186	832	522	310
Machakos	431	145	210	79	864	563	301
Kitui	439	112	123	121	795	395	400
Meru	491	206	147	131	975	625	350
Embu	514	256	183	239	1,191	638	553
Nyeri	489	172	191	149	999	699	300
Murang'a	323	186	159	192	860	611	249
Kirinyaga	351	240	158	227	975	587	388
Kiambu	282	185	351	168	986	722	264
Nyandarua	682	275	155	258	1,369	600	769
Nakuru	373	62	141	43	618	480	138
Nandi	639	96	225	60	1,020	494	526
Kajiado/Narok	1,389	50	191	44	1,674	668	1,006
Kericho	556	103	156	37	852	433	419
Uasingishu	545	101	178	62	886	488	398
Trans Nzoia	519	53	227	34	834	463	371
Baringo/Laikipia	545	71	104	24	744	502	242
W. Pokot/E. Marakwet	318	87	165	67	637	357	280
S. Nyanza	232	102	104	57	496	441	55
Kisii	302	265	158	241	965	442	523
Kisumu	183	104	172	77	536	479	57
Siaya	202	69	43	64	379	377	2
Kakemega	229	100	140	130	600	474	126
Bungoma	407	107	258	69	842	511	331
Busia	238	109	94	120	561	362	199
Average income	399	140	177	114	829		

Source: GOK, Economic Survey, 1988.

pattern is fairly stable over holding sizes, income levels and characteristics of head of household.

Regarding the income structure by per capita income quintiles, Nyanza shows a falling share for food crops as incomes increase, which is what one would expect. This is not the pattern in Central, however. In both provinces, absolute per capita food-crop income increases by income quintiles. Since the proportion of food crop sold does not increase by quintile, this implies that the better-off households in Central grow more of their food themselves and/or that they are better fed than the poorer households. Cash-crop income increases both absolutely and relatively from lower to higher quintiles. Livestock income is almost equally important for all quintiles.

Smallholders generally diversify into self-employment in Nyanza, while in Central it is more important for the top quintiles. For wage incomes the pattern is reversed. Wage income is a strongly differentiating factor in Nyanza, while in Central all quintiles seem to obtain a similar share of their income from wages. Finally, remittances are equally important to all quintiles in Nyanza, while they seem to matter somewhat more to the poorer households in Central.

In Central no significant correlation could be found between holding size and per capita income, but there seems to be a positive correlation in Nyanza. This may be due to the fact that it is easier to use surplus household labour outside the holding in Central than in Nyanza, and that it is less of a drawback to have a low land/labour ratio. Income patterns reveal, as expected, that households with large holdings draw a large share of their income from farming, while those with little land have a higher proportion from non-agricultural sources.

Migration is very extensive in rural Kenya, with, as noted earlier, a distinct difference between male and female migrants. The reason for male migration is mainly to look for a job or to take up a job offer, and the more educated the migrant the more important these reasons become. For the less well educated males, land shortage and marriage also matter a great deal. For female migrants, on the other hand, marriage is the dominant reason, although job search is important for those who are well educated.

Remittances are the major economic consequences of migration. Temporary migrants remit more than permanent migrants, which is hardly surprising since they have retained their ties with their households and expect to return home. Temporary migrants are reported to have remitted 21% and 17% of their income respectively for Central and Nyanza. Those in the top quintile remit larger sums in absolute terms, but the percentage does not vary systematically by income quintile; the remittance of something like a fifth seems to be fairly general.

One of the main concerns of this study is the extent to which the rural economy is monetized or commercialized. Bevan et al. (1989) found that in Central 45% and in Nyanza 56% of crop income is consumed on the farm. The percentage for livestock is also very much higher in Nyanza, but its measurement is uncertain. As one would expect, the subsistence element is larger for the poorer households.

The discussion so far has been confined to sedentary farmers. There is far less information about pastoralists. However, studies have been carried out in some areas; for instance, Herren (1988) has done a study of pastoralists in Laikipia district. He finds that 45% of all households are very poor (less than five cows), 11% are poor (5-10), 23% are in a medium category (10-20), 13% are rich (20-80), and finally 7% are very rich (over 80 cows). He also shows the extent of the losses incurred in the 1984 drought, ranging from 72% of the erd for the rich to 86% for the poor. Even in 1987 the herds of the rich were 42% smaller than before the drought, while those of the poor were 77% smaller. The community has not yet recovered and the income differentiation has increased, since the poorest were hardest hit.

Given the reduction in income subsequent to the livestock losses, there has been increased diversification of income sources, although the process was already under way before the drought. Poor households, in particular, must look to other sources of income. Local activities like brewing, charcoal burning and petty trade are quite common, and there is some limited scope for work in the local administration. However, labour migration has increased dramatically, especially since the drought. As many as 27% of household heads are absent, and remittances and non-herding income now dominate the income of many poor or very poor families. What this will imply for their future as cattle keepers is difficult to say. Herren expects that the next drought will further entrench these trends; it will then be impossible to help the poorer strata in the district through measures aimed at the pastoral sector.

A major policy dilemma in Kenya concerns the arid and semi-arid lands (ASALs). These make up the larger part of the country and contain about 20% of the population and 60% of the livestock herd. Land pressure in the more fertile areas is gradually pushing more people to this land. The ecology of the area is fragile, and it can not easily bear sedentary agriculture.

The burning issue is how to approach this problem. People living in the area are poor and need support. On the other hand, the more support the region is given, the more it attracts new migrants, and the harder becomes the pressure on resources. So far, no satisfactory answers to this dilemma are available.

The government has hopes that as much as 30% of future growth will come from this area. The elements of a strategy would probably contain measures aimed at upgrading the skills of the labour force and land and water resource protection and reclamation, coupled with improved technologies for dryland agriculture and grazing. The planners talk about dryland farming systems development, pastoral systems development, small-scale irrigation development, and local non-farm enterprise development. The World Bank (1988) reports, however, that projects in the region have had only limited success. This issue will be one of the major challenges in the 1990s.

The rural labour market

A recent report (Central Bureau of Statistics, 1990) gives some results from a rural labour force survey undertaken in 1988. Although the conceptual and measurement problems are considerable in the rural areas, an attempt has been made to apply the traditional methods. Work activities include wage work, work on the family farm, and work on non-farm business. It was found that virtually everybody was engaged in some form of work during the week of the survey. The participation rate for the 15–64 age cohort was 91.8% and 77% of children aged between 8–14 did some work during the period. Practically no open unemployment was reported, which may suggest that the traditional concept of unemployment is not so relevant in the rural areas.

About three-quarters of the respondents reported farm-related work during the survey period, while 21% of the males and 13% of the females reported wage work. It was further found that 11% and 8% respectively had worked in some non-farm own-business activity during the week.

The working week for the core group was about 40 hours for both men and women. Collection of firewood and water-fetching were included, but other household chores mainly done by women were excluded. Many members of the labour force reported that they would like to have another job, but that they were no longer searching. The main reason given was that there are no jobs available – normally referred to as the discouraged worker effect.

Access to land

There is a strong correlation between holding size and household income as shown in Table 2.10. It should be borne in mind, however, that there is also some correlation between holding size and family size which means that these figures overstate per capita discrepancies. It should also be noted that the group with no holding at all is not on average worse-off than those with little land; it also comprises people who have good jobs in the rural areas.

Table 2.10 also shows that land is the major differentiating factor, but that, on average, income from non-farm enterprises and remittances follows the same pattern. This implies that households with larger holdings diversify their activities. With regard to wage incomes, however, the picture is more omplicated, since this is the major source of income for those with little or no land. To bring about improvements for this category jobs must be created, a large part of which are, however, made up of work on other people's holdings, therefore a thriving agriculture also benefits this group indirectly. Smallholders are also dependent on what is happening in the urban areas. If the urban economy is flourishing they tend to receive more remittances, and there may also be some reduction in the labour force obliged to find an income in the rural areas.

Access to productive assets varies very much with the household's location in relation to major towns and with the level of agricultural development. For example, the purchase and use of agricultural inputs, which are highly correlated with productivity, are heavily dependent on the potential of the area. In high potential areas like Central and Rift Valley large quantities of inputs go into agricultural production.

Table 2.10. *Average net household monthly income (cash and kind) by source and size of holding (Ksh)*

Size of holding (acres)[a]	Farm Enterpr	Non-Farm Enterpr	Salary and Wages	Other Sources	Total
No holding	305	63	359	6	733
0.1–0.9	171	88	298	76	634
1.0–1.9	255	89	145	101	590
2.0–2.9	295	102	118	101	616
3.0–3.9	341	149	129	123	742
4.0–4.9	371	162	128	156	817
5.0–6.9	416	174	126	147	861
7.0–9.9	462	195	152	158	966
10.0–19.9	633	202	185	142	1,162
20 and over	1,100	265	219	185	1,770
Average income	399	140	177	114	829

Source: GOK, *Economic Survey*, 1988.
Note: (a) 2.47 acres = 1 hectare.
     The sample was about 2.8% of the rural population.

Consumption patterns

It is noteworthy that smallholder consumption varies much less over time compared with income. Of course, it is income from agriculture in particular that is unstable. We note, for example, from the Integrated Rural Survey that although incomes varied from negative (due to livestock losses) to over 8,000 Ksh, the total outlays varied only from 1,611 to 6,505 Ksh. Smallholders were obviously able to consume more than their income by running down assets or borrowing, while those with high incomes saved for investment or for bad years in the future.

A household's consumption expenditure pattern is influenced by the relative prices of goods and services it consumes and its income level. There are price differentials across regions because of transport costs, size of markets, and the marketing regulation of some commodities. There are also inter-regional differences in costs of production due to differences in, for example, rainfall, soil type and altitude.

With regard to the structure of rural consumption one finds that half of food consumption is purchased, and half own-produced. This is to some extent because smallholders do not produce all the kinds of food they consume, but with regard to, for example, maize, farmers are both buyers and sellers. In Central province the ratio between purchases and sales is 0.31 and in Eastern it is 0.36 (Akonga et al., 1987: 111). Smallholders do not often have storage capacity to keep their produce on the farm, but have to sell it immediately after harvest and buy it back later. According to 1974/5 estimates they spent 75% of their income on food, compared with 64% for rural households in 1981/2. Since the samples are different, it is not possible to say anything about the time trend.

The Household Budget Survey of 1981/2 showed a high degree of uniformity in the consumption structure across income categories. Food and non-alcoholic beverages took the lion's share of expenditure, followed by household goods, such as furniture, bedding, television sets, radios, and cooking stoves.

There are considerable subsidies for consumers in Kenya. They come in the form of subsidies to parastatals which are forced to sell at a loss. It is estimated that over the period 1979–84 they totalled Ksh 2 billion (Cleaver and Westlake, 1987: 32). The subsidy on maize meal is to be phased out as parastatal losses are reduced.

In 1987 both producer and consumer prices for beef were decontrolled. The retail subsidy on tea was reduced by 50%. There are still implicit subsidies on maize meal and vegetable oil.

The rural institutional structure

Price regulation is a central ingredient in agricultural policy. The Ministry of Agriculture undertakes annual price reviews for the major products, on the basis of which the government fixes prices at all points in the marketing chain. The Fourth Development Plan 1979–84 was the first explicitly to recognize the importance of agricultural prices as incentives. The need to use the parity pricing principle was mentioned as well as the importance of considering the long-run development of world market prices. The issue was again discussed in Sessional Papers No. 2 on *National Food Policy* and No. 4 on *Economic Prospects and Policies* of 1982, but the role of prices as a means of bringing about efficient resource allocation was hardly mentioned. However, in the Fifth Development Plan for 1984–9 (p. 178) the need for prices which guide the allocation of resources in the appropriate direction and the use of export or import parity pricing principles were explicitly recognized.

In recent years there have been improvements in the government's methods of setting prices for domestically consumed crops, which now satisfactorily reflect the principles of export and import parity agreed earlier. Official producer prices are now set at export or import parity price (mostly closer to import parity prices) plus transport costs. The inefficiency of the parastatals has meant, however, that producer prices have been squeezed. To remedy this parastatals could either be made more efficient or subsidized or consumers could be taxed. As already noted, the alternative of subsidies has been the course mainly pursued.

The fact that producer prices were previously kept low meant that production was held back. In 1980 weighted producer prices (except for sugar) were 24% below import parity prices, and this meant that farm incomes were 7% below what they would have been with import parity prices (Cleaver and Westlake, 1987: 26). This income loss accrued to the consumer in the form of lower prices and to the government in the form of reduced subsidies to the parastatals. However, by 1986 weighted producer prices (with the exception of sugar) were only 7% below import parity prices, which means that there has been a real shift in policy to the benefit of farmers.

Cleaver and Westlake estimated a model for agricultural production for the period 1972–84. They found that agriculture grew by 3.1% a year on average, and that the main positive factors were land expansion which accounted for an increase of 2.4% and producer price increases accounting for a 1% increase. They estimated that distorted prices had reduced farmers' share in GDP by 2.4% in 1980, but by 1986 this loss was down to 0.5%. Price distortions have thus been almost eliminated.

It is noteworthy that at the outset of the coffee boom in 1975–7 the estates produced more coffee than the smallholders, but ten years later the smallholders were producing two-thirds of the output. Smallholders thus reacted to the boom by increased planting, which in turn raised their production drastically by 1980/81. Since then there has been no trend towards increased output.

Land. At independence there were considerable areas of unused agricultural land in Kenya, and the impressive performance of agriculture since then has largely been based on an increase in the hectarage. There is scarcely any new land now available; increases in production in the future must therefore come mainly from increases in the output of existing land. To achieve this and to absorb the rapidly increasing population there is a need for increased specialization.

With regard to *marketing*, one can distinguish a formal and an informal system. Where food crops are concerned, the most important market outlets for smallholders are the local markets or small-scale traders, in other words, the informal system. For the major cash crops, only the official marketing channels matter. Most farmers in major smallholder areas like Central, Nyanza, and Western provinces have fairly good access to local markets and transport facilities.

Some 15 parastatals are involved in the marketing of agricultural output. The co-operatives are also engaged, and there are also a lot of private traders. The existing system of control has been criticized for its operational inefficiency and its distortions of resource allocation. Efficiency problems are particularly acute with regard to the internal food marketing system and the distribution of inputs. The distribution system for export produce is easier to operate and functions more efficiently than that for food crops.

The marketing boards have different roles for different crops. In some markets – for instance, coffee, tea, cotton, pyrethrum, tobacco, and wheat – the authority acts as a monopolist in processing or resale. Others – dairy products, sugar cane and maize, for example – fall short of the monopoly/monopsony position. The typical pattern when boards are involved is that the board takes delivery from traders, co-operatives or large farms, and then delivers to the processors and wholesalers.

A major element in the government's strategy to improve smallholder agriculture is the development of the *co-operative system* for marketing and provision of credit and inputs. In the 1960s and early 1970s co-operatives were concentrated in the central and more productive areas such as Central and parts of Eastern province. Since the late 1960s, loans to smallholders in Central province, for example, have to a large extent come from the co-operatives. It has been more difficult to get loans from the Agricultural Finance Corporation, but it has also played a role. Banks are of minor importance to smallholders. From the mid-1970s several largely donor-financed integrated rural development programmes have been implemented, for example the Farm Input Supply Scheme, the Smallholder Production Services and Credit Programme, the Integrated Agricultural Development Programme, the Machakos Integrated Development Programme, the Smallholders Coffee Improvement Programme and the Arid and Semi-arid Lands Development Programme. These have been concentrated in low-income regions such as Western and Nyanza provinces.

A study by Gyllstrom (1988) shows, however, that the co-operatives in the poorer regions have had considerable problems. It is only those in regions with a good agro-ecological environment and a developed infrastructure that have survived. In addition, co-operatives with a monopsony status, such as the coffee unions, have done much better than those that face competition. Coffee makes up as much as 75% of smallholder production delivered through the co-operatives.

The government has thus built up a vast organizational structure in the rural areas, but between 1971 and 1983 the co-operatives lost ground as marketing organizations. Their share of the value of marketed smallholder output fell from 48 to 43% in total and from 25 to 10% for non-coffee products. When turnover is small or the co-operative is inefficient, the proportion deducted to cover running costs becomes large, and this hurts smallholders in poorer regions, in particular.

Credit for smallholders does not always have a positive impact. The problems connected with loan schemes may actually slow down market integration. Defaulters may try to avoid dealing with the societies, which means that they are obliged to cease producing the output which has to pass through this marketing channel. Furthermore, because of the inefficiencies and irregularities of co-operatives members' confidence in them may dwindle, and they will not trust them to serve their interests. In the Lake Victoria region, the government interventions, for example in the cotton-growing areas, have led to administratively inflated co-operatives which have practically ceased to operate, an enlarged regional government bureaucracy and indebted smallholders. Administration of the credit programmes has been very costly, and there may well be cheaper ways to support smallholders.

Gyllstrom finds, on a realistic assessment of the assets of the co-operative unions, that half of them should have been liquidated, but support from the government, the Co-operative Bank and donors has enabled them to survive. The main problem has been the poor rate of debt repayment, which varies for the various programmes between 10 and 40%. Another factor is the high costs at the local level, which has meant that funds provided by the Co-operative Bank have not been lent to smallholders but used to cover running expenses. For western Kenya in 1983 between 10 and 50% of loan funds had been consumed in this way. The viability of the co-operatives is critically dependent on the soundness of their loans to members, and the situation is serious, at least outside the coffee unions.

Gyllstrom concludes that co-operatives have been successful only in regions where the environment favours high productivity and where the rural economy is sufficiently differentiated to keep transaction costs low. Organization of co-operatives in itself does not generate agricultural development. They cannot be a substitute for other measures such as land redistribution, investment in rural infrastructure, and more efficient markets.

The major change in *marketing* arrangements is the reform under way to improve the efficiency of the National Cereals and Produce Board, whose deficits have been a heavy burden on the government budget in recent years. In future, budget allocations to the NCPB will be limited to its requirements for maintaining food security and stabilizing markets. Apart from this, marketing is to be operated on a commercial basis. About 65% of the NCPB's buying centres were closed in 1987. Private traders and co-operatives have been licensed to trade in maize, and the monopoly position of the NCPB has thus been eliminated. The process is gradual, however. In 1988 the private sector was allowed to take up to 20% of the secondary market, and this percentage is being increased under the second Agricultural Sector Adjustment Operation due to be signed in 1991. The NCPB may then eventually become a buyer of last resort.

With regard to other parastatals the government has divested from the Uplands Company and the Kenya Meat Commission. Plans similar to the changes in the NCPB have been drawn up for the South Nyanza Sugar Company and the National Irrigation Board. These changes will be undertaken over the next few years, and money is allocated in the budget to liquidate old debts.

A crucial ingredient in the strategy of structural adjustment is an improvement in marketing efficiency and in particular the speeding up of payments. Many observers consider that promptness in payment is as important as the price itself in determining farmers' production decisions. Cleaver and Westlake (1987) give several examples showing that farmers respond vigorously to delays in payment, which have been up to 15 months. There were very large drops in production of both cotton and pyrethrum following long payment delays.

There have been moderate improvements in the payments from the Kenya Co-operative Creameries to milk producers. Farmers are now paid within a month of delivery. In the smaller rural dairies, however, they are paid on delivery. In coffee serious delays have continued and it is quite common for farmers to have to wait over a year for their payments; the bottleneck is said to be at the union level. Cotton farmers now have to wait up to six months, which is a slight improvement on earlier periods. It is only the private ginneries in Kitui and Kilifi which pay on delivery. For maize the situation was really serious in 1987 because of the economic difficulties caused by the bumper crop of 1986 but there has been some improvement since. Finally, with regard to pyrethrum there have been some improvements in recent years and farmers are now paid within a month.

IV.   TRENDS IN INCOMES AND DISTRIBUTION

Rural incomes and income distribution

In this section we first present estimates by Bevan et al. (1989) drawn from the Integrated Rural Survey 1974/5 (IRS1), which is national, and the 1982 survey of Central and Nyanza provinces, the most recent dates for which data are available. Since only two regions are covered, we need to be cautious about generalizing to the whole of Kenya. Nevertheless, there should be an indication of the trends in other rural areas (excluding the special problems of North-Eastern province) and the difference in the experiences of the two regions gives an indication of the inter-regional diversity in production changes. Moreover, together they constitute about half the smallholder population in Kenya.

Table 2.11 gives the percentage changes in income composition and the trends in real incomes in the two provinces between 1974/5 and 1982. The reliance of Central province on agriculture is rather below average, while in Nyanza it is above average. However, in 1974/5 both had a per capita income level about 16% above the national average for smallholder households.

The table shows that the relative importance of farm income declined and that of wage incomes increased in both provinces but especially in Nyanza. This suggests that agricultural development was very poor in Nyanza during this period. One possible explanation is that farm income was overestimated in 1974/5. Another is that agriculture really deteriorated in Nyanza, which is probable considering the fact that it is more exposed to droughts than Central province. The 170% increase in the share of remittances would confirm this. Moreover, the subsistence percentage, which was as low as 38% in 1974/5, had increased to 59% by 1982; this kind of trend is normally a sign of agricultural decline. The same percentage in Central province was as high as 72% in 1974/5, but by 1982 had declined to 43%, suggesting that agricultural development in this region has been better and that farming has become more market-oriented. Wage income increased its share in Central also, but at a much lower rate, and the share of remittances even declined.

The data on changes in income structure thus suggest that economic development in Central province has been quite good, while the situation in Nyanza has declined. This is borne out by our estimates of per capita income development. While per capita incomes increased by 6% for Central province smallholders, they declined by as much as 18% in Nyanza. In Nyanza there is relatively little of the major income-generating cash crops, tea and coffee, while it is largely these that have enabled smallholders in Central to improve their situation over the period. In 1976, 70% of coffee and 21% of tea were grown in Central province, as compared with 4 and 7% respectively in Nyanza (Bigsten, 1980). The crops extensively grown in Nyanza are pyrethrum, cotton, and sugar, which generate much less revenue than coffee and tea. There have also been major problems in the pyrethrum and cotton boards leading to large production declines.

From information from these two regions alone, the period up to 1982 would seem to be one of increasing economic differences between rural regions. Since 1982, however, the pattern of development has changed. Agriculture in general has fared

Table 2.11. *Percentage changes in smallholder income composition and trends 1974/5–82*

Income Component	Central	Nyanza
Farm income	−11.4	−30.7
Own business inc.	+3.9	−6.5
Wage income	+22.1	+91.8
Remittances	−10.0	+170.0
Trends	1974/75	1982
Central	100	106.0
Nyanza	100	82.2

Source: IRSI estimates from Bevan et al. (1989).

better and relative price changes haveworked to the benefit of the farmers producing food crops.

In another study Herr (1989) has used the Household Budget Survey of 1981/82 to analyse the structure of income and welfare of rural inhabitants. He uses expenditure rather than income as a measure of levels of living, assuming this to be an indicator of permanent income. He uses the budget share of food as an indicator of welfare, assuming that this will fall as households get more prosperous. Comparing the Integrated Rural Survey 1974/5 with the 1981/2 Rural Household Budget Survey he finds that there was such a fall (pp. 23 and 51) between these two dates, suggesting that smallholder families experienced an improvement in welfare over this period. This therefore gives a relatively optimistic picture.

It is obvious that wage incomes and other non-farm earnings are very important for the welfare of smallholder households as well as their scope for purchasing farm inputs which can improve their agricultural operation. According to the Rural Household Budget Survey 1981/82 about half of the households had some wage income. In other words, 1.2 million people in the rural areas were engaged in wage employment either in the formal sector as teachers and civil servants, or in the informal sector or in wage employment within agriculture. There were also 670,000 households engaged in self-employment. These figures show that the labour market in the rural areas is quite varied.

Generally there are considerable difficulties in saying anything definite about changes over time in income distribution. One attempt at measurement has been made by the World Bank (1988). It does not take into account the impact of changes in the distribution of the labour force among activities, but simply looks at changes over time in real income within categories. Real wages in both private and public employment fell between the first oil shock and 1985. Incomes in the informal sector increased up to 1979, but fell during the period of domestic deflation. By comparing the rural surveys of 1974/5 and 1981/2 it concludes that smallholder family incomes increased over this period.

If we accept these estimates, it seems that from the mid-1970s to the mid-1980s both the urban-rural gap and the formal-informal sector gap have declined somewhat. This suggests that income distribution within the group of wage-earners and smallholders may have become more even, but it is not easy to say whether poverty has decreased or not. Growth in per capita incomes has been very modest.

What, then, can we say about income distribution between wage-earners, small-holders and capital-owners? The factoral income distribution seems to have remained fairly constant. The number of employees has increased and this has been associated with falling real wages. Nothing is known about the number of people drawing income from capital. There are some indications that owners of large farms saw a more favourable development of their income from agriculture than smallholders after 1979.

During the 1980s, cash-crop producers, who are mostly the better-off, appear to have had smaller price increases than food-crop producers. Thus, it is possible that the poorest farmers benefitted. However, as already noted, Kenyan smallholder families do not live only on income from their own farms. Wage employment has increased substantially since 1979, while wages have fallen. Employment in the modern sector, which is of particular importance to smallholder families, in fact fell up to 1983, but then increased again to above the 1979 level. The income gain from rural activities in the formal sector may have been the factor that helped rural families to protect their income levels. The evidence on this is still fragmentary, however.

There are thus some tendencies towards improving income distribution, while others point in the opposite direction. Smaller gaps between urban and rural areas and between formal and informal employment reduce inequality, but at the same time it is possible that owners of capital and land (other than smallholders) have done better than employees and smallholders. At present it is not possible to say the direction in which inequality may have changed. The implied changes may, however, have been beneficial from the point of view of poverty alleviation, although there is still no solid evidence to prove this.

Some welfare indicators

Between 1979 and 1987 the share of education in the recurrent budget increased from 27.3 to 34.5%, and in the development budget from 2.8 to 4.9%. The low figure for government investment in the sector arises from the fact that parents now have to contribute directly to the building of schools, while the government pays only for teachers and basic facilities. Provision of facilities is skewed in favour of wealthier districts and urban areas; wealthier districts are able to construct more schools, thereby attracting a larger budget allocation. Expenditure on education has thus increased rapidly, but the intake has increased even faster, and many people are worried about the quality of education (Court and Kinyanjui, 1988).

Table 2.12 provides a provincial breakdown of enrolment figures. It should be pointed out that pupils cross provincial borders to get education, so the estimates are likely to be somewhat biased. Nevertheless it is probably fair to say that primary education is now virtually comprehensive, with the exception of Coast and North-Eastern provinces. With regard to secondary education, however, there are more significant differences. The most developed of the rural regions, Central, is considerably better provided with secondary school places than the others, and there are differences between the more populous regions. Nevertheless, if there is any tendency over time it is towards interregional equalization. One must therefore conclude that, in spite of the macroeconomic adjustments, educational expansion has been extremely rapid in the agricultural regions also. If anything, one would have to question whether the economy can cope with such a high rate of expansion. The government has also concluded that there has to be a slowdown (Sessional Paper No. 1, 1986).

Table 2.12. *Primary and secondary enrolment by province 1983–86 (in '000s)*

	Primary schools:				Secondary schools:			
	1983	–84	–85	–86	1983	–84	–85	–86
Nairobi	107.7	110.9	123.6	127.5	38.5	31.7	27.5	31.0
Central	741.3	750.4	828.3	822.7	119.5	124.8	98.5	101.7
Coast	273.2	281.9	300.2	321.6	28.6	26.9	24.5	27.6
Eastern	807.9	812.8	847.3	901.5	84.4	89.6	70.0	75.9
North-E	15.5	16.3	19.9	23.5	1.5	1.3	1.4	1.9
Nyanza	835.8	833.1	907.6	911.8	86.9	80.0	73.7	72.1
Rift Valley	931.5	959.2	1021.6	1061.7	68.6	80.8	82.5	9.0
Western	611.1	615.2	653.9	673.2	65.7	75.0	59.1	59.5
Total	4323.8	4380.2	4702.4	4843.4	493.7	510.9	437.2	458.7

Health services are concentrated in the urban centres, where only 15% of the population lives. Urban facilities are used by rural ones on a referral basis, but this has proved inadequate owing, among other things, to communication problems (Mwabu, 1987). The spending pattern of the Health Ministry has been highly inequitable and the health status of the rural population may have worsened. Another problem in recent years, as in other parts of the public sector, is an acute lack of funds for supplies. In 1982/3 hospitals received 69% of the allocation, while the rural health service received only 11%. The situation has not changed substantially since then.

One important aspect to bear in mind with regard to the health situation in Kenya is that it varies a lot across the country owing not only to differences in facilities, but also to ecological and climatic differences. For example, child mortality varies from 49 deaths per thousand live births in Nyeri district to 214 in South Nyanza district.

The first nutritional survey was carried out in 1977, followed by others in 1979 and 1982. These showed some increase in malnutrition for the under-fives, with the most severe stunting in Coast province followed by Nyanza. Greer and Thorbecke (1986) attempted to measure the proportion of households with a calorie consumption below the recommended daily allowance, and came up with the figure of 39% of smallholder households.

South Nyanza has the highest child mortality rate in the country. Kennedy and Cogill (1987) analysed the effects of a shift from maize to sugarcane production, the hope being that a move to commercial agriculture would both increase smallholder income and improve the health status of the population. They found that the incomes of farmers participating in the scheme rose significantly, and much of the extra income went on non-food expenditure such as housing and education. But the increased income also had a positive nutritional impact; a 1% increase in sugar income increased household calorie intake by 24 calories. The study also stressed the need for upgrading health and sanitation; what is suggested is a concentration on low-cost low-technology innovations.

Finally, we come to the issue of rural water supplies, where the relative share of government investments has increased significantly since 1983. Previously government schemes tended to concentrate on the districts with better access to water and particularly benefitted richer households with larger land holdings (GOK/CBS/UNICEF, 1984). There seems to have been an increased emphasis on poorer regions in recent years, though the coverage ratio of water to rural population is still highest in Central province, where *Harambee* (self-help) water schemes were started in the early 1970s and then taken over by the government after the creation of the Ministry of Water Development.

V. CONCLUSIONS

Economic changes for smallholders

This chapter has demonstrated that the period 1979–89 can be divided into three phases. During phase 1 (1979–82) the relative prices of tradables fell, which hurt agriculture – the major producer of exportables. During phase 2 (1983–8), however, this trend was reversed, and the price changes were more favourable for agriculture. A major explanation of the change in the development of relative prices after 1982 was the liberalization of trade and the exchange-rate depreciations. Finally, during phase 3 (1989), the positive price changes for agriculture were reversed by falling export prices.

Real agricultural output fell by about 10% in per capita terms over the decade. The agricultural terms of trade fell rapidly between 1979 and 1982, and remained approximately constant from 1982 to 1989. Since this meant a decline over the period as a whole, the real decline in income from agriculture was larger than 10%, though the figure varied between different kinds of producers, with cash-crop farmers generally experiencing larger falls than maize producers.

Smallholder families have a range of other income sources, but it is difficult to estimate changes in supplementary incomes without access to survey data. We have only very partial information on this. The wage labour market in the modern sector shows that employment has increased at the same rate as population over the decade. It is mainly public sector employment which has expanded, while the agricultural wage labour market has stagnated. The wage level in employment as a whole, on the other hand, has fallen by about 10%, while real wages have remained more or less constant in agriculture. It is not possible to say if the access of smallholders to these jobs has changed, but it seems reasonable to assume that their income from wage employment has fallen slightly in real terms.

It thus seems likely that the sum of income from agriculture and wage employment has fallen by approximately the same percentage as the income from agriculture, that it is by some 10%. To what extent smallholder families have been able to make up for this income loss by increases in own-business incomes is not possible to say, since no survey information is available. There are, however, indications that the informal rural sector has expanded significantly. Overall, one might perhaps venture to say that smallholders in particular have come through the crisis years with their income levels almost intact.

The welfare of smallholders is also dependent on their access to public services, and we have found that aggregate government spending, in particular on education, has increased more rapidly than population growth between 1979 and 1989. This suggests that, at least with regard to education, there has been no decline at all. Agricultural services have grown only slowly. In cost terms the development of public services thus seems quite impressive. However, there is evidence that inefficiency in part of the public services is increasing, mainly because of the problem of recurrent costs. Cuts have reduced the working capital needed to run the services, while cuts in personnel costs have been smaller. This is an area worthy of more detailed study. Given the deterioration in the quality of the public services, it is rather difficult to put a value on them.

Policy conclusions

An important finding of this study is that most smallholder families have a variety of income sources. This means that attention should not be confined to smallholder agricultural activity only, although this is still very important. We have also emphasized the importance of public services to the welfare of smallholders. At least three areas for policy intervention can be identified: first, policies aimed at supporting the agricultural output of smallholder families; second, policies to increase the access of smallholders or the rural landless to other economic activities; and third, policies to improve the usefulness of public services to the rural population.

With regard to agricultural policies, it should be noted that there have been definite improvements in pricing. There are, however, still large administrative problems in the marketing of agricultural produce as well as in the supply of inputs and credit. Many of the parastatals are inefficient, and the positive impact of co-operatives outside the coffee areas has been limited. Lack of promptness in payment has been a serious problem for smallholders although some improvements have been made recently. Delays in payment are equivalent to price reductions and they also create uncertainty, which may have strong disincentive effects. The question is whether it is possible to reform the parastatals and co-operatives to minimize these defects. If this turns out to be impossible, dismantling of the inefficient part of the apparatus might be considered and allowing marketing to be taken over by private agents. The same argument can be made regarding the supply of credit and inputs. The question of whether there are cheaper and more efficient ways of organizing these functions needs to be considered, particularly in the less developed regions.

We have argued that both credit and extension advice may have positive effects on agricultural productivity. However, the supply of credit in a way that leads to widespread defaults is counter-productive. Credit therefore needs to be channelled through institutions that can effectively reclaim the money, such as the coffee co-operatives which are allowed to deduct the money from the coffee revenue, or through other institutions with professional competence in the handling of credit. Credit from government or donors allocated to smallholders free of charge only hinders the development of an efficient marketing system. It could be better invested in rural infrastructure.

Smallholder families take part in a variety of income-generating activities. Even pastoralists are moving in the direction of increased income diversification. It should also be borne in mind that there are landless people in the rural areas, who have to rely on different sources of income.

In order to raise income levels in the rural areas a varied economic structure needs to be developed. Smallholder families have access to modern sector incomes through migration, but the development of activities in the rural areas themselves could further enhance this access. Government activities aimed at supporting small-scale industry in rural areas are therefore seen as a step in the right direction, although it is not possible here to go into any detail about how such a policy might be organized. A good supporting infrastructure is essential and probably easier to organize than direct support in the form of credit, etc.

The third policy area is the provision of public services. In aggregate terms the maintenance and development of services has been quite impressive. We have not looked in any detail at the content of the services, but anecdotal evidence suggests that the quality is deteriorating. One major problem here is the lack of money to cover recurrent costs which is partly due to the employment policies of the government. For political and other reasons public sector employment is allowed to expand in spite of the fact that many of the newly hired are superfluous from the point of view of production. The donor community also needs to reconsider its policies. Donors prefer to support investment, but in a situation where the government cannot effectively use the existing structures this seems ill-advised. Money might either be used to cover some recurrent expenditures, or if donors are only interested in investment, might go to investments that do not significantly increase the pressure on the recurrent budget.

We thus argue for policies which improve efficiency in the markets where small-holders trade, which support increased economic diversification outside the major economic centres, and which improve the efficiency of existing public institutions.

References

Akonga, J., Downing, T.E. et al. (1987) 'The Effects of Climatic Variations on Agriculture in Central and Eastern Kenya' in M.L. Parry, T.R. Carter, N.T. Konijn, (eds), The Impact of Climatic

Variations on Agriculture. Vol. 2. *Assessments in Semi/Arid Regions.* Reidel, Dordrecht.

Bevan, D., Collier, P., Gunning, J. with Bigsten, A. and Horsnell, P. (1989) *Peasants and Governments: An Economic Analysis.* Oxford University Press, Oxford.

Bevan, D., Collier, P., Gunning, J., with Bigsten, A. and Horsnell, P. (1990) *Controlled Open Economies.* Oxford University Press, Oxford.

Bigsten, A. (1980) *Regional Inequality and Development. A Case Study of Kenya.* Gower, Aldershot.

Bigsten, A. (1985) 'What Do Smallholders Do for a Living? Some Evidence from Kenya', in M. Lundahl (ed.), *The Primary Sector in Economic Development.* Croom Helm, London.

Bigsten, A. (1988) *Smallholder Circular Migration in East Africa.* Memorandum No. 112, Department of Economics, Gothenburg University.

Central Bureau of Statistics (1990) 'Rural Labour Force Survey', Nairobi.

Cleaver, K. and Westlake, M. (1987) *Pricing, Marketing and Agricultural Performance in Kenya,* draft for Lele and Meyers, MADIA study.

Collier, P. (1988) *Macro-economic Policy, Employment and Living Standards in Malawi and Tanzania, 1973–84.* WEP Research Working Papers, International Employment Policies Working Paper No. 18, ILO, Geneva.

Collier, P. and Lal, D. (1980) *Poverty and Growth in Kenya.* World Bank Staff Working Paper No. 389, Washington DC.

Court, D. and Kinyanjui, K. (1988) *Education and Development in Sub-Saharan Africa: The Operation and Impact of Education Systems.* IDS Discussion Paper No. 286, University of Nairobi.

Dornbusch, R. (1974) 'Tariffs and Non-Traded Goods', *Journal of International Economics,* 4(4).

ECA (n.d) *Agricultural Pricing Policies in Africa: The Kenyan Experience.* Joint ECA/FAO Agriculture Division, Addis Ababa.

Government of Kenya, *Development Plan,* 1966–70, 1970–4, 1974–8, 1979–84, 1984–9.

Government of Kenya, *Economic Survey,* annual.

Government of Kenya, *Statistical Abstract,* annual.

Government of Kenya, *Integrated Rural Survey 1974–75,* Nairobi.

Government of Kenya, *The Integrated Rural Surveys 1976–1979.* Basic Report, Nairobi.

Government of Kenya (1982) *Statement by President Moi on the Current Economic Situation in Kenya,* 21 September.

Government of Kenya CBS, UNICEF (1984) *Situation Analysis of Children and Women in Kenya: Some Determinants of Well-being,* Vol. 1, Nairobi.

Greer, J. and Thorbecke, E. (1986) *Food, Poverty and Consumption Patterns in Kenya.* ILO, Geneva.

Gyllstrom, B. (1988) *State-Administered Rural Change. Agricultural Cooperation in Kenya.* University of Lund (mimeo).

Hecox, W.E. (1986) *The Role of Structural Adjustment and Donor Conditionality in Reshaping Kenya's Industrial Development Strategy.* Industrial Research Project, University of Nairobi.

Herr, H. (1989) *Aspects of Agricultural Development and Consumer Demand in Rural Kenya 1987/82.* USAID, Nairobi.

Herren, U. (1988) *Pastoral Peasants: Household Strategies in Mukogodo Division, Laikipia District.* IDS Working Paper No. 458, University of Nairobi.

Kennedy, E., and Cogill, B.T. (1987) *Income and Nutritional Effects of the Commercialisation of Agriculture in Southwestern Kenya,* Research Report No. 63, International Food Policy Research Institute, Washington DC., November.

Mwabu, G.M. (1987) *Health Sector Financial Analysis: A Survey.* IDS Working Paper No. 452, University of Nairobi.

World Bank (1988) *Sector Study: Kenya's Agricultural Growth Prospects and Strategy Implications.* Nairobi (mimeo).

Appendix Table 2.1. *Distribution by province of heads of household by main occupation, holding size, and holdings of cattle (1978/9)*

	Central	Coast	Eastern	Nyanza	R. Valley	Western
A. Heads of household by main occupation (%)						
Agriculture etc.	55.8	73.7	67.6	79.1	72.3	80.7
Administrative	6.2	7.1	8.0	6.8	7.5	3.0
Manufacturing	5.3	4.3	6.7	4.1	4.2	3.1
General labourers	10.8	1.0	2.9	3.5	3.0	3.7
Transport	5.2	2.4	1.0	1.4	2.5	2.1
Armed forces	0.2	0.0	0.6	0.0	0.0	0.0
No occupation	6.7	5.2	3.5	2.6	2.9	4.2
B. Holding size (%)						
0 hectares	21.8	29.0	19.7	15.6	36.8	8.7
0.01–0.9	47.4	29.2	40.5	58.1	29.2	54.3
1.0–3.9	26.9	31.0	33.3	22.6	19.7	31.9
4.0 +	3.9	10.8	6.5	3.5	14.3	5.2
C. Number of cattle (%)						
None	55.9	88.4	52.0	58.1	50.9	60.8
1–5	35.9	4.0	29.4	18.9	9.7	24.0
6–10	6.0	4.6	11.5	13.7	12.2	10.6
11–20	2.2	1.7	6.1	7.2	15.4	4.6
21 +	0.0	1.3	1.0	2.1	11.8	0.0

Source: Integrated Rural Survey (4), 1979.

Appendix Table 2.2 *Factor incomes 1976 (K£m.)*

Rural Households	Factors:				
	1	2	3	4	5
Holding under 0.5 ha; little additional income	1.0	0.2	0.2	0.3	16.6
Holding under 0.5 ha; substantial additional income	5.4	0.8	0.8	1.3	12.3
Holding 0.5 ha–1.0 ha; little additional income	0.6	0.1	0.1	0.2	31.8
Holding 0.5 ha–1.0 ha; substantial additional income	5.4	0.8	0.8	1.3	14.4
Holding 1.0–8.0 ha	32.3	4.9	5.1	7.3	215.6
Holding over 8.0 ha	1.1	0.2	0.2	0.2	13.4
Other rural	32.2	15.6	17.9	39.2	30.3

1 – Unskilled and semi-skilled workers
2 – Skilled workers
3 – Office workers and semi-professionals
4 – Professionals
5 – Self-employed and family workers

Source: Social Accounting Matrix (1976).

Appendix Table 2.3.   Percentage distribution of heads of household, type of employment and household income type (1974/5)

Type of Employment	Income Group:								
	1	2	3	4	5	6	7	8	9
None	84.01	89.01	86.74	83.75	78.06	76.30	75.02	61.40	80.08
Operating another holding	0.00	0.00	1.53	1.30	2.03	1.07	0.02	0.42	0.96
Labour on another holding	0.00	3.28	1.63	2.88	3.15	0.81	1.13	1.05	1.84
Other rural-work	9.43	3.56	3.88	8.18	6.59	12.00	9.14	15.04	7.99
Teaching/government employment	1.81	0.94	2.87	0.86	1.30	5.65	11.35	13.50	4.42
Urban employment	4.75	2.48	3.36	3.02	8.71	4.17	2.19	8.80	4.60
Other	0.00	0.00	0.00	0.00	0.17	0.17	0.00	0.13	0.11

1 – Below 0 Kshs
2 – 000– 999 Kshs
3 – 1000–1999 Kshs
4 – 2000–2999 Kshs
5 – 3000–3999 Kshs
6 – 4000–5999 Kshs
7 – 6000–7999 Kshs
8 – Over 8000 Kshs
9 – Total

Source: Integrated Rural Survey, 1974–5.

Appendix Table 2.4.   *Comparison of provincial smallholder incomes (1974/5) (% and Kshs per month)*

Income components	Central	Coast	Eastern	Nyanza	R. Valley	Western	Total
Farm income	50.0	24.9	54.8	71.3	67.4	47.6	57.0
Own bus. inc.	7.7	18.8	14.1	9.3	6.6	5.1	9.7
Wage inc.	30.3	27.8	20.7	13.4	20.3	29.0	22.4
Remittances	12.0	28.5	10.6	6.0	5.6	18.3	10.9
Per cap. inc.	610.2	413.6	517.2	594.4	609.5	335.2	524.0
Relative inc.	116.5	78.9	98.7	113.4	116.3	64.0	100

Source: *Integrated Rural Survey 1, 1974/5* p. 56.

3

MADAGASCAR

ADRIAN HEWITT*

I. BACKGROUND

Several important features distinguish Madagascar from the other country studies in this book. Madagascar has a geographical and linguistic unity which is rare on the mainland of Africa and almost unknown among the post-colonial successor states of sub-Saharan Africa. Although for seventy years until independence in 1960, it was managed, like Niger, as a French overseas possession, moving from protectorate through colony to member of the French Community, it stood apart from the rump of French West and Central Africa.

Madagascar's detachment was more than just geographical. Its record of (albeit suppressed) nationalistic opposition, notably the 1915 Menalamba plot and the 1947 rebellion in which perhaps 80,000 were killed, is quite unlike that of the more docile Francophone African colonies in the sub-Saharan region and resembles more the South-East Asian or North African response to French colonialism. Similarly, Madagascar's inclusion in the West Africa–dominated Franc Zone (until 1973) and associated bilateral trading arrangements with France proved to be an anomaly. Its natural trading region was Eastern Africa, the Middle East and South Africa, while direct demand for two leading exports, vanilla and cloves, was located in the United States and Indonesia respectively, and hardly needed to transit via the 'mother country' at all.

Madagascar's robust though often threatened political pluralism provides another contrast with the rest of Africa. Madagascar has generally avoided the African addiction to coups d'état as a method of changing government. The resignation of President Tsiranana in 1972 and that of Ratsiraka's government in 1991 (although the president himself hung on) were both brought about by popular protest, organized opposition and street politics. (The other two regime changes, both in 1975, were, however, affairs largely internal to the military.) Crucially, throughout the post-independence period, Madagascar never allowed itself to become a one-party state. This was despite the expressed intention of President Ratsiraka in the 1975 constitution to outlaw all

* The author gratefully acknowledges the contribution of Maxime Rakotondramanitra, without whose fieldwork this analysis would not have been possible. Translations of extracts from the *Charter of the Malagasy Socialist Revolution* are by the author but page numbers refer to the French text which, with the Malagasy text published jointly, is the official version.

opposition to his 'socialist revolution'. That the Malagasy managed to sustain a form of multi-partyism even in the most unpromising circumstances ought to stand them in good stead so long as support for economic reform programmes is made conditional on adhering to particular nostrums of 'governance'.

Opposition parties have, however, often had to struggle to prevent their eclipse by the regime in power. The Parti Social-Democrate became so dominant at the end of the 1960s that only the (then) Communist Congress party, AKFM, survived in active opposition. Later, Ratsiraka advanced the AREMA (Avant-Garde de la Révolution Malgache) into a Leninist leadership party within a revolutionary National Front (FNDR) threatening to ban all opposition, even though the party was recognized as little more than a vehicle for the military in power. This failed and the continuing existence of opposition parties was recognized and entrenched in reforms in 1990.

Madagascar is, like the other African countries in this study, primarily an agricultural economy. Over 85% of the population live in the rural areas. But it is only in recent years (including the period under direct consideration in this study) that the Malagasy have been obliged to acknowledge that they live in a poor country. Throughout the 1960s, Madagascar enjoyed food self-sufficiency (in rice) and a widely balanced range of exports; economic growth was steady if unspectacular. When the United Nations list of Least Developed Countries was drawn up in 1971, it would have been unthinkable to have added Madagascar (as it would then to have included Ghana).

Disruptions, mismanagement and policy changes which are the subject of this chapter, however, brought about economic setbacks as spectacular as those experienced by Ghana. In 1979, Madagascar was classified by the World Bank (*World Development Report*, 1981) as the thirtieth poorest country in the world with a GNP of $290 per head. By 1989, it had sunk to twelfth poorest, with GNP at $230 per head (*WDR*, 1991). Most of the decline occurred during the sixteen-year presidency of Didier Ratsiraka (1975–91) whose disarming attitude to adjustment and economic reform is illustrated in Pryor (1990: 406) by his 'declaring in his 1986 New Year's Speech to the nation that such measures [raising food prices and liberalizing rice marketing to benefit rural producers] had been pressed upon him by his advisors and that he had never really been in favour of liberalization'.

Unlike Ghana, there is no clear date at which one can say the economic reform programme began in Madagascar. Whereas the 1970s were spent adopting newer and ever more radical-sounding policies, throughout the 1980s the government spent much of its time resisting adjustment or failing to implement agreed measures. Madagascar holds the world record (with Togo and Senegal) for the number of adjustment credits it has taken with the IMF, with ten standby or similar arrangements over the past decade (see Table 3.1). It has also drawn four times on the Compensatory Financing Facility (now the Compensatory and Contingency Financing Facility) in addition to adjustment credits. Paradoxically, however, the standby and Enhanced Structural Adjustment Facility arrangements are designed to provide 'temporary' support to governments seeking to restore viability to their country's balance of payments; Madagascar could therefore be said to have violated the intent of the facilities in practice by claiming an almost uninterrupted succession of temporary drawings.

Even though the first IMF programme dates from 1980 and was followed by a succession of drawings and several sector adjustment loans from the World Bank, the earliest (small) signs of an economic recovery began only after the 1987 devaluations, while the *implementation* of most of the economic reforms had to await the political changes of the early 1990s. Thus, added to the familiar problem of disentangling the effects of adjustment on rural producers from the effects of the recession itself, there

Table 3.1. *IMF arrangements and World Bank adjustment operations with Madagascar, 1980–89*

Type of arrangement/facility	Date approved	Approved amount
IMF arrangements and special facilities		**(SDRm.)**
Standby (2 years)	27 June 1980	64.5
Compensatory financing facility	15 July 1980	29.2
Standby (14 months)	13 April 1981	109.0
Standby (1 year)	9 July 1982	51.0
Compensatory financing facility	9 July 1982	21.8
Standby (1 year)	10 April 1984	33.0
Compensatory financing facility	27 June 1984	14.4
Standby (1 year)	23 April 1985	29.5
Compensatory financing facility	28 May 1986	16.1
Emergency assistance	28 May 1986	16.6
Standby (18 months)	17 September 1986	30.0
Structural adjustment facility	31 August 1987	46.5
Standby (10 months)	2 September 1988	113.3
Enhanced structural adjustment facility	15 May 1989	76.9
World Bank adjustment operations	**(US$m)**	
Industrial sector adjustment credit	15 January 1985	60.0
Agricultural sector adjustment credit	5 August 1986	60.0
Industry and trade adjustment credit	30 June 1987	100.0
Public sector adjustment credit	29 June 1988	127.6

Sources: IMF, Treasurer's Department, and World Bank, *Statement of Development Credits*, December 1990.

is in Madagascar's case the contention that the adjustment process was still inchoate after a full decade.

II.   RECENT ECONOMIC POLICIES

The economy has seen major policy shifts as well as changed allegiances over the past thirty years which have a bearing on the livelihoods and potential of farmers, other rural producers and the rural poor.

(a) The liberal neo-colonial era, 1960–72

The French handed over power, without any struggle, to their appointee, Philibert Tsiranana, who was president from 1960 to 1972. During this period the economy's growth rate averaged 3.1% merely by continuing most of the basic French colonial policies unaltered. For instance, the system of poll and cattle taxes to ensure revenue from peasant farmers, and their participation in the national economy, was not abolished until 1973. Yet Tsiranana prided himself on being the son of a simple cow-herd and did increase state spending on agriculture. This in a favourable world economic environment improved output and exports, although control of the latter was left in French hands through the continuation of post-colonial trading houses and the

Franc Zone payments system. Apart from setting up local co-operative movements – the Syndicats des Coopératives – (largely as a method of raising funds for the PSD party) and widening technical and capital assistance to include the European Development Fund and other donors, hardly any policies were changed. The Tsiranana government, though nominally socialist, certainly did not nationalize property or cut any of the umbilical links with France. Economic policy advice was taken almost exclusively from France and remained liberal with a thin veneer of inconsequential planning. Resentment against this lack of change rather than suffering from increasing deprivation was probably the proximate cause of Tsiranana's overthrow in 1972, although by then the government was confronting a number of short-term problems including a drought in the south, a cattle-plague in the west, a more than normally severe cyclone, and a split in the party on a number of issues, including the president's dialogue with South Africa. The natural hazards caused a fall in agricultural output which rapidly translated into price rises for urban consumers and consequent discontent on the part of the urban bourgeoisie. Of all the peasant farming interests, only the Antandroy of the South-West and some Merina villagers in the Central Highlands were actively opposed to the Tsiranana government; most farmers initially considered that the government had been captured by urban, military and even aristocratic interests which were unlikely to act in their favour.

(b) Interregnum 1972–75

Power was handed over to the armed forces chief, General Ramanantsoa, who legitimized his position by gaining 80% support in a popular referendum. Ramanantsoa's three-year presidency, and that lasting six days of Colonel Ratsimandrava who succeeded him (he was assassinated in office in 1975), now look like a mere interregnum between the twelve years of continuity under Tsiranana and the sixteen years of radical change under Ratsiraka in what was declared later in 1975 the Second Republic or Democratic Republic of Madagascar.

But the Ramanantsoa government itself introduced major changes. It withdrew Madagascar from the Franc Zone in 1973 (although, paradoxically, the parity with the French Franc was to be maintained for another nine years at great cost to the economy). It introduced a new investment code limiting foreign participation in prescribed sectors of the economy and restricting repatriation of profits. It introduced foreign-exchange rationing and import quotas and established production and marketing parastatals which the successor government was able to use to take over the foreign trading houses, and also established domestic crop-purchasing authorities to do the work of individual middlemen, not all of whom had been Malagasy. Some foreign-owned agricultural estates were brought back into national ownership. The changes were portrayed as nationalistic and with hindsight do mostly appear to be a delayed reaction to Madagascar's retrieving its sovereignty. They appealed to the urban Merina interests (from which Ramanantsoa himself hailed) and were of little benefit to the rural producers. Agricultural output stagnated and total exports (which were over 90% agricultural) began to fall, only recovering briefly when the OPEC price rise induced a brief commodity boom affecting Madagascar's coffee exports.

(c) The Second Republic 1975–91

Ratsiraka took power as a Frigate Commander in 1975, though he legitimized his position by winning presidential elections three times for seven-year terms. (He also promoted himself to Admiral.) He nationalized the banks, the insurance companies, the French trading houses and most of the foreign-owned manufacturing sector. New firms were encouraged to be worker co-operatives. In the agricultural sector the intention was to set up production co-operatives drawing, if necessary, land from expropriated estates. Marketing and input supply became directly controlled by state corporations. A new revolutionary constitution (1975) was followed by a charter of socialist enterprises (1979).

The aims of the new government, as regards agricultural policy, were stated in the Charter of the Malagasy Socialist Revolution (1975):

- The main aim of the agrarian revolution at this stage of the national democratic revolution is the development and extension of socialist co-operatives ... It is therefore a matter of recovering land through the implementation of appropriate laws regarding absenteeism; limits on property and transformation of the colonial property rights to socialist ones, with a free redistribution to the peasants by creating co-operatives that demonstrate group interests according to the principle of free consent. (p. 65)
- Land redistribution to the peasants implies the obligation to exploit it. Failure to do so will lead to sanctions involving even the withdrawal of the plot and its re-allocation to another beneficiary. (p. 63)

And in the secondary and services sectors:

- At the same time as nationalization, we must reorganize the industrial sector through the creation of national companies comprising all industries in the same branch of activity (sector-based enterprises). Evidently and as far as possible, they will be granted a monopoly over their production ...
- However, if creation of these companies is seen as useful, they, in turn, must obey the laws and principles of socialist enterprise rather than of the capitalist market (once again production must satisfy first the Malagasy people's basic needs). (p. 72)
- Therefore, the Supreme Council of the Revolution took the historic decision on 16 June 1975 to nationalize all banks and insurance companies. The second stage which involves nationalization of external trade and control over distribution is a necessary accompanying measure. (p. 75)

Up to 1978/9, however, it was claimed that domestic savings were able to meet national needs. This implied a substantial drain on the agricultural surplus, although farmers were considered the main source of effective demand.

- The funds necessary for our industrialization can come only from domestic savings. As a developing country, we have no other choice but to sell our industrial products in the domestic market of our large country (because they are not competitive on the world market); in particular, in the rural markets where 85% of the population live. Thus, our farmers will see an improvement in their standard of living and will become sole consumers of our industrial production. (p. 60)

They did not – and not only because of the economic illiteracy of the previous paragraph. The failure of this policy led the government (apparently encouraged by the World Bank which, according to Pryor, criticized the low investment rate in 1975–8) to introduce the policy of invest to the hilt or 'investir à outrance' (1978–80), which was financed by Central Bank loan advances to the state as well as by short-term external borrowing.

Despite the popular revolutionary flavour of the regime, it proved to be fundamentally biased against the agricultural sector. Although the colonial head-taxes on peasants had been abolished, Ratsiraka found new ways of exploiting the peasantry, even employing the military in crop collection and credit control. The agricultural parastatals were urban-based and reflected urban interests. A direct programme of bank lending to smallholders called the FMR which Ramanantsoa began in 1972 quickly became perverted and the state bank responsible for rural development, the BTM, allocated less than 50% of its loans to rural producers, and hardly any to small farmers.

This period saw a fall in agricultural output. Between 1972 and 1979, output of food crops had increased only slightly, the world coffee boom was mishandled, while production of industrial export crops (groundnuts and sisal) fell significantly. After that, food production per head fell severely. The FAO's index of food production per head (1979–81 = 100) fell to 91.5 by 1988, recovering a little subsequently.

Rice production increased as a result of an increase in cultivated area (on average by 0.6% per annum according to the World Bank's *Economic Memorandum* of 1986) but this did not match population growth. Besides low yields, the main constraint was poor marketing, which explains (bearing in mind the importance of rice in the Malagasy diet) the large increase in imports from 25,000 tons in 1971 to 170,000 tons in 1977, accounting for 40% of the total supply on the official market. Rice imports often exceeded 100,000 tons in the 1980s until foreign-exchange shortages reinforced by IMF agreements curtailed what was little more than an urban subsidy and a manifestation of bias against traditional surplus-producing farmers. Imports of oils and fats also increased.

Foreign policy entered a 180° turn. Ramanantsoa had introduced distance to Madagascar's traditional relations with France and ended links with South Africa. Ratsiraka established alliances with the USSR and North Korea. This had little tangible effect in terms of eliciting economic (as opposed to military) assistance, although Madagascar was able to purchase crude oil at Soviet 'friendship prices' until 1987. It did have the effect of depressing aid, as well as direct investment. To this were added other legal and political impediments to private investment.

But the use (albeit perverted) of the Soviet development model of the planned economy did cause another major policy shift with consequences throughout the 1980s. In 1978, anti-agricultural bias was further reinforced by the introduction of the policy of 'investir à outrance' under which Madagascar borrowed massively on world capital markets for several ill-considered industrial ventures. This, with the sudden rise in world interest rates after 1979, had the effect of quadrupling the foreign debt and raising debt service which by 1985 had reached 43% of export earnings. The balance-of-payments problems which have dogged the Malagasy economy ever since set in as early as 1980. The stock of external debt became larger than Madagascar's GDP in 1986 ($2.4 bn) and by the end of 1989 debt had risen to $3.6 bn.

There was no evidence of any positive effects on production. The following are some examples in the agricultural sector of physical investment in white elephants resulting from the new strategy. (The distorting effects of policies, though less spectacular, were more far-reaching for farming.)

- the Z-Ren naphtha-based fertilizer plant whose financing was estimated at Fmg 50 bn in 1977: the enterprise never succeeded because of high running costs, particularly for imported inputs, inappropriate design and inadequate quality control at installation. It never produced any marketable fertilizer before being taken over by Nigerian interests at a distress price in 1991.
- the Antsirabe flour-mill, similarly designed to run on imported inputs for a declining consumer market. No wheat is produced by Malagasy peasant farmers.
- the Mamisoa soya mill which absorbed state funds for no apparent consumer benefit at the output stage; the soya beans had to be imported.

Most investment projects, even outside agriculture and agro-industry, proved difficult to implement while those which were completed, such as the purchase of a single Boeing 747, had a low or negative rate of return. However, the programme favoured almost exclusively industrial development and operated at the expense of the rural population and the agricultural sector. As a result, there was a crisis of growth and investor confidence between 1979 and 1982, when real GDP fell by 10% in real terms as debt service quadrupled. Self-induced adjustment had propelled the economy in precisely the wrong direction. Externally-imposed adjustment from the IMF as early as 1980 was initially robustly resisted, and later rather more surreptitiously avoided.

Some argue that the economic reform programme began with the earliest attempts of the IMF and World Bank to get stabilization and adjustment policies adopted in 1980-2. These were, however, more than customarily offset by countervailing policies and it was not until 1987, when Moscow expressed its exasperation about debt arrears on its own crude petroleum account, and effectively exited from peripheral parts of the African scene, and when domestic opposition to the government began to be voiced following a new famine in the south, that serious economic reforms, marked by a major devaluation of the currency, began. Implementation of the new investment code and full liberalization of agricultural production and marketing did not occur until the end of the decade, by which time agitation for a new constitution redefining property rights and civic freedoms was already altering the balance of power.

Madagascar's decline from its position as a country enjoying modest agriculture-based prosperity to abject poverty and indebtedness seems to be more attributable than most countries' experience to inappropriate policies. Yet Madagascar was also one of the earliest objects of intensive adjustment attention by the World Bank and the international creditor institutions. Only when spontaneous domestic political changes began to occur did the economic reforms begin to be taken seriously. Until such programmes had the mark of local 'ownership', it proved easy for a nationalistic government to resist them regardless of the ensuing detriment to the economy, and despite the fact that the government only poorly represented the interests of the numerically dominant small-farmer constituency.

III.   THE REFORM PROGRAMMES

Two IMF standby agreements during 1980–82 were suspended, and a 'bilateral' import support/economic reform programme signed with France's Caisse Centrale de Coopération Economique (CCCE) succeeded only in maintaining a modest flow of bilateral trade. The third IMF standby in 1982 began a series of Malagasy franc devaluations and established ceilings on the budget deficit, the growth of domestic credit and of public sector salaries and on the size of the current account deficit (Tables 3.2 and 3.3). Later, World Bank programmes in conjunction with the IMF introduced price liberalization, notably in agriculture, and extended general import compression to the establishment of specific targets for rice (food) imports. Despite limits on new foreign borrowing, repeated rescheduling of existing debt has been necessary to keep the debt-service ratio within manageable proportions. Features of the three subsequent IMF agreements are outlined in Table 3.2. A seventh agreement, in the form of a Structural Adjustment Facility using Trust Fund resources, was signed in 1988 and an ESAF (Extended Structural Adjustment Facility) was agreed in May 1989 and will complete its disbursement in 1992 if the new government can implement the terms of the agreement.

Supply-side adjustments have been engineered sector by sector through a series of conditional loans from the World Bank starting in 1985. These were for industrial rehabilitation and adjustment ($40m., 1985); the agricultural sector ($60m., 1986: this helped usher in the liberalization of rice marketing); a trade and industry adjustment loan ($83m., 1987); and a $125m. public sector reform programme starting in 1988. The consequent redundancies arising from this last programme were to be alleviated by (a) an IDA agreement for $22m. for social programmes in 1989 and (b) Madagascar joining the World Bank SDA (Social Dimensions of Adjustment) Programme which offers social compensation. All sectoral adjustment loans were IDA credits. More recently, they have been joined by social programmes, proposals for expenditure on environmental protection and a relaxation of the ban on food subsidies via a publicly owned rice buffer stock. In 1991, the first World Bank structural (as opposed to sectoral) adjustment loan was in preparation, although the government of Prime Minister Victor Ramahatra resigned before this could be agreed. Despite the previous lack of cross-sector structural adjustment loans, the World Bank does classify Madagascar as one of the twenty-five Early Intensive Adjustment Lending Countries (World Bank, 1990), and in September 1991, World Bank Vice-President for Africa Edward Jaycox cited Madagascar (with Ghana, Guinea, Tanzania, Togo, Malawi and Kenya) as 'economic miracles' whose 'successful implementation of structural reforms' stood in stark contrast to other named non-reforming African countries which were, according to The Guardian (19 September 1991), 'stuck in the long grass'.

Despite some painful economic reforms, including a 46% devaluation in mid-1987, and the introduction over the period 1988–90 of a new investment code offering incentives and guarantees to foreign firms, sustained economic recovery has proved elusive without fundamental policy change. The period 1982–5 was little more than a stabilization phase, yet by 1989 the current account deficit was still stuck above 11% of GDP, the budget deficit over 5% and until 1988 economic growth rates had been consistently below the rate of population increase. Since the main agricultural sector reforms date only from 1987, it is too soon to expect many of the effects of adjustment to feed through into the incentive system. While there are signs that the policy bias against agricultural producers (especially smallholders) is being redressed, and marketed output appears to be increasing, there is as yet little convincing proof that poorer farmers are becoming better off, but strong indications that intermediaries are capturing many of the benefits of liberalization.

The means

Exchange-rate policy has been hesitant ever since the departure from the Franc Zone. Despite devaluations of 10–15% in the period 1982–6, the Malagasy franc remained grossly overvalued, reducing other incentives to export. Then the largest devaluation (46%) occurred in June 1987. Since then, the Malagasy franc has stabilized at around

Table 3.2. Main characteristics of IMF agreements completed

3rd (1982–3)	4th (1983–5)	5th (1985–6)	6th (1986–7)
1) Reduce current account deficit to 13% of GDP.	1) Reduce public sector deficit to 5.5% (1984).	1) Reduce budget deficit to 4.7% (1985).	1) Initial 25% devaluation (later devaluation equivalent of 46%).
2) 15% devaluation.	2) Debt rescheduling.	2) Limit domestic credit expansion.	2) New system to allocate forex to exporters (RIL).
3) Reduction of budget deficit to 9.4% (1982), 7% (1983).	3) Ceiling of 100,000 tons on rice imports.	3) Strict limits on new foreign loans.	3) Rice market liberalisation.
4) Domestic credit expansion limited to 20%.	4) Raise producer prices of rice and export crops.	4) Controls on domestic credit.	
5) No new short- or medium-term foreign borrowing.		5) Producer price rises of 11% for rice, 14% for coffee.	
6) Public sector salary increases to be limited to 4.5%.			

Table 3.3.   *Economic performance under the 1980s reforms*

	1980	1985–7 (average)	1987	1989
Current account deficit as % of GNP	−19.5	−11.0	−13.8	−16.0
Deficit in state budget as % of GNP	−13.9	−5.1	−5.3	−7.1
Real GNP growth rate %/annum	0.8	1.8	2.25	4.9
Inflation %/annum	30.5	18.4	30.0	9.0
Index of real exchange rate (1980 = 100)	100	78.9	58.6	54.1
Minimum lending rate %/annum	5.5	11.5	11.5	11.5
External reserves (except gold) $m	26	116	185	245

Source: Author's calculations.

$1 = Fmg 1,500, despite periodic adjustment. The black market in foreign exchange has practically disappeared, while the large profits enjoyed by importers have been reduced. In December 1988, the IMF's Managing Director announced that there was no need for further devaluation, although in January 1991 there was a 13% devaluation against the French franc, just before the dollar began to harden.

Fiscal policy was made more robust by external conditionality. All standby agreements concluded with the IMF have aimed at a reduction in the budget deficit. In 1982, operation LOVA aimed at raising national savings, and the balancing of the budget through the sale of Treasury bonds. Nevertheless, by 1990 the budget deficit was again over 5% of GDP following general and presidential elections in 1989. The government's recurrent expenditure alone that year was Fmg 464 bn.

Incomes policy had the declared aim of improving rural-urban income distribution by increases in agricultural producer prices. Wage increases, particularly for civil servants, were reduced to curb inflation. Since 1988, this policy has been followed by the abolition of certain posts in both administrative and parastatal organizations, using an IDA credit of $125m.

Monetary policy was inactive. Real interest rates were often negative. Moreover, the Franc Zone minimum lending rate was still maintained long after Madagascar had opted out (although these rates offered no positive incentives to savers). In 1987, real interest rates were still minus 18.5%.

Constraints

Prices and quotas for many of the country's exports, notably coffee, are fixed externally, although Madagascar has had some success with regional oligopoly pricing of vanilla and, until recently, cloves. The collapse of coffee quota arrangements and other international agreements has further limited Madagascar's scope for altering its net barter terms of trade, at least on the export side. Debt servicing accounts for an increasing share of the balance of payments deficit, and this constrains export promotion and capital equipment renewal.

The search for budgetary balance, via reductions in government spending, has had a negative impact on public investment and caused cuts in operating expenditures. The fall in public investment was a harsh blow for a country like Madagascar which has had little success in attracting foreign private investment since 1979 (if not 1972).

A further constraint on adjustment in the agricultural sector was the fact that the state removed a substantial share of agricultural producers' income through a levy of the National Product Equalization Fund (FNUP) which centralizes the profits of the stabilization funds before allocating them to state expenditure. Furthermore, the road infrastructure was in such a poor state of repair that the imposition of spending cut-backs represented a real obstacle in isolated areas. Collectors of produce who replaced the state occupy a monopsony position, offering low prices for producers' goods. This has led to the phenomenon of farmers producing food crops for sub-sistence only.

Agricultural reforms

Trade and tariff policy reforms have encouraged the liberalization of external trade to stimulate the output of tradables. Formalities with regard to exports have been simplified, but until recently required that almost all foreign-exchange earnings had to be retained. In 1987, the RIL (Liberalized Import Regime) came into effect for allocating foreign exchange. In 1988, the state disengaged further with the implemen-tation of the Liberalized Import System (SILI) as a means of moving towards introduc-ing an open general licence for imports, which was near to achievement in 1991.

External creditors' demands to reduce rice imports were resisted and in the period 1984–8 these often exceeded 100,000 tons. In 1986 the World Bank recognized that some state intervention in the rice market could be politically acceptable. It finally co-operated with the government to establish a rice buffer-stock, theoretically serving both rural and urban areas. Gradually rice output has expanded (to 2.5m. tons of · paddy) and rice imports have reduced, though not yet below 50,000 tons (the estimated level for 1991: Thailand is the major supplier).

Liberalization was felt only gradually in the rural areas, the objective being to increase production and marketing of produce, following increases in producer prices. The danger lies in the poor functioning of rural markets. Formally launched in 1982, the liberalization policy took off in 1986 with total liberalization of the marketing network (except for rice imports and vanilla exports); the abolition of the stabilization funds; the removal of rice subsidies; and a new investment code initially proposed in 1987, but only implemented against great domestic political opposition in 1990/91, aimed at freer markets in all sectors including agriculture.

Crucial to this was state disengagement (and the removal of the military from a con-trolling interest in agricultural trade). In 1983, some state monopolies were abolished but this did not include products of the stabilization funds and other special cases, such as price control over six products (including cement). 1986 saw the end of mono-polies on coffee, cloves and pepper. Vanilla retained its 'special' status. Also impor-tant for rural producers and the operation of markets was the 1986 privatization of road haulage and passenger transport services. This was accompanied by a freeing of tariffs and allowing greater profit margins for efficient operators.

The liberalization of the rice market can be analysed to help assess the above deci-sions. In 1985, the producer price was only Fmg 90/kg, but it was five times higher for consumers. With the 1986 liberalization, the increase in the producer price was 10 times higher than the rise in retail price: the beginning of a 'wild' liberalization. Dur-ing the tide-over (soudure) period (i.e. the 'hunger gap' between the consumption to exhaustion of farmers' own-grown crops and the following harvest), consumer rice prices reached Fmg 900/kg, resulting in shortages and hunger in the rural areas. Later in 1986, buffer-stocks enabled the maintenance of a remunerative price for producers and a fairer, albeit subsidized, price for those consumers who had access to rationed subsidized supplies; these were primarily in the urban areas.

In Toamasina (December 1986 to April 1987) the average free market consumer price was Fmg 500/kg, while that for the buffer-stock was Fmg 400. This compares with the tide-over period when the producer purchased rice at Fmg 900–1000/kg as against a producer price of Fmg 90/kg at harvest a few months earlier. In contrast, the world price for rice imports was only Fmg 100/kg. The result was slow recovery in production in 1987, but there were encouraging signs with increases in downstream activities such as local mills and collection agencies. Increased input prices as a result of devaluation were seen as a setback. In February 1989, consumer prices were about Fmg 600/kg and producer prices, before the beginning of the 'soudure' tide-over period, Fmg 150/kg. Even the latter was still above the world price, although the large domestic market for rice in Madagascar means that border prices need not be the sole determining factor of agricultural efficiency. Moreover, although Madagascar has yet to become a world exporter of the commodity like Thailand, rice has, over the period of initial adjustment, returned to the position of a 'tradable product'. This has occurred both internally – when restrictions on the transport of rice across regional borders were relaxed in the mid–1980s – and internationally when in 1988/9 Madagascar restarted exports of de luxe rice varieties.

Pre-structural adjustment institutional reforms had included the creation of the 'Bankin ny Tantsaha Mpamokatra' (Rural Development Bank, known as the BTM), purportedly specializing in agricultural finance. This did not solve the problem of lack of rural credit. The small agricultural credit operations launched in 1977 failed, with poor utilization leading to repayment problems. Between 1977 and 1980, the recovery rate slumped from 88% to 40%.

In 1981, the BTM stopped dispensing credit to small farmers, and in due course it left agricultural lending almost entirely. It attempted to find new avenues such as small equipment credit. A substantial part of these loans was extended to urban customers in the industrial and services sectors purporting to be farmers. These loans also proved difficult to collect when they fell due, and as a result the BTM was by 1991 in the worst difficulties of all the three state banks. The other two (BFV-trade and BNI-industry) were being prepared for privatization, but the BTM's balance sheet made it unattractive to potential investors.

A Decree of 2 April 1986 established free competition in the prices of agricultural goods. Freedom to export then applied theoretically to all commodities except vanilla, thus virtually ending the state's (SONACO's) monopoly. Since then, the stabilization funds have been wound down. However, even in 1987, the FNUP recorded substantial revenues. The abolition of SINPA's monopoly in the purchase of rice from the farmers and the introduction of free movement in rice marketing between regions are also indicative of liberalization. But it must be borne in mind that these reforms were only just beginning in the agricultural sector at the end of the 1980s, despite almost a decade of rhetorical adjustment preceding them.

IV. IMPACT OF THE ADJUSTMENT PROGRAMME ON MACRO-MICRO LINKAGES

Adjustment and stabilization programmes designed primarily to restore external balance, to reduce the role of the state in the economy (and the consequent weight of public spending) and to induce supply-side reforms aimed at a more efficient allocation of resources, may not have an immediate or direct effect on small farmers. The latter often operate in a specific micro economy where many of the parameters are unsusceptible to perceived change. But macroeconomic reforms, not only those prescribed for and implemented in the agricultural sector, are transmitted to farmers as signals, requirements and alterations to norms and practices in a number of ways. Linkages are effected through the use of the various markets for land, credit and finance, and labour; for non-factor items such as farm inputs and services; and crucially, for the produce of the farmers themselves. Also important, as well as markets, is the economic and social infrastructure enabling the agricultural sector to perform. Given Madagascar's diversity and the different economic, climatic and political conditions which farmers in different regions face, it was important for this study to consider these macro-micro linkages through the perspective of three different (albeit not wholly representative) groups of small farmers typical of different agricultural production regions of the country.

Assessment of the consequences of these reforms on macro-micro-economic links is fundamental to an understanding of how the adjustment programme reaches the rural population and its specific groups.

Factor markets

Land reform has not been a significant element in Madagascar's adjustment policy. There is not much of a market in land, although the increasing subdivision of family plots, pressure on land availability in the highlands and observations of larger numbers of near-landless are factors indicating that this situation may change. State-sponsored settlement schemes in the middle-west were a feature of the 1960s, while the 1975 Charter promised a radical reform of attitudes to land ownership, in future to be governed by 'rational exploitation', an extension of squatters' rights. However, such policies were only executed with respect to the expropriation of former French colonial concessions and not used subsequently. Constitutional reforms were being proposed in 1991 which were likely to eliminate many of the Marxist-Leninist elements of the 1975 constitution and restore private property rights.

Rural financial markets have so far been poorly served by formal sector institutions. One of the three state banks, the BTM, which was nominally charged with rural credit provision, in fact allocated only between 32% and 29% of its lending to the agricultural sector in the 1980s. Most of this went for export-crop marketing on the part of major bodies. Of the remainder, much of the credit to smallholders financed food production rather than export-crop development. Given the limited scope of banking institutions, informal credit, often at very high interest rates, continues to oil the wheels of the rural economy. Reforms of the banking sector began in 1989, with the reintroduction of foreign banks and private ownership. The state agricultural bank, the BTM, will be the last bank to be privatized, however, owing to its weak portfolio and the manifest difficulty of its specific task if left unsubsidized.

The labour market: rural incomes have only recently begun to rise at a faster rate than urban wages. However, one-third of all smallholders owning less than 10 ha use paid non-family labour during some seasons. As the reforms have yet to raise farm incomes appreciably, there are no firm signs of this market for labour expanding further.

Madagascar has a labour surplus which was only recently being addressed by expansion in manufacturing, notably through fiscal policy directed at the creation of export processing zones. Before this, the surplus, estimated to be increasing by

Table 3.4.   *Minimum wages and farm incomes 1984–7 (Fmg)*

	1984	1985	1986	1987
Minimum annual wage (urban)	211,200	243,600	261,600	276,000
Rice – 1 ha	157,500	175,000	315,000	236,250
Coffee – 1 ha	115,500	138,250	210,000	280,000

Source: Ministry of Agricultural Reform (MPARA) and the State Statistical Repository (DGBDE).

200,000 per year, was necessarily absorbed largely by the agricultural sector, thereby cheapening wages without increasing efficiency or productivity. Formal sector employment grew by only 5% between 1983 and 1987, whereas in 1987 the much larger stock of private agricultural employment grew by 4% compared with 1983. Minimum wages, as compared with the income of farmers with 1 ha under rice or coffee, as shown in Table 3.4, do indicate that, though farm incomes are erratic, the gap between rural and urban wages has narrowed under adjustment. This effect has been enhanced since 1987 by further imposed budgetary stringency, invalid only in the election year of 1989.

The urban minimum wage is higher but its growth is low compared with that of agriculture. The numbers in paid employment also grew more rapidly in agriculture than in manufacturing over the period 1983–7, but faster still in the public service. However, informal employment is far more important in the agricultural sector.

The rural informal wage-earning population

Informal employment featured prominently in the 1985 Agricultural Census, which put the economically active population in agriculture and rural activities at 5.3 million. Informal work is usually undertaken by smallholders on a casual basis. Almost one-third (32%) of traditional agricultural holdings (according to the Census those of less than 10 ha) use hired labour at least once in the year, but this varies from province to province. Antananarivo Province hired the most (54%) and Toliary the least (19%). Although the need for casual labour increases with the size of the plot, all categories use it.

The bigger the farm, the more work is required and the more hired labour is introduced to complement both family labour and mutual help. Only 4% of livestock-breeders, however, resort to hired labour because of the small scale of the enterprise.

When farm work is unavailable, a fairly large percentage of these casual labourers find employment as craftsmen, usually for a period of three to six months during the tide-over period. Broadly speaking, it is the poorest (some 18%) who tend to engage in casual employment to make up a rice deficit or simply to earn some money during the tide-over period. Wages, often including lunch, vary according to sex, with women's wages generally 25% lower.

Because demand for labour often exceeds supply during the cultivation period, a large number of farmers engage in paid employment then in order to employ casual labour later on. To allow a profit margin, they try to employ labour at the lowest possible rate while, in turn, working themselves for higher wages in the same regions or in others.

According to the Census, more hired workers are employed in the predominantly rice-producing areas than in those producing export crops (such as coffee), which are less labour-intensive than rice. Thus, the shift to production of tradables is not particularly conducive to expanding wage employment.

Non-factor markets

The market for agricultural inputs.   Fertilizers and pesticides supply has been increasingly put into private hands. Before 1979, it was the monopoly of the rice-marketing parastatal, SINPA; from 1979 to 1982 such imports were purchased directly by the Ministry of Agriculture, MPARA; by 1988, they were three-quarters privately supplied, with 100% target by the early 1990s. Yet the steep rise in foreign-exchange costs of inputs has meant that the price of fertilizer (input) relative to paddy (output) has risen for the average farmer, over the period 1982-8, except in 1986 when rice prices were exceptionally high. The benefits of increased efficiency in supply and fewer import restrictions have yet to be felt by the smallholder end-users of farm inputs, although import volume data do show that national chemical fertilizer purchases have increased five-fold from 13,320 tonnes in 1982 to 66,000 tonnes in 1987.

Fertilizer is widely used but farmers lack draught oxen, partly owing to the prevalence of cattle theft. The main obstacles to the use of insecticides and pesticides remain shortage of supply and poor technical advice. Inputs are in short supply because of foreign-exchange shortages and poor substitution policies. The plough has long been encouraged by the extension services but is used by only a minority of farmers.

As noted above, the Ministry of Agriculture and Agrarian Reform (MPARA) was in sole charge of input sales to farmers in the 1979-82 period. Supplies were irregular and farmers were unable to acquire fertilizers, insecticides and pesticides when they were most needed. Under adjustment, MPARA has progressively passed over to private operators the task of supplying inputs to the rural areas; the transfer is supposed to be completed by the early 1990s. It has been facilitated since 1987 by the entry of various private companies or parastatals to take charge of input distribution. Theoretically, this should have eased farmers' access to inputs. Nevertheless, two problems have emerged:

- reach: private operators deal only with stores supplying a maximum number of clients at the lowest cost; that is, those with easy access and a high potential of purchase. This militates against small farmers in the remoter areas.
- price, since the state cannot control profiteering on the part of entrepreneurs.

From the onset of liberalization in the input trade in 1982, prices have continued to rise (the price of fertilizer NPK 11-22-16 is used as a reference because of its relatively wide distribution) to reach six times the original level. As a ratio, the paddy/fertilizer relationship follows a more acceptable trend (see Table 3.5) though it indicates a declining trend from 1982. The rise from 1978 to 1981 was due to stable prices for fertilizers compared with the continuous increase in the paddy price. The exceptional figure for 1986 only illustrates the exceptionally high paddy price in that year; otherwise farmers have faced increasing costs since 1981.

Effective competition between suppliers in the field ought, however, to ensure a more efficient approach to input use on the part of farmers. Instead of MPARA's monopoly over input distribution with only 500 centres, more than 20 companies now

Table 3.5.   *Fertilizer paddy prices 1978–88*

Year	Price per kg NPK 11–22–16	Index	Paddy price	Paddy price/ NPK price	Index
1978	62	100	35	0.56	100
1979	62	100	39	0.63	112
1980	62	100	43	0.69	124
1981	62	100	47	0.76	126
1982	100	161	60	0.60	107
1983	140	226	65	0.46	83
1984	180	290	90	0.50	89
1985	180	290	100	0.56	99
1986	210	339	180	0.86	153
1987	280	452	135	0.48	86
1988	375	605	150	0.40	71

Source: Calculations on the basis of MPARA data.

perform this task. On the one hand, donors continue to supply fertilizer and farm equipment and MPARA invites bids from local operators to cover customs clearance, distribution and marketing costs. On the other hand, the policy of structural adjustment has led to the implementation of specific lines of credit coupled with a new import system. This should enhance input availability on a national scale.

The policy of structural adjustment has thus facilitated better input availability and a liberalized distribution network. But the real problem lies at the level of demand which seems dominated by a marked decline in producer prices relative to those of inputs. Such imbalances need time for the requisite price signals to work through the system. Time is not, however, a commodity readily available to farmers living on the margin of subsistence.

Support services: extension and research

Madagascar has a long experience of agricultural extension services. Overall, there are two kinds of services: diffused: i.e. scattered and generally provided by specialized officials from the Ministry of Agriculture; and intensive: i.e. carried out in the context of specific projects (e.g., the Rice Development Operation (ODR), Wheat and Soya Operations) and generally financed from outside the state budget directly by donors. Support services also include agronomic research currently undertaken by a body attached to the Ministry of Agricultural Production, FOFIFA. This was established to succeed the French research agency ORSTOM. Extension services, which were never very successful in reaching smallholders, have been cut back as a result of budgetary stringency.

The lack of attention to publicly funded agricultural support services is reflected by the agricultural ministries' falling share of the budget in the 1978–88 period from 9.9% to 5.1%. But the inappropriateness of much of the extension service outside specific project perimeters and the misguided focus of local agricultural research have meant that for small farmers the withdrawal of publicly funded support services was hardly noticed.

The market for produce: rice, coffee, vanilla and cloves

An index based on the first year of the 1978–87 period indicates a higher prices index for paddy than for coffee and cloves from 1981 onwards. Coffee recovered briefly in 1987. Vanilla remained higher for the whole period except for 1986-7, whereas clove prices remained by far the lowest. Prices in constant terms indicate a general decline from 1980. Paddy and coffee started to recover in 1983. Producer prices tended to increase more slowly than general prices except in 1979 and 1980 for vanilla and 1986 for paddy.

Two conclusions can be drawn. First, there has been an overall deterioration in farmers' incomes since 1978-9. And second, the impact of the adjustment process, gradually implemented since 1981, emerges only in 1986 and especially 1987 with the reverse tendency in favour of agricultural exports. In the overall development of producer prices in constant terms from 1982 to 1986, rice seems to hold the greater attraction. It was almost as if the initial impact of adjustment was to encourage a return to subsistence production. Appendix Tables 3.1 and 3.2 illustrate the evolution of various relative prices.

Relative prices.   As producer prices rose less steeply than consumer prices in the traditional sector, real incomes of smallholders will have declined during the 1980s without a considerable volume response. It is striking, however, that only after 1986, and particularly in 1987, did a reversal of the tendency against export crops reveal itself in the relative price indices. Before this, the incentive was to return to subsistence, or at best to market food output (rice) through informal local channels. Although the first rice liberalization measures started as early as 1983, the watershed was 1987, when the major agricultural reforms began. Since 1986/7, all export-crops marketing of interest to smallholders has been liberalized except for (a) sugarcane (because of the lucrative but highly limited quota arrangements with the European Community and the United States) and (b) vanilla (which because of the nature of the product and the dominance of two trading houses is also permitted to continue with fixed price regulations). But it cannot yet be said that there has been a major response in the rural areas to price signals.

Urban areas are considered as rice consumers; export crops concern them only marginally. Rural areas, on the other hand, are both rice consumers and producers of the four commodities analysed. Changes in the price of paddy relative to the consumer price depict the producers' situation in which decreasing returns are advantageous to the downstream sector (collectors, processors, and huskers). This was the case when returns decreased from 63% in 1978 to 37% in 1988, with the lowest point of 28% in 1985. When producer prices are compared with export prices (fob), the situation is not the same for the three products studied. In 1987, coffee producers received 28% of the export price, but those producing cloves and vanilla received only 12% and 1.5% respectively. Moreover, there has been a continuous deterioration in these three crops since 1981, the theoretical start of structural adjustment.

Theoretically, adjustment was designed to develop export crops in order to increase foreign-exchange earnings and to provide farmers with better incentives to allocate more cultivated areas to crops. In the case of Madagascar, the recovery of the coffee price over that of paddy began to illustrate this trend only from 1987, after nine years of decline, and then world market prices turned against coffee producers. Only in 1987 and 1988 were coffee revenues higher than those of rice. Thus farmers' choice of crops grown is influenced by factors such as soil, climate, marketing, credit and technical advice at least as much as by price.

Table 3.6. *Agricultural exports '000 tons*

	1978	1979	1980	1981	1982	1983	1984	1985	1986	1987
Coffee	55	63	69	57	53	50	51	42	45	52
(index)	100	114	125	103	96	90	92	76	81	94
Vanilla	1.45	0.43	0.41	0.64	1.06	1.1	0.83	0.63	0.69	1.1
(index)	100	29	28	44	73	75	57	43	47	75
Cloves	14.76	13.39	4.36	7.71	10.47	2.97	6.27	12.03	10.18	3
(index)	100	91	29	52	70	20	42	81	68	20

Source: MPARA.

Because of stockpiling and (irregularly) quotas, there is no *a priori* connection between output and exports; higher agricultural output does not necessarily mean higher exports (see Table 3.6). With the best output performance of + 63%, vanilla exports reached only 75% of their 1978 level. Coffee exports have stagnated at 7% below the 1978 level. And clove exports are as irregular as their production, which follows a four-year cycle. Even with products in which a supplying country can influence world prices directly (vanilla and traditionally cloves in Madagascar's case: the reverse being true for coffee), adjustment cannot simply consist in allowing suppliers to rush into what seem to be the most lucrative markets.

Thus, prices alone do not yet offer adequate incentives for farmers to switch production. Although some export prices are improving, difficulties remain at other levels. Production is stagnant except for maize and cassava, while exports do not vary with production (and efforts to strengthen Madagascar's position on the crucial world coffee market prove particularly ineffectual). However, liberalization of marketing has only very recently been completed, and only the downstream services sector seems to have benefited from the present stage of adjustment. This had its own political backlash when middlemen, and particular ethnic groups, were credited with extracting the benefits from the reform process. The situation was further exploited by politicians both in power and in opposition. Nevertheless, farmer numbers are so important (as producers, consumers, suppliers of export or non-tradable goods, wage-earners, sharecroppers, landless, migrants) that an assessment of the situation of specific types of small farmers is needed. To this we turn in Section V.

Social and economic infrastructure

Highly dependent on public spending, this is an area which suffered from budget cutbacks in the 1980s. Results such as the massive return of malarial infection in the highlands (documented by WHO and UNICEF), an outbreak of bubonic plague in 1990, and the increasing insecurity of the rural areas are difficult to attribute to adjustment as they derive at least initially from wider factors including the recession itself. While the degradation of the road infrastructure (not least rural roads) is manifest, economic indicators such as the volume of diesel fuel and gasoline consumed show a fall by 1985 to 85% of the 1981 volume. Recovery in this indicator began in 1986 (as imports were also being liberalized, and so imports rose despite price increases to reflect the foreign-exchange cost more closely), as did the rise in sales of spare parts in the same year.

By 1991, the UNDP in its second *Human Development Report* was attributing to

Madagascar a glowing record on all the social indicators which, in its composite index, provide 'a more realistic statistical measure of human development than simple GNP per inhabitant'. In the report Madagascar is ranked 13th highest in Africa, ahead of Cameroon, Côte d'Ivoire and Nigeria, with a composite human development coefficient (made up of life expectancy, literacy and purchasing-power-parity-adjusted income per head) of 0.371. (In contrast, Sierra Leone's human development indicator (HDI) coefficient, the lowest, was a mere 0.048; Mauritius, the highest in Africa, had 0.831.) More striking still was the assertion that Madagascar's HDI rank was 31 places higher than its 'normal' unadjusted per head income would suggest. This was the highest upgrading on account of human development factors (as measured by the UNDP) in the whole of Africa. However, scepticism about the methodology by which the adjustments were arrived at (and the method of weighting the three criteria into a composite index) is increased when one considers that the other countries challenging for Madagascar's ' + 31 places' adjustment record include Tanzania (29 places better in human development indicators than in economic performance), Ethiopia (+ 18 places), Malawi (+ 16), Mauritius (+ 16) and Mozambique (+ 14). Some African countries, such as Gabon (– 49), were massively downgraded by this HDI ranking system. Moreover, the UNDP Report claimed that Madagascar's human development had increased over the period 1970–90 and only suffered a slight setback in 1991.

Health care. There are many centres of primary health care but these lacked the bare essentials in the 1980s. By contrast, there was a rapid expansion in the numbers of doctors and paramedical staff (between 1975 and 1985 the number of doctors rose from 543 to 1,218) which greatly reduced the Ministry of Health's budget for equipment and medicines. All patients in hospitals have had to pay for their medicines for a number of years.

In the rural areas, one of the signs of this deterioration has been an increase in malaria. In 1985, the Ministry reported 490,000 cases and 6,200 deaths; in 1987, there were 760,000 cases and 11,000 deaths. The main causes are insufficient preventive treatment (Chloroquine is considered too expensive to distribute) and insufficient anti-insect campaigns. It was only in 1988 that, thanks to many international donors, a proper antimalaria campaign was launched in Madagascar.

Physical infrastructure. Since it would be futile to try to increase output, intensify technical training and liberalize the marketing network without sufficient means of communication to ease access to market factors, transport plays an important part in the adjustment process. International aid donors have focused particularly on the road sector. The World Bank devotes 30% of its loans to transport and, of this, 60% has been invested in the road infrastructure.

Many problems still remain. In the 1986–90 plan, the transport sector as a whole was seen as still unable to satisfy demand despite the partial resolution of the appalling situation of the early 1980s. Apart from the basic paucity of the road network, poor co-ordination among the various rehabilitation programmes over the past few years has also been a problem. Of approximately 50,000 km of roads, only one-tenth have

Table 3.7. *Madagascar: human development indicators 1991*

Life expectancy 1990 (years)	Adult Literacy (%)	Real GDP PPP-adjusted ($)	HDI coefficient	GNP less HDI rank
54.5	76.9	670	0.371	+31

been asphalted; this gives very low density (15 km per 100 sq km) and is unequally distributed among the provinces.

The rail network, which barely complements the roads, includes two independent systems – the Northern network (Antananarivo-Moramanga-Lac Alaotra-East Coast-Antsirabe) and the Southern network (Finarantsoa-East Coast).

Airways provide the only means of servicing the isolated areas. Some airports are, however, hampered by too short runways and insufficient ground equipment; of 57 airports only 27 have all-weather runways.

Since the country is an island, shipping is fundamentally important not only for external trade but also for internal communication with the isolated regions. Unfortunately, harbour facilities are seriously dilapidated and this slows down activities and increases the operating costs. Madagascar has about 3,500 km of navigable canals and rivers. The Pangalanes canal which stretches along more than 400 km of coastline, and is the most commonly used waterway, has been under rehabilitation since 1981.

Transport infrastructure policy under the adjustment phase was used for three overriding political motives: to ensure food self-sufficiency, first in rice, then in oil and cereals; to promote activity in the regions producing export crops (in order of priority, these are coffee, vanilla, sisal, cape peas, meat and mining products); and thirdly, to develop the infrastructure supplying industry. Thus, agricultural priorities ought to have been among the most important considerations under adjustment. Yet even the primary target of food self-sufficiency was not remotedly achieved during the 1980s.

Some regions remain entirely inaccessible; the roads may be unfit for use but the high transport tariffs since liberalization also make produce collection unattractive. Social disparities between regions are widening: when and if disadvantaged areas sell their produce, the prices will be low (collectors want to ensure a profit to cover transport costs and/or their monopsony position), and manufactured goods from urban areas, in turn, are sold to them at high prices. The slow development of the infrastructure thus determines the relative impoverishment of certain regions within the context of structural adjustment. The situation would hardly have been any better if the pre-adjustment framework, with controlled collection, controlled consumer prices and a disappearing vehicle fleet, had prevailed; these regions would simply have had neither collectors nor consumer goods.

In absolute terms there has been some improvement even in the isolated areas. In relative terms, though, the situation has worsened compared to the privileged areas (namely those closer to the roads). Clearly, the implementation of an adequate infrastructure policy necessitates a judicious distribution of means as well as overall targets because of its very high cost and regional sensitivities, but it is not certain that a strategy which radically reduces the role of the state in infrastructure spending decisions can succeed in making the optimal allocation of infrastructure investment for the nation as a whole.

V.   THE IMPACT OF ADJUSTMENT ON SMALLHOLDERS AND THE RURAL POOR

Analysis is based on data gathered in the 1984/85 National Census of Agriculture, which became available in 1988, and the supplementary findings and smaller surveys relating to the years immediately before and after the date of the Census. The Census estimated a total *rural* population of 8.6 million (of which 8.3 million were *agricultural*), growing at 3.1%. The agricultural population was formed into 1.46 million farm units of which 99.95% had holdings of less than 10 ha. The *average* landholding was only 1.5 ha, and 76% of rural families had 0.75 ha or less.

From the Census this impact study adopted the following three groups, from different regions and with different production mixes.

Rice farmers of the central highlands

This is the densely populated rice-farming Malagasy heartland, mostly within easy access to the capital, Antananarivo, and the major plateau towns. The smallholders of this region ensure their subsistence through the cultivation of food crops (mainly rice, cassava and maize). Their monetary needs are satisfied through marketing of their surplus and other small transactions. This region represents half the rural population of the country.

In general, the producer price of paddy has remained low despite the fact that the rice produced in these rural areas also supplies the urban areas. For most of the 1980s, the government's policy was to try to safeguard urban interests, and so did not allow the price of rice to fluctuate according to supply and demand. As a strategic variable, the producer price for paddy was controlled. Prices of other produce were low because they are relatively abundant in the rural markets. With peasants remote from export channels, and transport infrastructure in a state of disrepair, such products do not yet count as export crops.

Production takes place on smaller-than-average farms, where irrigation remains a problem most of the time, and where there is a low use of chemical and even natural fertilizer (relative to the required level). Thus, the volume of output remains low and there is little scope for any major development without additional infrastructure investment, research and extension. However, price liberalization was expected to have its most immediate effects in the high plateau rice farming hinterland near the capital.

The problems of the poorer farm families are exacerbated by population growth (with the average size of plots becoming smaller), and rising prices of inputs and manufactured consumption goods. Farmers are forced to sell more rice (the product in highest demand among food crops) to face such increases. Less rice is then available for consumption, leading to a rice deficit over often two to three months in the interstitial 'soudure' season. The main solutions therefore are a reduction in consumption or resort to informal credit. While the latter can incur debt-service obligations which contribute to the smallholders' gradual impoverishment, the former puts the farmer's family at some physical risk and reduces capacity for physical effort.

Smallholder export-crop farmers of the central east coastal region

Here, coffee is produced alongside rice but with marked differences, depending on which area is allocated to which group (e.g. high hills, low slopes, marshes, or alluvial valleys). Although coffee is still the main source of cash earnings, the trees are so old and their upkeep so limited that the yield is constantly diminishing. The region is over-populated and farms are very small, and this too perpetuates low incomes. An important issue at the root of the increasing poverty is the dynamic behind the allocation of areas for rice and coffee production.

In the 1970s, the relatively high price of coffee encouraged farmers to give up food crops on the grounds that coffee would be sold to buy rice. In the early 1980s, the rise in the price of rice and the increasing difficulty in its supply meant that farmers tended to divide the area between the two crops as best they could to allay such difficulties. But the coffee price proved highly unpredictable and reached a fifteen-year low in the late 1980s. Yet the areas are too small to allow producers to be self-sufficient in rice. Instead, they face diminishing returns from coffee and an increasing rice deficit.

Subsistence farmers and herders of the Androy region of the dry south

Characterized by drought, the smallholders of the Androy specialize in food crops (maize, cassava and, in a smaller way, rice). Yields are low because of the harsh climate and the very limited use of fertilizer. Here, water poses a fundamental problem not only from the production but also from the consumption point of view (the existence of water merchants indicates how close to the margin farming is as an occupation). Cattle breeding is well-developed, though often not for cash, and the area has a high emigration rate (both temporary and permanent).

Apart from the climate, the region's main difficulty is that it is poorly integrated into the interregional trade and commerce. This influences farmers' attitudes, limits the extent of markets and keeps prices low. Livestock are kept as a reserve that can be sold but, here again, with supply exceeding demand, prices remain low. The region suffers from very poor infrastructure and precarious health service provision and has a low literacy rate.

The results of surveys conducted among farm families in 1988 compared with data collected in the Agricultural Census in 1985 reveal that the impact of adjustment policies had yet to prove positive for the farmers in each of these three diverse groups, or even to redress the dominant bias against rural production that had reigned since the mid-1970s.

In the *central highlands*, 77.5% of farmers still had a rice deficit, some for up to five months of the year. Average consumption of milled rice was down to 147 kg per person per year, and overall consumption of animal products was only 110 kg per farm family (average household size in the census was 6.78 persons). But the receipts of the typical farm family had already diversified: while 41% was from the sale of agricultural products, 29% was from craft activities and labour hire and a further 12.2% from the sale of local goods and services. Other external resources, including urban-rural income transfers, usually within families, made up the remainder.

Broadly speaking, the central highland rice producers were concentrating on ensuring their family's subsistence in the face of increased input and consumer goods costs. This came before expanding marketed output. Yet this is the region most favoured by its geographical situation (in or near the main transport arteries, close to the capital and other urban centres). The farmers continued to shun formal credit because it seemed inaccessible or available in the wrong part of the season, and they foresaw problems in repaying it, given the rise in living costs. Instead, they tended to hoard cash or make distress sales of produce in order to buy rice at much higher market prices (now unregulated) during the interstitial soudure season.

Liberalization of fertilizer supply has coincided with substantial price increases (especially on those few farmers' consumer and intermediate goods which are imported). The farmer has little idea of the price his crop will reach when he purchases the fertilizer, and has as yet few years on which to place any confidence in the swings and roundabouts of liberalization. The smaller farmer, especially, prefers to avoid risk, limit his indebtedness, and do without. Many of the farmers are unfamiliar with the new fertilizers now being offered. Liberalization is thus forging ahead of the extension services. However, it does appear that a market for agricultural labour is developing in the central highlands.

In the *central east coast region*, farmers have a clearer choice between food and export-crop production. Characterized by traditional agriculture, strong demographic pressure and unreliable climate, this is a rice-deficit region. Poor soils, combined with low potential to extend cultivable area, emphasize food insufficiency and encourage migration. Farms are small, the majority with less than 1 ha. A rice-coffee combination is practised by nearly all farmers. Some cultivate rain-fed rice as well as fruit (especially bananas).

During the economic crisis which Madagascar experienced in the 1980s, the main problems facing coffee farmers was securing payment, at remunerative prices, for the coffee crop. Uncertainty on this account led to a lack of care in cultivation, an ageing of plant stock, and subsequently low yields.

On the other hand, the main problem preventing an increase in rice production is poor water control. A sudden heavy rainfall can provoke floods and prevent the second rice crop. Without better control over water, all the advantages of an eventual intensification policy (selected seeds; use of fertilizer (note that the region does not use manure); use of draught animals) are drastically reduced. Farmers suffered directly from cutbacks in infrastructure spending and maintenance on the part of the public authorities. This was, however, at least as attributable to generally poor management of the national budget as to the prioritization of expenditures which had to occur under adjustment.

The final blow came when world coffee prices fell to historic lows in the period 1988–91. By then, adjustment was beginning to be taken seriously and border prices were beginning to be reflected in purchase prices; this was hardly to the advantage of farmers.

For coffee producers in the east, the enduring problems of limited landholdings, old coffee bush stock (and lack of working capital to renew it) and a near-absence of extension support remained. Farmers in this group might be expected to switch between rice and coffee again. But the complete liberalization of coffee marketing is so recent (1988) and the lead time so much longer that the price and market effects of a more general adjustment process over six years cannot yet be asserted. Most farmers will keep some food production in any case. There is as yet little sign that they are using large factor inputs such as credit, labour or fertilizer.

The Antandroy of the semi-desert *southern Androy region* own nearly 32% of Madagascar's total cattle stock. Crops account for, on average, only 25% of their income. There is as yet no evidence that the reintroduction of markets has stimulated their economic activity, at least with respect to cattle-raising. Most Antandroy keep cattle as capital and cull a minimum number, usually for trade within a very restricted locality.

The poor southern Androy farmers, who are geographically more remote than the other two groups, are also quite literally further removed from the process of adjustment. They continue to suffer from a political decision of more than a decade ago not to supply formal rural credit to the region. Adjustment has, however, probably begun to stimulate emigration as a market for agricultural labour has developed elsewhere. There is a risk, however, that such an exodus of the fitter heads of households may render a poor region even poorer overall, even if remittances are taken into account.

VI. CONCLUSIONS

If these three farming regions can be taken as at least partly representative of Madagascar under what was clearly the early stage of an as yet not-too-intensive adjustment programme, and before the major political upheavals of 1991, a few general conclusions can be drawn.

The impoverishing effects of adjustment, initially increasing the price of purchased food and consumer goods, persist. Neither the market incentive mechanisms nor concerted action by the remaining state-run bodies have clearly benefitted agricultural producers as opposed to intermediaries. Yet when political disruptions, leading to the fall of Prime Minister Ramahatra's government, began in June 1991, it was the urban middle classes who felt their relative impoverishment more and who drove the rebellion. When in August 1991 demonstrators were massacred outside the presidential palace, President Ratsiraka used Antandroy farmers to support his presidential guard against an essentially urban-based opposition.

As the nation as a whole has experienced a decade of declining real incomes, smallholder farmers have moved closer to the margins of poverty where their family's very survival begins to be at stake. Their capacity to take risks and even to respond to otherwise highly attractive incentives has been much reduced. Those effects of reforms that are so far visible are partial and inchoate.

While the relative incentives may have switched in favour of certain exportables (notably coffee), even this product has barely recovered to its real incentive price of a decade ago, before the adjustment reforms. However, over the period 1981–6, the price of paddy rice rose faster than prices for urban manufactures used by farm families, such as candles, soap, cloth, and white sugar. Some farmers may see the rural-urban terms of trade moving in their favour (even without producing one of the privileged export crops). Yet the majority perceived the 'risk' of market-oriented reforms largely in the relationship between the price they receive for rice paddy (at harvest time) and that which they have to pay when shortages occur. The difference between these two prices has widened under liberalization. For the poorer farmers who cannot set aside food stocks from their own production, this is a threatening development rather than a stimulus.

It is too soon to see the full results in agriculture, and on smallholders and the rural poor, of the reforms. Whereas stabilization policies began nearly a decade ago, major agricultural liberalization is only now feeding through to producers. Farmers have become more risk-averse because they have had a long experience of declining incomes and are closer now to absolute poverty. They do not therefore respond with alacrity to market stimuli.

The common distinction between food as a non-tradable and export crops as tradables does not apply to rice, which is beginning to be traded internationally again. In any case, one of the most significant agricultural reforms under the structural adjustment programmes was the liberalization of the *domestic* market for rice: until recently it was prohibited to transport rice across regional borders or to sell it privately from a food-surplus to a food-deficit area.

Within each region there are types of farming families which are more impoverished than the general run of smallholders; the landless, female-headed households, and recently arrived distress migrants are among the more disadvantaged still. Though not fully representative of the rich diversity of Madagascar's agricultural economy, the three regions studied nevertheless provide reliable evidence on how different types of smallholders, facing very different physical farming conditions and enjoying varying traditions and differing levels of political attention or hostility, responded to the process of economic reform during the 1980s.

Judgements about the results of the reforms need to recognize that Madagascar was still being affected by recession throughout the decade (notwithstanding its association with the IMF through the stabilization programme from 1980 and the claim that 'adjustment' started in 1982). In fact, it would be better to start from 1986 (with the sectoral loans and the liberalization of output and transport) or 1987 (the only major devaluation) or 1988 (liberalization of marketing for the export trade, except for vanilla; first adjustment loan throughout the entire public sector, accompanied by a social subsidy loan) or even 1989 (liberalization of the financial sector) before deciding whether or not the recovery process is really in motion. A survey of household data and the 1985 Agricultural Census helps shed light on farm family behaviour but these data tend to be mixed up with the general effects of recession. Even rural insecurity, in terms of cattle theft (almost a tradition) and thefts of food and export products from the fields (an important phenomenon of the 1980s), has been a major consequence of the recession, reflecting the increasing poverty of the landless and the lack of public spending on security services (see, in particular, Jureco, 1988).

The recession and the apparent bias against farmers (especially against marginal groups and marginal populations, such as the Androy farmers who were forced to emigrate) have been so continuous and have lasted so long that it will take a long time for income to recover to former levels, let alone for farmers again to trust price and market indicators. Their absolute and relative incomes have declined so drastically that compensatory programmes, coupled with firm adjustment policies, are necessary. Nonetheless, the most important of these (for medicines; anti-malarial drugs; a rice buffer-stock; and programmes to employ graduate civil servants during the reform of the public sector) are not directed towards the smallholders. These programmes lack any rural dimension, such as credit at accessible rates during the tide-over period; temporary subsidies for imported fertilizer or that eventually mixed locally by Z-ren at a high resource-cost; effective extension services; agricultural projects funded by donors targeting the smallholder; subsidies for road infrastructure (and repairs) including rural tracks, also aiming at smallholders. The latter would also help reinforce the rural-urban link in production as well as exchange.

Rice is again becoming much more widely traded, both internally and externally. The example of the Androy demonstrates this, for there rice is considered as a luxury good to be exported, once it is allowed, to other markets in the interior of the country. The coastal farmers both produce and consume rice but, in allocating their factors of production, they choose between rice and coffee. Although they were not self-sufficient in the 1980s, it makes sense for the Malagasy to regard rice as an export product as from the 1990s. Recent increases in paddy production following market liberalization will increase its domestic marketing. This does not prevent rice being both tradable and for consumption, thus respecting the food security policy. With a population growth rate of 2.8%, only an increase in agricultural productivity and the stimulus of more open export markets can determine both roles in the future.

Finally, the progress of liberalization in general and of economic reforms targeting agriculture, in particular, faces some obvious constraints. Among the most important are:

At the level of sectoral implementation. The abolition of state services in the rural areas does not guarantee that a private entrepreneur will materialize to fill the gaps. Those dependent on the state, and with no interest in terms of short-term profitability for the small private traders, will remain. Even if this were not the case, ethnic frictions between producers and traders could be either exploited or exacerbated.

At the national level. It is now acknowledged that Madagascar has an ecology problem. Sponsored by the World Bank, the 1988 report, *Environmental Action Plan*, acknowledges the problem and advises long-term investment and protection measures which go against the first stabilization programmes.

At the global level. Currently at $3.68 bn, Madagascar's long-term external debt, and its increased service burden (up to 1989), hampers any long-term recovery. External disequilibrium originally necessitated the stabilization and adjustment programmes. Debt servicing required exceptional measures to tackle the external imbalance over the 1980s. It would be a mistake to penalize smallholders for the accumulation of costs not only during 3 years (1978–80) of misguided excessive investment but also nearly 10 years of adjustment policy, by formulating agrarian and macroeconomic policies which extract too large an agricultural surplus at the expense of rural welfare. Measures to write off a large portion of the state's unwisely incurred public debt, together with a recognition that Madagascar's balance-of-payments problem was less delinquent than the underlying budget problems, would ease matters for the rural economy considerably.

Some of the most crucial reforms still have to be put in hand at the level of domestic politics. A more representative government would be likely to take the process of economic policy reform and implementation more seriously. It has been, after all, in political posturing on matters which affected the livelihood of millions of poor farming families rather than in implementing agreed adjustment policies that Madagascar has shown ingenuity over the past fifteen years. But there are now signs of change. In June 1991, the then Economy and Planning Minister announced a number of firm commitments which overturn many of the xenophobic or pseudo-marxist features of the 1975 constitution and the Charter of Socialist Enterprises. The state was to withdraw from 'most' productive sectors of the economy; all state monopolies were to end before the end of 1991. Every effort was to be made to render the Malagasy franc fully convertible; exchange controls were to be loosened. A 1977 decree preventing foreigners owning rural property in excess of 20 ha was to be repealed; a 1973 decree prohibiting the closure of any company without government permission was to be struck out; import licensing was to be run down and tariff reforms were to result in a five-step simplified and transparent system from 10% to 50%. Together with the deregulation of agricultural marketing and the withdrawal of the state (and the military) from most production and trade in the sector, Madagascar's farmers could now face fewer policy distortions than at any time over the past decade of structural adjustment. But these economic reforms were enough to encourage the opposition parties to seek the political kingdom also. The last six months of 1991 were a period of near anarchy as ever more implausible coalition partners formed short-lived governments and more and more economic sectors went on strike. From the mayhem a Third Malagasy Republic is bound to emerge, but its government will have to initiate a major new programme of economic reforms.

References

Andriamananjara, Rajaona (1974) *The Investment Code 1973*. Antananarivo: Imprimerie nationale.

Archer, Robert (1976) *Madagascar depuis 1972: La marche d'une révolution*. Paris: l'Harmattan.

Bates, Robert (1984) *Markets and States in Tropical Africa: The Political Basis of Agricultural Policies*. Berkeley CA: University of California Press.

Deleris, F. (1987) *Ratsiraka: Socialisme et misère à Madagascar*. Paris: l'Harmattan.

Hugon, Ph. (1988) 'Madagascar: le riz et le pouvoir', in Jacques de Bandt et Philippe Hugon (eds) *Le Tiers-Monde en mal d'industrie*. Paris: Economica.

Jureco S. A. (1988) *Paysans sans Terre et Accès à la terre à Madagascar*. Antananarivo: UNDP/FAO.

Madagascar Ministry of Agricultural Production and Agrarian Reform/UNDP/FAO (1988) *Recensement National de l'Agriculture: Campagne Agricole 1984/85*. Antananarivo: MPARA/UNDP/FAO.

Madagascar Government (1979) *Charte des Entreprises Socialistes*. Antananarivo: Imprimerie nationale.

Madagascar: Banque des Données de l'Etat (1987) 'Enquête sur les budgets des ménages – milieu rural'. Antananarivo, mimeo.

Pryor, Frederick (1988) *Income Distribution and Economic Development in Madagascar: Some Historical Statistics*. Washington DC: World Bank Discussion Paper No. 37.

Pryor, Frederick (1990) *The Political Economy of Poverty, Equity and Growth. Madagascar and Malawi Compared*. Washington DC: World Bank.

Rajoelina, Patrick (1988) *Quarante Années de Vie Politique de Madagascar (1947–1987)*. Paris: l'Harmattan.

Ratsiraka, Didier (1975) *Charte de la révolution socialiste malgache: tous azimuts*. Antananarivo: Imprimerie d'ouvrages éducatifs.

Tronchon, Jacques (1982) *L'insurrection malgache de 1947*. Fianarantsoa: EFA.

UNDP (1991) *Human Development Report*. New York: UNDP.

World Bank (1986) *The Democratic Republic of Madagascar: Country Economic Memorandum*, Report No. 5996-MAG. Washington DC: World Bank.

World Bank/AID/Coopération Suisse/UNESCO/UNDP/WWF (1988) *Madagascar: Plan d'Action Environnementale*. Washington DC: World Bank.

World Bank (1990) *Adjustment Lending Policies for Sustainable Growth*. Policy and Research Series Paper No.14. Washington DC: World Bank.

World Bank (1991 and 1981) *World Development Report*. Washington DC: World Bank.

Appendix Table 3.1.   *Producer prices 1978–87, current Fmg/kg*

	1978	1979	1980	1981	1982	1983	1984	1985	1986	1987
Paddy	35	39	43	47	59.8	65	90	100	180	135
Green Coffee	180	185	215	250	260	280	330	395	600	800
Cloves	340	385	395	430	435	435	435	435	525	600
Vanilla	305	500	600	700	700	1000	1000	1000	1100	1200

Source: MPARA.

Appendix Table 3.2.   *Producer prices 1978–87, constant Fmg/kg*

	1978	1979	1980	1981	1982	1983	1984	1985	1986	1987
Paddy	35	34	32	27	26	23	30	30	47	30
(index)	100	98	91	76	74	67	85	85	134	87
Green Coffee	180	162	159	142	112	101	109	117	156	180
(index)	100	90	89	79	62	56	60	65	87	100
Cloves	340	337	293	244	188	157	143	129	136	135
(index)	100	99	86	72	55	46	42	38	40	40
Vanilla	305	438	445	398	302	361	329	297	286	270
(index)	100	144	146	130	99	118	108	98	94	89

Sources: DGBDE and MINCOM.

4

MALAWI

ELIZABETH CROMWELL

I. ECONOMIC OVERVIEW

At Independence in 1964, Malawi was an extremely poor country with few resources other than fertile land and abundant labour. The new government decided that the country's economic future lay in export-oriented agriculture and provided little protection or support for industry. Apart from textile production, it remains centred almost exclusively around the processing of food, tobacco and tea; together these account for over 95% of manufactured exports. The sector has been characterized by a high degree of monopoly power, low capacity utilization and the dominant role of a number of quasi-public bodies. Contrary to the popular image of Malawi, state participation – in particular, the operations of the quasi-public company Press (Holdings) Ltd and its subsidiaries – has, until recently, been prolific in all sectors of the economy.

Meanwhile, agriculture was the specific focus of development policy. The key feature of the sector at Independence was its division into two distinct sub-sectors: large-scale commercial tobacco and tea estates and a large number of semi-subsistence smallholdings. This was subsequently reinforced by legislation in two specific areas. First, the 1965 Land Act, which provided four classes of rural land tenure: public land, freehold land, leasehold land and user rights to customary land allocated to smallholders by Traditional Authorities (hereditary tribal leaders) (Pachai, 1978). Under the Act, estates operate under freehold or leasehold tenure and smallholder agriculture on customary land; as the Act permits the granting of leases or freehold tenure on customary land, it has allowed rapid expansion of estates at the expense of smallholder cultivation. Second, the Special Crops legislation of 1968 dictated the crops that may be grown in the two sub-sectors – the more lucrative flue-cured and burley tobacco being reserved for estates and oriental and fire-cured tobacco and cotton being the monopoly of the smallholder sector.[1] Wages and incomes policies have further favoured the estates by keeping down minimum wages.

Whilst estate development policy concentrated on the provision of preferential access to economic assets, policy towards smallholders centred on the maintenance of key support services. In 1978 the National Rural Development Programme (NRDP)

[1] Although, as part of the 1990 Agricultural Sector Adjustment Credit, burley production is now to be opened up to smallholders.

was inaugurated. Its primary objective is to improve rural standards of living through the establishment of country-wide extension, credit and marketing facilities for smallholder farmers. This has involved the creation of eight socio-ecologically demarcated Agricultural Development Divisions (ADDs).

In terms of physical emplacement of facilities, the NRDP has been a valuable mechanism for coherent intervention in the rural economy. Malawi had an impressive market infrastructure, prior to the liberalization of agricultural marketing in 1987; seasonal credit funds averaging MK44m. (US$18m.) (World Bank, 1987); and extension worker:farmer ratios of 1:500. However, this investment has not benefitted the majority of poor farmers and has had little positive impact on production (maize yields have increased by only 0.8% per annum on average – and production has actually declined quite substantially in some ADDs (Fischer, 1988)). Over-emphasis on the extension of technologies appropriate only for larger semi-commercial smallholder farmers (in particular, large credit packages for monocropped hybrid maize) has precluded the participation of the majority of smallholder population.

With respect to macroeconomic development, for over a decade after Independence growth was rapid, with outstanding achievements in capital formation and its financing. Both government and private domestic savings rose faster than investment and government savings became positive in 1971. Concerted efforts to increase tax revenues were effective and manufacturing output expanded. However, agriculture's share of GDP declined, reflecting slow growth in the smallholder sector. As well as its preferential access to economic assets, the estate sector's rapid growth was facilitated by a high implicit tax on smallholder cash crops, in the form of low producer prices offered by the agricultural marketing parastatal ADMARC, with the resulting profits being channelled into the estates. This latter policy was an important contributory factor explaining the slow growth in smallholder output during the period.

The impressive overall performance was in large part due to government economic policies that encouraged export-oriented agricultural production, provided a favourable environment for foreign capital and enterprise, maintained low tariffs and minimal quantitative restrictions on imports (so discouraging uneconomic import substitution) and promoted wage restraint in order to keep Malawian goods internationally competitive. Exchange-rate competitiveness was also maintained by a series of devaluations. As a result domestic inflation was held down. Malawi also benefitted from highly favourable world prices for its internationally traded commodities and substantial migrant worker remittances – the second most important source of foreign exchange after agricultural exports. And the President's long term of office and strong personal control have brought a political continuity which is lacking elsewhere in sub-Saharan Africa.

However, by the end of the 1970s growth was clearly slowing down. Domestic investment and savings rates were halved between 1979 and 1981. The banking system's assets fell sharply, although domestic credit expanded – loans to government being the major component. The worst manifestation of the crisis was the explosion of the balance-of-payments current account deficit; the debt-service ratio also jumped in the last three years of the decade. The profitability of the large parastatal sector reversed from MK33m. profit in 1977 to MK7m. loss in 1980 and the government deficit increased. Inflation also rose dramatically.

The chief causes of this downturn were external. By 1980 Malawi's international terms of trade were 59% of their 1970 level owing to a substantial reduction in the world price of tea and tobacco, increases in the cost of imported fuel and fertilizer as a result of the world oil price rises, and substantially increased external transport costs (the cif margin on exports reached 28% by 1980), resulting from the closure of the rail line to Nacala because of the escalating civil war in Mozambique. The war also resulted in Malawi hosting a large number of Mozambican refugees; despite international assistance, this has imposed a very substantial burden on the domestic budget, estimated at 1% of GDP in 1989 alone (World Bank, 1990a).

Remittances also declined dramatically as the result of a general reduction in migrant employment opportunities in neighbouring Zambia and Zimbabwe and a three-year ban on migration to South Africa by the Malawi Government, following an air crash in 1974 in which a large number of Malawian mine labourers were killed. In addition, a partial drought in the southern part of the country in 1979 reduced foreign-exchange earnings from agricultural export sales and necessitated the allocation of dwindling forex reserves to the purchase of imported food.

Domestic mismanagement also contributed to the crisis. During the 1970s an annual government deficit equivalent to around 10% of GDP had been covered by external borrowing. This debt began to mature at the end of the decade; interest payments created a rapid expansion of the deficit which was then financed by commercial loans and drawings on reserves. The problem was exacerbated by the award of large pay increases to the civil service in 1977. Government borrowing then began to crowd out the private sector. And some of the activities of the quasi-public institutions had been highly unsound both financially and economically. Secondly, the export base had been allowed to remain heavily concentrated on three commodities: tobacco, tea and sugar (accounting for more than 70% of total exports). When international commodity prices declined sharply towards the end of the decade, foreign-exchange earnings were dramatically reduced.

Thirdly, this concentration had a disastrous impact on overall growth when the estates developed severe structural problems at the same time. The rapid expansion of estate agriculture during the 1970s had been largely due to the official encouragement – including preferential access to bank loans – given to the creation of tobacco estates by senior members of the Establishment. With favourable international prices, and the market opportunities provided by Rhodesia's Unilateral Declaration of Independence in 1965, these estates prospered: by 1980 lending to tobacco estates comprised 54% of the commercial banks' loan portfolio. With the deterioration in the international trading environment at the end of the 1970s, a combination of poor technical management and high gearing forced many of the estates into bankruptcy and precipitated a near crisis in the banking sector.

Thus, although in the 1970s international donors held Malawi up as a shining example of what could be achieved by a small resource-poor country through free market policies and an efficient bureaucracy, at the beginning of the 1980s this reputation as the economic miracle of Central Africa was somewhat tarnished. The naiveté of the donors' prior perception of the Malawian economy became apparent. Attempts to restore equilibrium using available domestic resources – through devaluation and improvements in agricultural producer prices in 1979 – proved inadequate. Therefore, in mid-1980, the government entered into negotiations with the International Monetary Fund for standby funds. An earlier Compensatory Financing Facility had proved inadequate for the necessary major restructuring of the economy. The IMF standby agreement came into operation in 1980 and the first structural adjustment loan was agreed with the World Bank in 1981. Since then there have been an IMF Extended Financing Facility (1983) and two more structural adjustment loans (in 1982 and 1985) as well as two sectoral adjustment credits, for trade and industry in 1988 and agriculture in 1990.

Malawi's experience of economic reform merits some attention as the country represents a special case among the cluster of African nations now involved in donor-financed structural adjustment programmes. Its initial position in 1980 was one of only moderate destabilization compared with many countries in sub-Saharan Africa. Coupled with this, the loan conditions did not involve basic changes in a government ideology of fiscal conservatism and economic efficiency. And the President's effective control of political and economic power allowed reforms to be pushed through that have foundered in other countries through lack of popular support. On the other hand, the external environment continued to deteriorate during much of the 1980s with respect to both the persistent decline in international terms of trade and increased transport dislocation, as a result of escalating insecurity in Mozambique, and this has made the achievement of macroeconomic equilibrium something of a moving target.

These special features have meant that few of the standard policy prescriptions, such as correcting overvalued exchange rates, have been applicable in the Malawian context. This explains the relatively mild conditionality of the early loans and why some of the reforms have had only limited success. It has also made Malawi a testing ground for new approaches – such as sectoral adjustment credits, started by the World Bank in Malawi in 1988, and the IMF's Enhanced Structural Adjustment Facility, of which Malawi was, in July 1988, the first beneficiary.

Numerous studies have examined the macroeconomic dimensions of Malawi's reform and hypothesized about its implications for the national economy as a whole (Collier, 1988; Kydd with Hewitt, 1986; Kydd and Hewitt, 1986; Kydd, 1988; Winter, 1984). However, virtually nothing has been written about the distributional consequences of adjustment for particular social groups. Of particular concern for all agriculturally-based economies such as Malawi's, is the economic and social impact on poor peasant farmers; the evidence in this chapter may therefore have wider relevance for other land-locked and land-constrained countries in sub-Saharan Africa.

II.   THE ECONOMIC REFORM PROGRAMME

Macroeconomic reforms

In terms of broad economic strategy, Malawi is unusual among sub-Saharan countries in that the direction previously pursued was broadly in sympathy with the new orthodoxy advocated by donors lending for economic recovery. Reform has therefore not involved dramatic changes in economic philosophy or policy.

IMF support for the reform programme has continued, with only small interruptions, up to the present. Throughout, it has been conditional on fiscal and monetary restraint and exchange-rate depreciation. However, the initial lack of success in meeting balance-of-payments objectives, coupled with the apparently deep-seated structural causes of disequilibrium, led to the negotiation of a series of more concessional structural and sectoral adjustment loans (SALs) with the World Bank. Conditionality associated with these has varied. The first required only a commitment to raise charges made by parastatal enterprises and to decontrol prices. The second was more stringent, requiring substantial increases in the producer prices of export commodities and reform of the quasi-public sector. Arrangements for the third loan departed from the previous format in that they included funding from bilateral donors. Conditionality was more relaxed and revolved around a concern to improve the performance of parastatals. In particular, there was pressure to raise the productivity of the estate sector and to improve the efficiency of agricultural marketing through, inter alia, the privatization of a number of ADMARC's activities. Emphasis was also placed on diversifying production, particularly of exports.

By the mid-1980s the external environment was deteriorating further owing to considerable increases in international freight costs, leading to a reassessment of the appropriateness of the macroeconomic objectives of previous loans. As a result, a sectoral adjustment credit for trade and industry was agreed with the World Bank in June 1988, oriented to the liberalization of external trade, the promotion of domestic competition and support for small-scale industry.

The major objectives of the reform programme to date can be summarized as follows:-

a) to reform the tax system by broadening the tax base and increasing the proportion of revenue derived from income and company profits relative to trade;
b) to reduce the budget deficit in proportion to GDP through fiscal restraint and monetary stringency. In particular, to reduce government borrowing in order to encourage expansion of the private sector;
c) to institute greater cost recovery on the part of parastatals;
d) to decontrol prices and wages;
e) to maintain a competitive exchange rate and to institute a flexible foreign-exchange allocation system;
f) to establish a target debt-service ratio and improve control over the servicing of foreign debts.

The overall impact of this programme has been mixed. After an initial sharp fall in real GDP, due more to non-policy factors such as inclement rainfall patterns, nominal growth continued weak but positive through the mid-1980s, although with a sharp dip in industrial performance in 1987 as a knock-on effect of the stringent foreign-exchange controls applied at the time. The high rate of population growth, plus the influx of refugees from Mozambique, meant real per capita GDP was actually lower at the end of the decade than in 1980.

With regard to the sectoral growth pattern, the most striking factor has been the growth in government services which, contrary to programme objectives, was substantially faster than growth in the economy as a whole until the very end of the decade. Of other key sectors, only estate agriculture has recorded more or less persistent growth. Perhaps most worryingly, adjustment has been achieved primarily through contraction in aggregate demand rather than diversification of the productive base.

Trade and exchange-rate policy.   Almost alone among sub-Saharan African countries, Malawi has consistently maintained its currency close to the market value. This greatly simplified the implementation of reform, since the periodic devaluations were a continuation of previous policies. The data in Table 4.2 reflect effectiveness in this respect, in so far as the changes in the nominal rate mirror those in the real effective rate of exchange.

Currency depreciation has been a central instrument in correcting the severe balance-of-payments deficits of the late 1970s. Also important, however, has been the depressed demand for imports; it is this, rather than export performance, which contributed most to reducing the current account deficit and accounts for its resurgence after the start of import decontrol in 1987. The debt-service ratio grew to substantial proportions before rescheduling under the Paris and London Club agreements allowed a reduction in the late 1980s.

Mechanisms for the acquisition of foreign exchange have also been modified. Prior

Table 4.1. *Principal macroeconomic indicators, 1980–90 (annual growth per cent per annum)*

	1980	1981	1982	1983	1984	1985	1986	1987	1988	1989	1990
Real GDP[a]	−0.40	−5.20	2.70	3.60	4.40	4.30	2.60	−0.20	3.29	4.30	4.68
Real GDP/capita	−3.64	−8.17	−0.51	0.48	1.38	1.23	−0.81	−3.22	3.10	−2.79	1.43
Agriculture	−6.50	−8.20	6.40	4.40	5.40	1.10	0.10	1.90	1.98	3.45	5.09
of which:											
Smallholder	−8.50	−8.90	2.50	3.70	7.20	1.20	0.40	0.50	0.49	1.56	7.52
Estates	3.30	4.90	22.40	7.10	0.80	0.60	−1.10	7.20	7.13	9.58	−2.19
Manufacturing	0.30	3.60	−0.30	7.10	2.50	0.50	5.30	−0.80	3.27	7.87	6.03
Govt. Services	8.40	6.30	5.50	4.90	10.30	3.20	8.50	4.10	5.28	2.33	2.69

Note: (a) 1978 prices; new series introduced 1987.
Source: GOM, *Economic Report*, various issues.

Table 4.2. The external account, 1980–89

	1980	1981	1982	1983	1984	1985	1986	1987	1988	1989 (est.)
					[Kwachas per US dollar]					
Exchange rate:										
Nominal[a]	0.83	0.90	1.06	1.18	1.41	1.72	1.86	2.21	2.54	2.79
Real Effective	100.0	99.8	96.0	97.7	96.7	96.9	87.0	82.4	88.4	n.a.
Current account deficit	22.21	11.39	11.15	12.35	1.34	9.63	6.16	5.08	8.7	10.7
					(% of GDP)					
Balance of external account	−0.70	−3.31	−5.62	−9.00	+3.40	−6.26	−0.28	+1.21	+3.86	2.61
Debt-service ratio		27.9	20.4	23.3	21.9	28.5	31.6	37.2	38.1	
Exports (fob)	24.64	24.52	21.62	19.72	26.32	23.12	25.46	20.81	22.4	18.80
Imports (cif)	27.56	21.99	17.74	16.97	13.50	15.90	16.33	13.27	33.73	35.66
Commodity terms of trade Index	100	121	123	113	118	101	88	91	82	77
Income terms of trade Index	100	97	102	124	94	94	87	93	85	72

Note: (a) Period average.
Sources: IMF, *International Financial Statistics*; GOM, *Economic Report*, various issues; Kydd (1988); World Bank (1990a).

to the reform programme all importers were required to apply to the central Reserve Bank which allocated quantities of foreign currency for specific purposes on a non-transparent system. Following SAL-III in 1985 the need for prior Reserve Bank approval was removed for the importation of 75% of raw materials and spare parts. From February 1988, 25% of allocations were deregulated, and a further 50% the following September.

A number of measures have been taken to liberalize international trade, including reducing tariffs on some commodities and easing import procedures by decategorizing a number of goods formerly requiring prior foreign-exchange clearance. Both these measures have caused a rapid increase in imports as a proportion of GDP which has not been matched by exports.

Fiscal and monetary policy.   The growth of government deficits necessitated the mobilization of domestic revenue and more stringent control of public expenditure. The tax schedule was reorganized, many personal allowances were eliminated and marginal tax rates increased, with the net effect of diminishing the equity of the system. The objective of increasing the proportion of revenue from taxes on incomes and company profits was not noticeably fulfilled, however, given that parallel attempts were made to reduce that derived from international trade.

Attempts to control government expenditure met with greater success. However, reductions occurred primarily in development rather than recurrent expenditure, where the high salary component and the political implications of reducing the number of government employees raised problems. Aid flows to a great extent supplemented the development budget.

Attempts to restructure demand met with only limited success. As a proportion of GDP consumption changed little throughout the period, although there was some shift from government to private consumption. The main impact of austerity measures fell on investment, particularly private investment (see Table 4.3). Savings showed no particular trend.

Malawi's fiscal problems had been aggravated by the financial problems of the parastatals. These companies had not been able to service their debts and the government, which guaranteed their foreign debt, had incurred substantial costs in meeting their interest and amortization payments. The divestiture of a number of them and the increased efficiency of the remainder have proved beneficial in so far as many of them are now financially self-sufficient.

The objective of introducing greater control over monetary growth, and in particular over the rate of domestic credit expansion, was largely unrealized after the initial reversal of trend over the early part of the decade (Table 4.4). The hoped-for financial deepening has not occurred: the banks are still lending predominantly to their traditional clients. Although nominal interest rates have risen they have remained negative in real terms, except in 1985. Inflation rose dramatically to 31% in 1988.

Incomes and employment policy.   Traditionally Malawi has pursued a policy of keeping formal sector wages low in order to encourage employment and promote international comparative advantage for estate exports. The reform programme required a continuity of this policy: additional measures included the de-control of non-agricultural prices coupled with wage restraint, with the aim of encouraging private sector growth while maintaining a competitive export sector and control over the civil service wage bill. As a result the purchasing power of wage-earners has been seriously eroded in real terms (Table 4.5), although this must be attributed as much

Table 4.3. *National account variables, 1980–90*

	1980	1981	1982	1983	1984	1985	1986	1987	1988	1989	1990[b]
						(% of GDP)					
Govt. deficit	8.49	11.5	11.7	8.2	7.8	6.4	7.3	8.6	9.0	6.8	6.3
Govt. expenditure	35.4	35.7	35.5	30.9	30.1	29.5	30.7	27.1	30.0	26.5	26.4
Pvte. investment[a]	5.1	5.0	6.2	5.4	3.3	4.9	2.9	5.6	7.6	9.1	n/a
National savings	8.5	5.7	10.3	11.5	13.9	5.8	8.8	8.9	10.1	6.2	6.1
Development expend. (% of Total Govt. Expend.)	41.8	48.8	61.7	32.1	33.1	27.5	26.2	21.3	31.9	26.4	29.5
Income tax (% of total govt. revenue)	31.7	32.6	28.0	32.5	32.8	33.2	35.0	34.3	36.9	32.3	32.7

Notes: (a) Private investment refers to total investment net of investment by government and public corporations. Data from Kydd (1988) and World Bank (1990a).

(b) Estimate.

Source: GOM, *Economic Report* (various issues).

Table 4.4. *The monetary sector, 1980–89*

	1980	1981	1982	1983	1984	1985	1986	1987	1988	1989
% growth in M2	12.6	26.1	14.5	5.9	32.6	−1.0	25.4	22.7	40.1	5.5
Domestic credit expansion	12.0	29.0	17.7	17.1	2.3	13.0	23.6	11.0	−22.0	23.1
Inflation (%)	19.0	11.8	9.8	13.5	20.0	10.5	14.1	25.1	31.5	11.8
Interest rate (%)	7.90	9.75	9.75	9.92	11.75	12.50	12.75	15.75	12.75	n/a

Sources: IMF, *International Financial Statistics*. Inflation percentage derived from CPI. Interest rates refer to deposit rates. World Bank, 1990a.

Table 4.5. *Employment and wage indices, 1981-7*

	1981	1982	1983	1984	1985	1986	1987
				(1980 = 100)			
Employment							
Private sector	86	92	106	104	113	120	108
Government	100	100	104	104	106	109	119
Total	89	94	105	104	111	117	111
Real wages							
Private sector	103	104	89	81	77	75	73
Government	93	97	90	82	82	79	84
Total	102	103	89	81	78	76	75

Source: GOM, *Economic Report* (various issues); Kydd (1988).

to past policies as to the reform programme per se. In 1989, an attempt was made to rectify the situation by doubling minimum wages, unchanged since 1986.

Employment indices in the formal sector, on the other hand, reveal a more encouraging picture with employment expanding over the period as a whole and, until recently, mainly in the private sector.

Agricultural sector reforms

In the agricultural sector the crisis of the early 1980s manifested itself in stagnating production, declining food security and falling export earnings caused by a deterioration in the international terms of trade for Malawi's traditional export crops. The early adjustment loans therefore addressed the need for: increased and diversified agricultural exports, by means of producer price incentives and, for the estate sector, an export credit facility; and a restructuring of ADMARC and the liberalization of domestic trade in agricultural commodities. Concern that deep-seated structural problems were constraining the ability of the sector to respond to macroeconomic reforms led to the negotiation of an agricultural sector adjustment credit (ASAC) in March 1990. The ASAC addressed structural constraints relating to access to land and fertilizer and credit use among the poorest smallholders, and the efficiency of estate land use.

The preferential access to land enjoyed by the estate sector has contributed to increasing pressure on customary land cultivated by smallholders. Thus the ASAC includes a freeze on further land transfer pending a full review of the tenure system and a doubling of leasehold rents to encourage more efficient land utilization.

Institutional reform and liberalization. The parastatal Agricultural Development and Marketing Corporation (ADMARC) has been one of Malawi's many hybrid organizations, expected simultaneously to operate according to commercial criteria and to carry out a range of development functions including price stabilization; market clearing and maintaining a national produce marketing infrastructure; farm input supply to the smallholder sector; and, originally, responsibility for national and household food security through financing the Strategic Grain Reserve and the consumer maize subsidy. In addition, it has had a range of less explicit development functions involving the financing of commercial agriculture and acting as an intermediary for venture capital for other quasi-public institutions (Pryor, 1987).

During the 1970s, ADMARC was able to fulfil this broad mandate as the surplus from profitable international commodity trading subsidized non-commercial activities, such as the implicit maize subsidy and the provision of development finance for the estate sector. However, in the early 1980s, ADMARC's financial position deteriorated dramatically owing to a sharp downturn in world prices, over-extension in development financing, operational inefficiencies and increases in the quantities of maize having to be unprofitably cleared from the market (partly caused by a 68% increase in the producer price in 1981). The Corporation was no longer able to carry out its multi-functional mandate and, in 1985, had to borrow $45m. to finance crop purchases and maintain the Strategic Grain Reserve. For the first time ever, it was unable to purchase all the produce offered. A World Bank report of the time described the Corporation as 'a fiscal time bomb waiting to explode' (World Bank, 1986).

Thus, as part of SAL III, a two-pronged programme of institutional reform was drawn up. First, the Corporation was to be financially restructured. Previous studies, carried out under SALs I and II, had identified its financial problems as being caused primarily by over-investment in illiquid equity capital, over-diversification out of agricultural sector investments and the poor performance of its chosen portfolio (which resulted in a negative cash flow of around MK3m. between 1984 and 1986). Since mid-1987 the Corporation has, with USAID support, pursued a programme of asset rationalization with the aim of achieving a smaller, more profitable and less illiquid core portfolio.

Secondly, the Agriculture (General Purposes) Act of 1987 provided the legal basis for liberalization. ADMARC's financial position was to be improved by closing down all points buying less than 60 tonnes of produce a year (about 20% of the total), although it was to remain the buyer of last resort, maintaining pan-seasonal and pan-territorial prices. Private traders were allowed to operate under licence at a choice of 1,139 points throughout the country. They were to offer at least the ADMARC purchase price and were to sell only to individual consumers or to ADMARC (with no maximum price limit on the former and a fixed margin of about 20% on the latter). Export licences were available at the discretion of the Ministry of Trade, Industry and Tourism and private trader activities were to be monitored through the licensing system.

From the beginning, liberalization has been fraught with difficulty. Its first year coincided with a particularly poor harvest, thus accentuating free market price increases and regional shortages. The influx of Mozambican refugees has also diverted private trader purchases to the relief programmes and out of domestic circulation. However, many of the problems are the result of poor initial planning and the lack of a clear concept of ADMARC's future role. This is reflected in the dearth of information currently available concerning the effect of the reform. There have been certain clear results. Large gaps in the marketing network have developed as the closure criteria took no account of smallholder access and private traders failed to move into the abandoned areas (it has been estimated that only purchases made within 65 km of a main ADMARC depot provide any profit to traders (Bowbrick, 1988)). ADMARC's financial position has improved but it is still under the constraint of maintaining food security, buyer of last resort functions and input supplies, with the result that it has to transport crops from and inputs to the remote areas unserved by private trade. The licensing system has proved unenforceable, with many traders buying at less than the stipulated floor prices and filing false purchase returns, making accurate national food security calculations impossible. Furthermore, many private traders now entering the market are inadequately financed and with insufficient storage capacity and technical expertise.

These difficulties do not necessarily provide a rationale for abandoning the liberalization policy. However, they do point to clear deficiencies in its implementation: in particular, the sequencing of the reform (the deregulation of the market before price liberalization, for example), the speed with which it was implemented and the failure to tailor policy design to the specific market circumstances of small, underdeveloped economies such as Malawi's, where support for the development of private sector trading capacity is an essential complement to liberalization.

Pricing policy.   Smallholder production has been encouraged by improving producer prices. This initiative pre-dates donor-assisted structural adjustment, with a 68% increase in nominal producer prices for maize in 1981. Subsequent movements (see Appendix Table 4.1) were initially designed to favour production for export, but when this resulted in a drop in food crop sales that threatened national food security, a more balanced approach was pursued. A reversal of the 1970s policy, which implicitly taxed smallholder producers in favour of the estate sector through the maintenance of low real producer prices (Kydd and Christiansen, 1982), has been the main method used to restore production incentives.

The real value of these nominal prices has been eroded, however, by inflation and, more importantly, by steep increases in the real cost of inputs. This latter has been of most influence on maize and groundnuts production (promoting groundnuts over maize) and on tobacco and cotton production (where sharp increases in the landed cost of pesticides have served to discourage production). A four-year Fertilizer Subsidy Removal Programme was introduced as part of SAL III in 1986, in line with the general move towards increased cost recovery. It aimed to achieve this through the substitution of traditional fertilizers with high-analysis equivalents at only marginally higher prices, so that farmers would get much more nitrogen at only slightly greater cost (see Appendix Table 4.1). However, the government strongly resisted this element of the reforms, maintaining that there should be no removal of a subsidy intended to benefit a key productive sector of the economy. The removal has now been re-phased to come into force only when acceptable high-yielding maize varieties have been developed and the external transport situation is regularized.

Inevitably, the direct impact of reforms in official producer price policy will be strongly influenced by the indirect market impact of the liberalization reforms, i.e. by the extent to which private traders take up the opportunities presented by ADMARC retrenchment and consequently develop a role in price determination.

Liberalization of the input supply for smallholders is now being addressed by the new ASAC. This is still at an early stage and the only concrete move has been to reconstitute the Smallholder Fertilizer Revolving Fund as an independent trust. Involving private traders in retail distribution is planned for a subsequent stage. Thus, for the time being, the subsidized prices set by the Ministry of Agriculture continue to exert the most influence on smallholder production decisions.[2]

Other reforms.   As noted earlier, the comprehensive agricultural support services supplied through the NRDP have not promoted broad-based growth, largely because they have failed to address the needs of the smallest farmers. The reform programme has not directly incorporated a change of direction in the NRDP. However, three World Bank/USAID-funded projects instigated under the fifth phase of the programme (1986–91) are designed to start this process, and some of these also form part of the ASAC. The Malawi Agricultural Extension and Planning Support Project, the National

[2] For 1990/91 the subsidy amounts to 30% of landed costs for fertilizer.

Agricultural Research Project and the Malawi Agricultural Research and Extension Project provide for the reorientation of the extension service towards the needs of smaller farmers, the revitalization of the national agricultural research system and the development of area-specific extension messages. At the same time, the recently launched Mudzi Fund (financed by the World Bank and the International Fund for Agricultural Development) is intended to provide small credit packages for the development of off-farm enterprises by the poorest smallholders. One of the most significant moves is the ASAC's addressing of crop-specific constraints to increased productivity on the smallest holdings. This has two elements: the ending of the prohibition on smallholder cultivation of burley tobacco; and support for research on the development of acceptable highyielding flinty (hard endosperm) varieties of maize. One of the major constraints to the uptake of existing maize hybrids has been that they are dents with soft endosperms unsuitable for traditional Malawian storage and processing techniques.

In relation to tariffs and trade policy, there has been little agriculturally-oriented reform so far. Malawi is unusual in that, as a result of the dual structure of the agricultural sector and ADMARC's de facto monopsony of product marketing in the smallholder subsector, smallholders have been little affected by explicit trade control measures. In relation to export taxes, the estate sub-sector has paid on an ad valorem basis for some time, and rates have recently been increased as part of the macroeconomic reforms. However, exports of smallholder produce have been handled entirely by ADMARC, rendering taxes inappropriate; instead, the claw-back has been less explicit, taking the form of substantial margins between the price paid to producers and the international sale price realized by ADMARC. At the beginning of the reform period this implicit taxation was substantially reduced as part of the move towards improved production incentives. But the decline in maize sales has forced a revision of this policy and a corresponding move back towards implicit taxation of smallholder export production.

Malawi's land-locked position makes it uneconomic to import agricultural commodities. The small quantities entering the country are mainly concessionarily financed by donors, chiefly for immediate food security purposes, and their distribution is controlled. Imports of inputs are similarly controlled for the smallholder sub-sector.

Malawi's experience with agricultural sector reform may be summarized as follows. Underlying structural constraints inhibited the sector's response to the price incentives included in the early reform programmes and performance fell short of expectations. In particular, the design of early reforms directed towards marketing liberalization and removal of the fertilizer subsidy does not appear to have been based on a sufficiently detailed understanding of the opportunities and constraints influencing the rural economy and, as such, limited their positive effect. However, although it is too early to assess their impact, the initiatives contained in the new ASAC that address the more fundamental factor constraints and related structural issues are likely to go quite some way towards enabling the smallholder sector to benefit from the more general restructuring of the economy.

III.   SOCIO-ECONOMIC CHARACTERISTICS OF THE RURAL POPULATION

Agriculture is the backbone of the national economy. In this respect, Malawi is similar to many other countries in sub-Saharan Africa. But there are also several important differences. On the positive side, reasonably regular and ample rainfall removes the threat of recurrent drought that has plagued agriculture in other parts of the continent. On the other hand, the high population growth rate (now 3.6% per annum) – coupled with limited land resources and strictly contained rural-urban migration – has created substantial land pressure. Population densities of 85 persons/sq.km. (NSO, 1987) are among the highest in rural Africa. In addition, there are now 800,000 Mozambican refugees in the border Districts of Central and Southern Region, currently equivalent to 10% of Malawi's population – the highest recorded percentage in the world. This high density, together with very limited access to capital because of low average per capita incomes, has resulted in a particularly labour-intensive pattern of production on smallholder farms. Perhaps the most significant feature, however, is the large degree of differentiation within the sector both between the estates and smallholder farmers and within the smallholder sub-sector itself.

The smallholder sub-sector is heterogeneous in a number of respects. As well as the ecological variation between Central plain, Northern plateau and lakeshore, higher population densities in the South result in smaller average sizes of holdings. Of the 7.5 million rural people in Malawi nearly half live in Southern Region, a further 40% in Central Region and 12% in Northern Region (NSO, 1987). And within regions, there is great variation in the household characteristics of larger and smaller farmers. The former make up an emergent commercialized group, relatively well integrated into the market economy, while the latter remain, for the most part, highly marginal subsistence producers.

Ecological conditions and cropping patterns

Between 40 and 60% of the total land area of 9.4 million hectares is cultivable (GOM, 1987a). Owing to land shortage, cultivation is already intruding into unsuitable fragile environments in all Regions.

There is a single growing season with an average rainfall of 1220mm falling between November and April. Extreme deviations from this average are infrequent but not unknown, the failure of the rains in 1979 and the severe flooding of 1988 being two cases in point. The predominance of hoe cultivation has accelerated degradation of the high natural soil fertility through insolation and leaching (Pryor, 1987), and nutrient depletion is now serious enough to have a significant impact on production potential in a number of areas. Agriculture is almost universally rain-fed although there is a small amount of dry season *dimba* (wetland) cultivation of vegetables.

Maize cultivation for food is the priority of most smallholders and this is clearly reflected in cropping patterns throughout the country. On the largest holdings, of 3 ha and above, maize occupies nearly 60% of available land (improved varieties accounting for 10%), with cash crops such as tobacco, groundnuts and cotton taking up a further 25%. The remainder is occupied by a variety of security food crops which, in different parts of the country, include millet, sorghum, cassava and pulses. Some intercropping (chiefly maize/bean mixtures) is practised and most holdings are continuously cultivated, resulting in the severe nutrient depletion mentioned above. On the smaller holdings of 0.5 ha and below (the majority), only about 3% of land is down to improved maize and local varieties account for more than three-quarters of the total cultivated area. On the remaining area cash crops – particularly tobacco – are relatively less important (10% of total area) and security food crops more so. Malawian farmers are renowned for their price responsiveness and this causes considerable intra-annual variation in cropping patterns on the larger holdings, but not for the smallest farmers for whom risk aversion determines a consistent emphasis on food maize production.

Regional variation in cropping patterns has, until recently, been entirely due to ecological variation, as ADMARC's policy of maintaining pan-territorial producer prices and guaranteeing to purchase all production offered for sale minimized regional variation in market accessibility. Thus in Southern Region cotton and mixed-stand millet/sorghum are the preferred cash and security food crops, whereas moving up the country groundnuts, tobacco and local maize are more widely grown, whilst on the lakeshore rice and cassava are locally more important.

The very low uptake of hybrid maize varieties compared with other countries in the region (the overall proportion of cultivated area planted to hybrids has remained static at 5% for the last fifteen years) is a major constraint to increasing smallholder productivity. A number of particular features of Malawi's smallholder economy are considered to have contributed to this (Kydd, 1989). The soft white maize hybrids that have achieved considerable success in Kenya and Zimbabwe are disliked because of their poor resistance to weevil attack when stored fully sheathed, Malawi-style. In addition, Malawians prefer maize porridge made from shelled maize – which can only be prepared wastefully from hybrid maize because of the difficulty of separating the husk from the grain – whereas in other parts of East and Central Africa milled whole maize is readily consumed. ADMARC's long-standing difficulties with providing timely supplies of hybrid maize seed and fertilizer have forced smallholders to rely on their own local maize seed, which does not require fertilizer to obtain an economic yield.

Resource endowments

Land.   The division between smallholder and estate land is defined by form of land tenure rather than size of holding; estates are found exclusively on freehold/leasehold land whilst customary land is reserved for smallholders. In 1987 440,000 ha of cultivable land was under freehold/leasehold tenure and a further 170,000 ha of *de jure* customary land (thus approximately 14% in total) was being used by estates in anticipation of the receipt of leasehold tenure (MOA Planning Division data). Nearly three-quarters of the estates are located in Central Region – the historical centre of estate activity (Mkandawire and Phiri, 1987).

There are significant political obstacles to change in a sub-sector historically linked with influential socio-political groups. However, the low land utilization rates on estates (estimates vary from 6% to 28% of leased land (Kydd and Christiansen, 1982; Mkandawire and Phiri, 1987)) represent a substantial under-utilization of resources. A point of some contention is the extent to which the estates' use of land is contributing to pressure in the smallholder sub-sector. In the 1970s government policies favouring expansion of the estate sub-sector resulted in 200,000 ha of customary land being lost (Mkandawire and Phiri, 1987). It has been argued (Mwakasungura, 1986) that this land should be returned. This would provide a short-term increase in per capita smallholder production, but continuing rapid population growth would soon absorb the land made available. With the freeze on further estate expansion, the increase in leasehold rents and the support of flint maize development, the new ASAC has made a start on tackling the issues of land reallocation and the constraints on smallholder productivity.

Land held under customary tenure now accounts for 79% of the total cultivable land. Available cultivable customary land per capita has declined by between one-fifth and one-third over the last ten years and now stands at between 0.46 and 0.70

ha. There is no uncultivated land at all left in over half the Districts of Southern Region and very little in the more densely populated Districts of the Centre and North (GOM, 1987a). At least 50% of families have less than 1 ha of land; a higher proportion (70%) of female-headed households are concentrated on these smaller holdings. Given present technology and levels of access to support services, holdings of 0.5 ha and below are not viable. Thus the large number of households with marginally viable holdings is an important feature of Malawi's rural economy.

Labour. Owing to the current low levels of technology use and the severe land constraint, the smallholder sub-sector is both a heavy user and a potential supplier of labour. Family labour availability ranges from an average of 1.62 Man Equivalents[3] in the smallest households to 6.4ME in the larger. In all Regions the modal availability is larger in male-than in female-headed households; however, there is some evidence (Peters, 1988) that labour availability in female-headed households varies significantly between households. The clear correlation between land and labour availability accentuates economic differentiation in the rural population, being particularly apparent in comparisons of different types of female-headed households.

Detailed information is lacking on how households allocate their available labour to different productive activities. One overriding influence is the desire of all smallholders to produce enough maize for family food self-sufficiency through the 'hungry period', between December and March and on to the next harvest. However, although it is the dominant criterion in resource allocation decisions, most families fail to achieve this goal and have to supplement own-holding production with income earned off the farm.

There are various distinct labour markets. Very little is known about the way the informal market functions except that both labour productivity and the relationship between productivity and remuneration vary widely between the different mechanisms (Chipeta, 1982). This would appear to provide evidence of factor allocation distortions in the rural economy. The most common mechanism is *ganyu* (seasonal labour remunerated in cash or kind). Ganyu is notorious for trapping participant families in the cycle of continuing production deficit described above. The market is oversupplied, owing to the large number of food-deficit households (one ADD reports families resorting to advance 'booking' of their right to perform ganyu labour on larger holdings (Mkandawire and Chipande, 1988)); wages – paid at piece rates in cash or food – are therefore low (in 1987 equivalent to about 70 tambala per day in Southern Region (AES, 1987) or, in other words, only just equivalent to the statutory minimum wage). Furthermore, the peak availability of ganyu employment – for land preparation and, later in the season, for weeding – coincides with the times when families should be working on their own holdings to ensure the next season's harvest. Thus ganyu labourers avert short-term crises in domestic food availability at the cost of further reducing household capacity to satisfy food needs from own-holding production in the longer run. Some estimates put the proportion of smallholders participating in the ganyu labour market as high as 50%. Certainly this vicious circle is a dominant and highly detrimental feature of Malawi's small farm sub-sector, particularly for the poorest families.

Another possibility is migration either domestically or regionally. The mobility of the rural population is a particular characteristic of Malawi's agricultural sector, with around 18% of adult males having been migrant labourers at some time, the

[3] Enumerated by the National Statistics Office as: one hour of adult male labour = one ME; adult female = 0.7 ME; child = 0.3 ME.

major motivation being to accumulate capital to invest in farming or, in certain areas, in *lobola* (bride price).

Wage labourers on agricultural estates number around 177,000 or about 2.5% of the rural population and are chiefly men from land-short areas and returned migrants unable to find customary land to cultivate. The low wage rates act as a considerable disincentive to families with other income-earning options, although available evidence suggests that they do conform to the statutory minimum wage in most cases (Kaluwa and Mkwezalamba, 1988).

In addition, there are about 12,000 visiting tenants (a Malawian adaptation of sharecropping) cultivating burley tobacco on estates. Under this system a married man is allocated land by oral agreement and on a seasonal basis, and is provided with production inputs on credit. To make full use of the provided inputs usually involves allocating the labour of wives and children to production of the cash crop. All production has to be sold to the estate. Payment is theoretically at a government-stipulated minimum price, less advances made. Nearly three-quarters of tenants come from the land-short Districts of Central and Southern Regions; they also gain access to inputs not accessible to the majority of farmers on small holdings. One of the most important incentives, until the latest ASAC, was the ability to produce a profitable crop prohibited by law to peasant farmers; in a 1988 survey 90% of tenant farmers stated this as their prime motivation for becoming tenants (Nankumba, 1988). However, circumstantial evidence suggests that many estate owners find ways of substantially reducing the eventual cash payment to tenants: net household returns of as little as MK100 per annum do not appear to be uncommon.

The other source of employment for smallholder families is self-employment in off-farm activities. Self-employment revolves around small-scale service functions such as sale of poles and thatching grass for house building, selling firewood, brick making, beer brewing, etc. These are all poorly paid and most families are constrained by lack of capital from participating on a large enough scale for significant income to be generated: less than 15% of their time is allocated to this type of work by families on holdings of less than 1 ha.

The proportion of the total labour force employed in agriculture (including smallholder farmers, estate labourers and government employees) declined only marginally – from 89 to 84% – during the 1980s. From the evidence presented above this would appear to be the result of the limited opportunities for smallholders to transfer to other sectors.

Capital.   The inability to generate investment resources or get access to credit with which to purchase improved inputs and equipment is a major constraint to increasing production for many rural families. There is little empirical evidence but field observation and anecdotal evidence point to three factors, in particular, contributing to this.

Firstly, investable surpluses from produce sales are minimal; secondly, a dearth of rural banking facilities and other savings institutions necessitates available savings being held in cash, the value of which is easily eroded by inflation and the knock-on effects of devaluation; and thirdly, the absence of a land market precludes the use of land as collateral for loans. By the same token, the shortage of banking outlets limits small farmers' access to formal sector credit, whilst informal moneylenders (*katapila*) charge extortionate interest rates – as high as 100% per month according to some sources. Loans of surplus land or for consumption needs (*kubwereka*) are made between kinship groups but on a very limited scale.

Therefore, the chief source of capital for smallholders is the NRDP agricultural credit funds. About 15% of farmers obtain this credit, although only 22% of funds go to households with less than 1 ha. There is substantial regional variation in access, partly reflecting differences between ADDs in donor allocations to credit funds, as well as the differing profitability of production opportunities in different regions. In the ADDs with operational credit funds, the proportion of women members of farmer credit clubs has been increasing steadily but still stands at less than 25% nation-wide (Murison, 1987). The bulk of loan funds are limited to specific purposes, typically for inputs such as fertilizers and seed, and are distributed on a seasonal basis through credit clubs, which have group responsibility for ensuring repayment. Repayment rates are high (typically 90% and above), but clubs achieve this by excluding farmers perceived to be a credit risk, i.e. those with very small holdings and women. For small numbers of *achikumbe* (progressive farmers) individual longer-term loans may also be provided for farm mechanization (work oxen, ploughs, etc). Commercial interest rates are charged on both types of credit.

It is estimated that only 10% of farmers on small farmers own ox ploughs or ridgers, with the remainder relying entirely on the traditional *jembe* (handheld hoe). *Annual Survey of Agriculture* data show that, in 1984/5 for example, only 20% of smallholders used fertilizer and, of these, 40% bought it using cash and a further 21% used a combination of credit and cash. The importance of the credit constraint is highlighted in the *National Sample Survey of Agriculture* of 1980/81 which indicates that the most important reason for not using fertilizer was unavailability of credit (cited by 65% of farmers). The corresponding figure for non-use of improved seed was also high (59%).

Given that at the same time MK20m. of donor-financed smallholder credit funds remain undisbursed, this suggests that it is not limited availability of funds but the inappropriateness of the NRDP credit clubs for the smallest farmers that is the major cause of low credit uptake – because they fail to take into account the heterogeneity of the smallholder sub-sector and, specifically, the need to devise membership criteria with which the smallest farmers can comply. Over MK44m. was available from this source in 1986 but it was almost entirely for hybrid maize and other cash crops – which small farmers do not grow – and in set packages for 0.4 ha which are too large in both quantity and price. In addition, repayment must be in cash which most small farmers do not have. A start on tackling this problem has been made with the recent launch of the Mudzi fund (see p. 126) which is targeted specifically towards the poorest households.

Access to services

The design of present support services would appear to restrict considerably the ability of the majority of the smallholder population to participate. The services with the most direct influence on their economic situation are input and produce marketing and agricultural extension. Until market liberalization in 1987, over 60% of the rural population had 'adequate' physical access to produce and input markets (GOM, 1987), as ADMARC maintained a network of 12 depots, 52 permanent markets and about 1,050 seasonal markets evenly distributed throughout the country, where pre-announced pan-territorial and pan-seasonal prices were offered. In 1987, as noted earlier, 20% of these markets were shut down, and private traders have not taken over ADMARC's produce-buying functions as hoped. This is likely to have a significant impact on market integration opportunities for smallholders, particularly those in the remoter areas.

Fertilizer is the input most widely marketed to peasant farmers and is used by about

25% of households nation-wide (but by only 9% of households with less than 0.5 ha) (World Bank, 1990b). Smallholder fertilizer sales had been growing at around 8% per annum until recent years, because of the promotion of fertilizer use by the extension service and price incentives for maize and tobacco (the major fertilizer-using crops); the rate of growth has now declined, reflecting the disincentive created by early attempts (now suspended) to remove the subsidy as part of the reform programme and by declining real producer prices. A subsidy of about 30% (1990/91) is applied to the domestic purchase price for peasant farmers, who obtain supplies through ADMARC's local distribution system; this results in leakages of about 25% of the total quantities of smallholder fertilizer to the estate sub-sector, which is supposed to pur-chase at the full price from private suppliers and bear the transport costs from Limbe or Lilongwe. Traditional single super phosphates and ammonium nitrates are being replaced with high-analysis diammonium phosphates and urea through the Small-holder Fertilizer Revolving Fund in order to reduce the cost per unit of nitrogen to farmers and thus facilitate the eventual removal of the subsidy.

Given the dangerous levels of nutrient depletion now being recorded, whether the subsidy should be removed or other channels for smallholder access to fertilizer (e.g. fertilizer-for-work schemes) should be introduced are issues that need immediate investigation and resolution. The design of appropriate interventions needs to be closely linked to the NRDP credit programme because the majority of the smallest farmers require credit to finance input purchases. A start on addressing these issues will be made as part of the ASAC, which includes a pilot targeted fertilizer subsidy and credit scheme for the smallest holdings.

Access to extension services varies between Regions and according to holding size. Central Region is best served, with about 40% of male-headed households having received some kind of crop husbandry advice. Southern Region is least well served, with only 15% of male farmers with less than 1.5 ha having received advice, the pro-portion rising fo 25% of farmers with more than 1.5 ha. In the North larger farmers are again better served and about one-third of male-headed families have had some crop husbandry advice. The proportion of female-headed households receiving advice is much lower in all Regions, ranging from 6% on smaller holdings in Southern Region to 25% on larger holdings in the North.

As regards social services, 63% of the rural population do not have access to an improved water source (gravity-fed, borehole or protected shallow well), as compared with 23% of urban families, and 44% have to walk more than 5 km to their nearest dispensary. Regional primary education participation rates of 72% in the North, 25% in the South and 37% in Central Region have been recorded. The North's high participation is partly explained by the Region being the historical centre of mission education. Rural illiteracy rates of 77% are 20% higher than in urban areas (Ministry of Health, 1986). There is a positive correlation between holding size and level of education, with less than one-third of farmers with less than 0.7 ha having any education (defined by the Ministry of Education as five years or more of primary education). This must partly be explained by the relatively high cost of education in terms of fees, uniform requirements and the opportunity cost of older children's on-farm labour.

Female-headed households

Women form just over half the rural population. In the matrilineal Chewa areas in the Centre-South of the country 30% of households are headed by women and 17% in the patrilineal Tumbuka/Tonga areas in the North. Female-headed households are thus an important sub-category of the smallholder population.

There are various reasons why households come to be headed by women and these, in their differential influence on household labour availability, have important implications for economic viability. Over 70% of female-headed households are headed by an unmarried woman, whilst about 20% are headed by a woman whose husband is absent (usually working abroad) and around 10% (predominantly in the North) by a woman whose polygamous husband is residing in another wife's household (NSO, 1983).

Wives of absent migrants can use remittance incomes to employ labour to substitute for absent family members, whereas single mothers and wives of absent polygamists face a shortage of labour to devote to own-holding production. As a result, the former tend to have larger holdings and are food self-sufficient, in contrast to the latter who are food-deficit and therefore rely much more heavily on off-farm income sources. However, these latter do not have the capital, skills or time to engage in the more remunerative types of self-employment (which would allow them to purchase the hired labour necessary to make full productive use of their holdings). Survey data show that female-headed households are clustered on the smallest holdings (70% have less than 1 ha, *Annual Survey of Agriculture*, 1984/5)) and have fewer family labour resources than other families (over 35% have only 1 or 2 members compared with the average family size of 3–5). At the same time, they earn less than half what comparable male-headed households do from off-farm businesses (CSR, 1988a).

The NRDP has operated a Women's Programme in recognition of the different requirements of women farmers and household heads. However, by concentrating on idealized household nutrition and hygiene practices, it fails to support women's important activities in food-crop production and the conflicting demands made on their time as farmers, home-makers and businesswomen. Moreover, as most rural households maintain separate conjugal income streams – most women have no access to their husband's income from cash cropping or other employment and therefore no means of starting up small businesses or offering collateral for loans – few women can take advantage of Programme credit.

Smallholder incomes and food security

Malawi stopped collecting comprehensive agricultural survey data at national level in 1984/5. Although absolute incomes will have changed in the interim, some idea of their order of magnitude and relative distribution between different sizes of households and activities can be obtained.

Table 4.6 shows that 60% of the rural population have an annual cash income of less than MK200 (US$128 at 1984 rates) – of which about 25% comes from sales of food crops, 7% from cash-crop sales, 8% from the sale of livestock, 30% from off-farm self-employment, 15% from wage labour and 15% from transfers (chiefly remittances from migrant workers). On the smaller holdings proportionately more income is derived from off-farm employment and less from livestock sales. Incomes are generally higher in the North.

Survey data suggest that average annual production of food crops per household varies from 240 kg (sufficient for the food needs of one adult) on holdings of 0.5 ha and less to 3,650 kg on holdings of 2 ha and above (1984/5 *Annual Survey of Agriculture* data). Available information on household food security supports these orders of magnitude which imply that, for the 55% of households with less than 1 ha of land,

Table 4.6.   *Average income by holding size (MK)*

Holding size (ha)	Total households	Agricultural income	Off-farm income	Remittances	Total income
0.5	298,543	60	26	5	91
0.5–1	419,560	136	23	6	165
1–1.5	258,236	236	20	8	263
1.5–2	141,604	320	18	5	343
2–2.5	81,603	432	21	7	460
2.5–3	45,431	521	22	6	549
3	54,889	782	14	9	805

Source: ASA 1984/5, Table 3.1 and Summary Table 5.
Note: Agricultural income includes sales of food and cash crops and livestock; off-farm income includes that from self-employment, estate wage labour, non-agricultural employment and ganyu labour; remittances are from non-resident members of the household in off-farm employment.

own-holding production is inadequate for subsistence needs. This proportion is higher among female-headed households and families in the South.

These families therefore have to depend on earning enough cash to make up the deficit with purchased food. Families with larger holdings of 1.5 ha and above derive 25–40% of their total income from wage labour and self-employment in small business (CSR, 1988a). They are able to use these proceeds to purchase agricultural labour at times of peak need; around 60% of families with annual expenditures of over MK30 on hired labour meet this cost with cash earned off the farm. As noted earlier, wives of absent migrants use remittance incomes in this way. Thus these families are able to grow higher-value but more labour-consuming crops such as hybrid maize, groundnuts, tobacco and cotton.

There is a clear regional variation in the proportion of household income earned from ganyu labour, ranging from 7% in the North to 28% in the South (CSR, 1988a).

Table 4.7.   *Calorie-deficit rural households in Malawi*

Holding size (ha)	Total households	Average household size	Calorific value prod. ('000)	Calorie needs ('000)	Food deficit (%)
0.5	298,543	3.6	948.22	2,759.40	66
0.5–1	419,543	4.4	2,412.18	3,372.60	28
1–1.5	258,236	4.9	4,188.70	3,755.85	(12)
1.5–2	141,604	5.1	6,041.62	3,909.15	(54)
2–2.5	81,603	5.7	8,527.93	4,369.05	(95)
2.5–3	45,431	6.1	10,303.65	4,675.65	(120)
3	54,889	6.4	16,284.63	4,905.60	(232)

Sources: Columns 1–3 taken from ASA 1984/85, Table 3.1; Column 4 from ASA 1984/5, Table 3.9A using UNICEF estimates of the calorific value of each crop; Column 5 uses UNICEF estimates of annual calorie requirement per person and Column 3; Column 6 equals Column 5 minus Column 4 i.e. the proportion of household calorie needs *not* satisfied by own-holding production. Figures in brackets equal production surplus.

The other source of off-farm employment is paid wage labour on agricultural estates. Here average monthly earnings are significantly lower than in the formal manufacturing sector – 35% of the all-industry average according to some estimates (*Malawi Statistical Yearbook*, 1984).

The importance of food sales as a source of cash income on even the smallest farms and the extent to which all rural families are dependent on non-agricultural sources of income are an important feature of the rural economy. It is often not easy for the smallest farmers to generate enough income from off-farm employment: between 75% and 95% are unable to make up food needs from other sources. Until 1987, the maintenance of pan-seasonal consumer prices by ADMARC was of particular benefit to these food-deficit households. As noted above, families on the smallest holdings are caught in a vicious circle of ganyu employment and food deficit; 30% of them have exhausted their own food stocks by September, just three months after harvest. As a result, Malawi has an exceptionally poor average level of nutrition among its rural population and 'nutritional deficiency is. . . . a principal or contributing cause for a dominant fraction of preventable mortality in Malawi' (Ministry of Health, 1986). Child stunting and wasting – closely correlated to poverty conditions – is particularly prevalent: 54% of the under-fives have low length-for-age and 27% have low weight-for-age[4] (CSR, 1988a).

Differentiation in the smallholder sector

By definition, the geographical distribution of vulnerable households mirrors that of small farms and is clustered in Southern and Central Regions, with relatively fewer in the North. In assessing the dimensions of their vulnerability, it is worth noting that these households have significantly worse access to both factor markets and support services than other rural groups in Malawi.

Figure 4.1 shows the great importance attached to food-crop cultivation by farmers on smaller holdings. Given the low land/labour ratios on these farms, it would be expected that, on the contrary, farmers would favour cultivation of labour-intensive cash crops. However, in Malawi, vulnerable households are highly risk-averse because of their restricted access to factor markets other than labour, and therefore food crops, where the farmer faces only production risks, are a better choice than cash crops where, in addition, (s)he faces price risks associated with both the crop and the food supplies (s)he must purchase for subsistence needs. In this context the preference of vulnerable households for food-crop cultivation appears quite logical. It also explains the relative unresponsiveness of smaller farmers to changes in relative producer prices.

Data on the proportion of production sold are not available, broken down by holding size. For most farmers the amount sold is a residual after their own subsistence needs have been satisfied; it will therefore vary between good and bad seasons. Circumstantial evidence shows, however, that even smaller farmers are highly integrated into agricultural product markets because so many of them are food-deficit and have low cash incomes: they have to sell crops in order to realize income for immediate cash needs and then buy back food later in the season. Many are in fact net purchasers of food. Vulnerable households are more likely than larger farmers to use private traders because they can sell their produce earlier (ADMARC markets do not usually open

---

[4] The former indicates chronic undernutrition and the latter seasonal malnutrition.

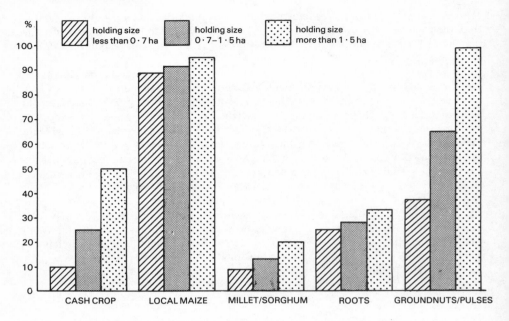

Figure 4.1. Percentage of households growing selected crops by holding size
Source: Quinn, Chiligo and Gittinger, 1988, Table A-1.

until the first week of July), thus obtaining cash sooner and avoiding the costs of on-farm storage. But they are also at risk of receiving lower prices.

Vulnerable households are at a disadvantage because the land tenure system prevents the use of land as collateral for credit which, given that smaller farmers have lower cash incomes, would otherwise be a valuable way of increasing their access to capital. In relation to NRDP credit funds, as noted earlier, it is the inappropriateness of the packages for small farmers rather than a shortage of funds which is the main problem. This inability to obtain capital acts as a severe constraint to maximizing labour productivity on small farms and is therefore a major cause of vulnerability in the rural sector.

The participation of households in the labour market clearly has a crucial influence on their vulnerability since, owing to the stunting of other factor markets in the rural economy, labour allocation is the only area of decision-making where they can exercise some control. Net labour outflow is much greater in vulnerable households. However, this statistic disguises the issue of seasonality which is of crucial importance in understanding the rural labour market: although family labour balances are on the whole positive on all farms, there is a seasonal constraint in December and January as a result of peak labour demand (for weeding) coinciding with the time of lowest labour productivity because of food shortage and malaria (Chipeta, 1982). As a consequence, even the smallest farms require hired labour at this time. Coupled with this is the need for vulnerable families to augment their small cash earnings from agriculture with off-farm employment. Structural rigidities in this employment result in those taking part being unable to tailor periods of off-farm employment with periods

Table 4.8. *Off-farm employment in the rural sector*

Holding size (ha)	Self-employed (%)	Paid agric. (%)	Paid non-agric. (%)	Total MDE
0.5	9	40	51	106
0.5–1	12	29	59	105
1–1.5	12	23	65	99
1.5–2	16	25	59	105
2–2.5	12	24	64	100
2.5–3	15	14	71	97
3	15	15	70	93

Source: adapted from ASA 1984/85.
Notes: MDE = man day equivalent; Columns 2–4 show percentages of total MDE shown in Column 5.

of low own-holding labour requirements. Own-holding production therefore suffers.

For vulnerable households self-employment is relatively less important because of their lack of capital and low levels of education. Lack of education also limits their ability to participate in non-agricultural paid employment as compared with families on larger farms; nonetheless employment in this sector is still their largest use of off-farm labour time, largely because of oversupply in the ganyu market. Only two-thirds of vulnerable households' income is derived from agriculture, in contrast to almost all larger farmers' income. Increasing the present limited employment opportunities would be of major benefit to them in terms of ameliorating their cash income constraint.

Vulnerable households are also socially disadvantaged in relation to the rest of the rural population. Table 4.9 shows that they are considerably worse-off in terms of education and nutrition levels. This further increases their economic vulnerability through influencing their labour productivity and earning potential.

Table 4.9. *Social characteristics of vulnerable households (%)*

Holding size (ha)	Education	Malnutrition	
		MHH	FHH
0.5	30	60	50
0.5–1	31	58	46
1–1.5	43	51	47

Source: adapted from CSR, 1988a/.
Note: Education = percentage of households with five years or more education.
Malnutrition = percentage of households with stunted under-fives; MHH = male-headed households; FHH = female-headed households.

IV. IMPACT OF REFORMS ON THE RURAL ECONOMY AND VULNERABLE FARM HOUSEHOLDS

The evidence presented so far points to the fact that major constraints to resumed growth in the smallholder sub-sector are Malawi's poor natural resource endowment (land shortage in particular) and the weakness of links between smallholders and the wider economy. While positive change in the macro economy may bring benefits to the estate sub-sector – which has adequate access to land and capital resources to expand production – it will thus be of only limited relevance to smallholders as long as these links remain weak.

Factor markets

Labour.   At the macro level, reform may be expected to create an increased demand for labour via its stimulation of economic growth. This appeared to be the case in the mid-1980s, although the expansion in private sector employment was reversed for a time as a result of the negative effect of stringent import controls in 1986/7. This was particularly damaging for an economy such as Malawi's where there is an urgent need for greater absorption of surplus labour from the agricultural sector.

The major impediment to the expansion of labour absorption by the smallholder sector itself is the narrow scope for diversification into labour-intensive crops in most areas, caused by the land constraint and poor access to other inputs. Both of these limit responsiveness to price changes by restricting small farmers to responding by reallocating existing land rather than by increasing total hectarage under cultivation. This is what happened between 1980/81 and 1986/7 when – because of increases in producer prices for groundnuts relative to those for maize – there was a continuous increase in hectarage planted to groundnuts at the expense of maize. Thus changes in the demand for labour in the small farm sector are likely to be muted – although positive. This will benefit households dependent on off-farm agricultural employment, but the concomitant increased labour supply because of continued population growth will limit the need for employers to offer higher wages. Lack of data prevents an empirical assessment of actual changes in the demand for labour and real earnings.

Job opportunities in the formal agricultural labour market are almost exclusively on the estates. Devaluation will increase estates' domestic currency earnings and this may be expected to elicit a positive production response, assuming it compensates for the negative effect on production of declining world commodity prices. Production techniques on the estates are not import-intensive, so devaluation will have little impact on the costs of production; instead, the labour intensity of production will result in increased employment opportunities (average labour:land ratios on tobacco estates are as high as 1:0.32 ha (GOM, 1987)). Real returns to estate labour are influenced by minimum wage legislation, movements in consumer prices and the supply and demand situation in the market. As the smallholder sub-sector is now severely limited in its ability to absorb the growing rural labour force, alternative rural labour markets, such as the estates, have for some time been oversupplied. This, coupled with the estates' continuing dependence on low wage rates for the maintenance of international competitiveness, has limited wage increases to the stipulated minimum: as discussed earlier, statutory minimum wages have been declining in real terms, as clearly demonstrated in Table 4.10. Furthermore, the discouragement of trade union activity has limited employees' ability to influence wage rates.

Thus the declining real wage bill, in combination with improved domestic currency earnings for employers in the sub-sector, is likely to have contributed to an expansion in employment opportunities. Table 4.11 shows that the real earnings of both employers and employees have declined dramatically during the 1980s, despite a positive trend in the early part of the decade. The latter group include some who had sought paid employment to escape food constraints associated with small holding size;

Table 4.10. *Changes in nominal rural minimum wage purchasing power*

Year	Rural wage (t/day)	Consumer maize price (MK/bag)	Monthly income (MK)	Purchasing power (%)
1981	50	9.90	12.50	21
1982	58	11.70	14.50	19
1983	58	12.60	14.50	13
1984	58	12.60	14.50	13
1985	58	12.60	14.50	13
1986	58	13.32	14.50	8
1987	77	18.00	19.25	7
1988	77	27.00	19.25	−29
1989	174	28.80	43.50	51

Notes: Rural wage = statutory minimum; Consumer maize price = ADMARC price per bag. It is estimated that the average family needs one bag of maize (90 kg) per month to satisfy basic calorie requirements; Monthly income = 5.5 day working week; Purchasing power = proportion of monthly income remaining after purchasing domestic maize needs.

Table 4.11. *Real annual earnings in private sector agriculture 1979–87 (MK)*

	1979	1980	1981	1982	1983	1984	1985	1986	1987
Nominal earnings	145	163	199	229	214	236	265	280	302
GDP deflator	85.0	100	116.3	127.2	141.8	161.4	172.8	219.4	275
Employers' real earnings	171	163	171	180	151	146	153	127	109
CPI (food)	80.1	100	109.8	114.6	132.3	153.1	167.1	293.3	245.2
Employees' real earnings	181	163	181	200	162	154	159	95	123

Sources: *Malawi Statistical Yearbook*, various years; *Monthly Statistical Bulletin*, various months; *International Financial Statistics Yearbook*, 1986; World Bank, 1990a.

Notes: 1987 is the latest year for which private sector earnings are available. Employers' real earnings deflated by GDP deflator; employees' real earnings deflated by Consumer Price Index food costs.

inflationary tendencies (partly due to increases in agricultural producer prices) have thus seriously eroded the benefit of this move.

Malawi's manufacturing sector may be sub-divided into large-scale agro-processing industry and medium-scale import-substituting manufacturing, the former dominated by tea and tobacco processing firms. As production of these crops is favoured by structural adjustment, employment opportunities may be expected to expand. Although most of the processing equipment is imported, and thus its increased cost post-devaluation might theoretically deter expansion, capacity utilization has been so low in the past (UNDP/MTIT, 1988) that in practice increased output can be achieved without substantial new investment in equipment.

The non-agro-processing sub-sector is, in contrast, oriented towards the domestic market and, since it relies heavily on imported raw materials, devaluation has increased production costs without a compensatory influence on revenue. Strict import controls until 1986/7 were a further impediment to growth. Given the limited initial movement towards the decontrol of domestic prices stipulated in the reform programme, firms' ability to recoup higher costs of production through price increases has been restricted until recently. Thus adjustment dampened incentives to expand and is unlikely to result in substantially increased employment opportunities. In fact, the failure of growth in employment opportunities in the formal sector to keep pace with the expansion of the labour force is now a severe problem.

Wage rates in both sub-sectors are in line with the statutory minimum which, as noted above, has been declining in real value as a result of the government's wage restraint policy (and the limited bargaining power of the labour force). This decline predated structural adjustment and has continued at much the same rate during it.

Public sector employment policy has an important indirect influence on the private sector labour market. The government has maintained a policy of achieving reductions in the fiscal deficit through natural wastage rather than redundancies; it is generally agreed that civil service over-expansion has not been severe in comparison with other African countries. The policy has been implemented by reducing the retirement age and limiting the establishment of new posts and has thus resulted in an excess of both middle-aged senior managers and school leavers in the open market. This is likely to increase competition for formal sector employment.

Land.   The growing land constraint has been one of the major factors inhibiting smallholders' response to the producer price incentives offered under the reform programme. However, as there is no functioning land market in Malawi, it is social and institutional rather than economic factors that have been the primary cause of the land shortage, particularly tenure law. The role of reform incentives in removing distortions in land allocation, in the absence of institutional reform, must therefore be limited.

Nevertheless, the most recent reform programmes have recognized the disadvantages of continued institutional promotion of land allocation to the estate sub-sector and include provision for restrictions on further expansion. This will undoubtedly ease the present pressure on customary land. However, continued high population growth is an equally important source of pressure which will make containment of the estate sub-sector only a temporary respite. Until the other structural constraints in the smallholder sector have also been addressed, there will be limited scope for the sector to respond adequately to recovery measures designed to promote resumed agricultural growth.

Capital.   There has been a gradual movement during the reform period towards positive real rates of interest for commercial bank lending, although the estate sub-sector benefitted from relatively lower rates as compared with the rest of the economy until 1989. In contrast to the smallholder sector, the estates make significant use of formal bank credit. This contrasts with the experience elsewhere in Africa where borrowers have enjoyed negative real rates for much of the recent past. While this movement is in line with the overall objectives of economic recovery, it may have an adverse impact on commercial investment.

However, the impact on smallholders is likely to be much less as their access to loans from the formal banking sector is restricted. Instead, institutional credit channelled through government projects and credit from informal moneylenders are their major sources. It is impossible to hypothesize about the likely effect of the reform programmes, as virtually nothing is known about the determinants of interest rates in the informal money market; in any case, this is a relatively minor source.

Agricultural project credit is largely donor-financed under the NRDP and, as such, has been protected from cuts in the government budget introduced under the reform programmes. But reform has not directly addressed its inappropriateness for the smallest farmers. As noted earlier, the recently introduced Mudzi Fund should go some way to improving the availability of credit to these farmers. Probably the reform's most significant impact on project credit is the increased difficulty in obtaining repayments after market liberalization. Previously project credit officers called up seasonal loans directly at the ADMARC markets where all smallholders brought their produce for sale.

Product markets

The impact of economic recovery programmes on the markets for smallholder agricultural products has been felt via reform of the official producer price structure and structural reform of ADMARC. Because of ADMARC's dominant role in the agricultural market place, devaluation and external trade liberalization have had a relatively much smaller influence on this area. In fact, in Malawi's situation any analysis based exclusively on an examination of changes in parity prices is of limited value: high and increasing external transport costs, in addition to high internal inflation and stagnant world commodity prices, serve to distort export and import parity prices substantially. Thus the analysis here is focused instead on changes in real producer prices.

Malawi's major smallholder agricultural products may be grouped into crops grown chiefly for cash (tobacco, cotton, hybrid maize, groundnuts and pulses) and those grown chiefly to satisfy household food needs (local maize, sorghum, millet, cassava). Some products are interchangeable, being grown for cash but consumable should a food shortage or changes in producer prices dictate. Hybrid maize, groundnuts and pulses fall into this 'intermediate' category.

Change in relative real producer prices is a major influence on the production decisions of smallholder farmers; the particularly high price responsiveness of the larger Malawian smallholders has been documented by numerous authors (notably Dean, 1966). Terms-of-trade indices for food and (export) cash crops (see Appendix Table 4.2) show that, although decline in real producer prices has been universal, for the most part cash crops experienced a price boom at the beginning of the adjustment period and declined only more recently, compared with food crops where decline has been more limited but also constant over time. However, the food/cash crop categorization cannot be used to distinguish a pattern of absolute real decline or improvement. This suggests that external market forces restrict the government's freedom to set prices to promote one category over another; certainly Malawi is a price taker for all major agricultural exports. For example, strong international markets for NDDF tobacco and pulses compared with those for the other tobaccos and for groundnuts may explain the relatively more favourable price profile.

Nonetheless, part of the most recent downturn in producer prices for export cash crops must be explained by the declining proportion of the export price passed on to producers by ADMARC: after a significant increase in the mid-1980s, this is now only a third higher – on average – than the 1981/2 level, when smallholder prices still contained an element of implicit taxation as a remnant of earlier policies.[5] In part this represents ADMARC's need to subsidize less profitable domestic trading in maize and other low value-for-weight commodities with the proceeds of export operations, suggesting that Malawian smallholders producing for export have not benefitted from increased earnings resulting from devaluation, owing to ADMARC's policy of protecting maize-deficit households.

Overall, therefore, it seems that the reform programme initially encouraged production of cash crops – in order to boost export earnings – but, because of the unacceptable decline in the production of food crops that ensued, has recently been reoriented towards a more balanced promotion of both product categories. For example, 1986/7 maize production was no greater than output in 1979/80 – resulting in a 210,000 tonne deficit compared with per capita consumption needs and creating a very real national food security problem. Policy objectives of protecting consumption of the maize staple via maintenance of low prices have therefore back-fired somewhat – particularly as a large proportion of poor net consumers are themselves producers – discouraging production and creating large deficits on ADMARC's crop trading account, which have fuelled the overall government deficit.

For Malawian smallholders, therefore, it is the change in the relative profitability of cash and subsistence crops that exerts the greatest influence on production decisions. Appendix Table 4.3 shows movements in real prices of smallholder crops since the beginning of the reform period and should be compared with Appendix Table 4.4 which shows production trends over the same period. Relative price changes – particularly for tobacco, maize, groundnuts and cotton – appear to have had an important influence on production decisions. For example, the earlier boom in tobacco and groundnuts was at the expense of maize and cotton production and, now that the period of policy bias in favour of cash crops appears to have ended, there is a corresponding move back towards maize production. Indeed, the promotion of maize production in the interests of food security has underlain the return to relatively low real prices for groundnuts for this very reason. Added to this has been the deterioration in world prices for Malawian export (confectionery) groundnuts owing to a change in consumer preference for smaller kernels.

However, it is not simply own price changes that have an impact. The most apparent feature is the absence of direct causality and the important influence of relative changes. Increases in the production of security food crops such as sorghum and millet appear to reflect the decline in maize production caused by falling real prices for this crop rather than real price increases for security food crops per se, as very little production is formally traded. Similarly, increased production of pulses has resulted from reduced (pure-stand) hybrid maize production in the face of falling maize prices (pulses are traditionally interplanted with local maize). Secondly, production trends for certain crops appear to have been significantly influenced by other factors; cassava production has been constrained by an epidemic of cassava mealy bug and cotton by problems with input supply, credit and marketing services.

In addition, where parallel product markets exist, the impact of changes in official prices is less than would otherwise be the case. For example, the majority of pulses production is sold at substantially higher prices on the parallel market, thus explaining increased production at a time of falling real official prices. Accordingly, ADMARC's share of pulses exports between 1982 and 1984 was less than 2% of the

---

[5] The substantial decline in oriental tobacco producer prices as a proportion of the export price realized by ADMARC is an exception and reflects official discouragement of this crop in recognition of the imminent end of a market for this heavy type of tobacco.

total. Similarly, it is estimated that up to one-third of groundnut production is disposed of in this way.

Finally, relative changes in the price of inputs as well as of products have substantially influenced farmers' decisions. With significant increases in the real price of fertilizer in the mid-1980s, as a result of the SAL III Fertilizer Subsidy Removal Programme then in operation, fertilizer-using crops (hybrid maize) became much less profitable in comparison with unfertilized crops (local maize and groundnuts). At the same time, sharp increases in the landed costs of pesticides for tobacco and cotton similarly reduced their relative profitability.

The liberalization of agricultural marketing in 1987 will, of course, have an extremely important impact on smallholder product markets. So far there is a remarkable dearth of comprehensive, quantitative evidence about the nature of the changes taking place; the major donors have apparently not felt it necessary to support an effective monitoring system whilst the Ministry of Agriculture is presumably constrained by lack of funds. Figure 4.2 illustrates one example of the increased fluctuation in crop prices that may be expected in the open market. Clearly the majority of net food-deficit households who sell at the beginning of the marketing season (June), and have to repurchase during the later food-deficit period (December), will face substantially reduced incomes and increased outlays. In addition, the regional distribution of markets will be affected; less profitable remote locations abandoned by ADMARC have never been attractive to private traders. Thus an increase in subsistence production would be expected in these areas. This would influence both the regional distribution of income and national food security (via the reduction in production of marketable surpluses).

Thus, a number of conclusions may be drawn concerning the overall impact of the reform programme on smallholder agricultural product markets. First, the major influence has been through changes to official producer and input prices, which initially favoured cash crops over food crops but more recently have promoted the latter. The previous decline in real smallholder producer prices has been limited under structural adjustment (smallholder crops are no longer the subject of heavy implicit

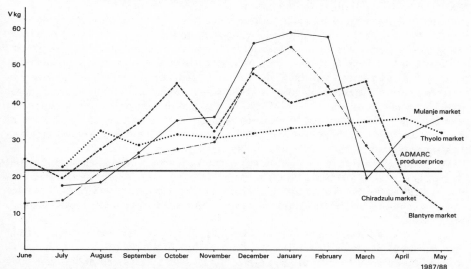

Figure 4.2. Maize price trends in liberalized markets 1987/8
Source: Blantyre ADD Evaluation Unit.

taxation). Second, farmers' production decisions are also affected by other factors – such as availability of extension advice, inputs and storage – that are only now beginning to be addressed by adjustment. Third, factor constraints limit the price responsiveness of supply such that it is manifested in changes in cropping pattern rather than in aggregate production. And finally, production decisions will be increasingly affected by the unofficial prices offered by private traders. At the moment this influence is substantial only for pulses and groundnuts and for maize for the net deficit and peri-urban households. However, the growing refugee population means that the activities of private traders in the first two markets is already having a significant impact on food availability, as a proportion of their purchases is leaving the domestic food circulation system to supply the refugees under aid contracts.

Economic infrastructure

As noted earlier, a major component of Malawi's economic disequilibrium has been the large government deficit and a major part of the reform programme has been focused on its reduction. Cuts have been most severe in the development budget.

As an export-oriented, land-locked country, Malawi is heavily dependent on international trade and cheap and reliable external transport links are therefore essential to the economy. Since before Independence the major link has been provided by the rail line to the Mozambican coast; however, escalating insecurity in Mozambique has limited utilization to 30% of capacity. Although one of the lines, to Nacala, re-opened in October 1989 the use that can be made of it is still restricted. In the meantime, international road haulage to the South African and Tanzanian ports has become much more important. As domestically-owned capacity is less than 100 vehicles, Malawi is incurring substantial foreign-exchange costs in employing hauliers from neighbouring countries; current outlays are equivalent to 7% of GDP (Harrigan, 1988). The disruption to Malawi's external transport routes resulting from the Mozambican conflict may be classed as one of the single most important causes of economic destabilization and barriers to recovery in Malawi today.

In an attempt to reduce these costs the economic recovery programme includes funding for the creation of a Northern Corridor route to the Tanzanian coast. However, this is handling only 8% of total external traffic at the moment (World Bank, 1990a) and is not due to come fully on stream until 1992. Meanwhile further investments in transport infrastructure will be limited by the need to reduce development expenditure, and the government budget deficit in general, as part of the reform programme.

On the domestic front, a key platform of the post-Independence government has been the uniform development of all three Regions of the country and the removal of spatial imbalances through investment in transport infrastructure. Accordingly, the transport vote has traditionally received as much as 30% of the development budget (GOM, 1988). However, the high cost of imported vehicles, spare parts and fuel and the passenger transport parastatal's monopoly of many of the more lucrative routes have restricted the use of vehicular transport in rural areas: Malawi's 20,000 vehicles are predominantly owned by urban dwellers and 90% of rural journeys are still made on foot (GOM, 1987).

The relative importance of transport expenditure in the government budget has not changed significantly as a result of the reform. Cuts in the overall budget will have affected the level of service offered but it is not clear whether rural services have been relatively more affected. Given the low use made of the formal transport infrastructure by the majority of the rural population, it is likely that changes will in any case have little impact on them. Of far more importance for many households is the withdrawal out of walking distance of ADMARC marketing facilities resulting from SAL III.

The government's agricultural sector support services as provided under the NRDP are being reformed outside the framework of the recovery programme, as we saw earlier. Given that they are substantially donor-funded, they are likely to be protected from budget cuts. Whether their reform will increase accessibility to small farmers remains to be seen.

Access to productive assets

As already shown, the estate sector has been expanding at the expense of customary land availability as the result of two separate developments. The first, which preceded the structural adjustment period, was the government's policy of promoting estate agriculture in order to increase export earnings; the second may have been a spontaneous reaction to currency devaluations which have encouraged further increases in export-crop production.

Apart from the resulting squeeze on customary land, an indirect spin-off, as far as land-constrained smallholders are concerned, is the expansion of employment opportunities for them in the estate sector. Circumstantial evidence suggests, however, that the poorest families may not benefit from these developments since it is the better educated small farmers who obtain such employment most easily.

The freeze on estate expansion in densely populated areas that forms part of the recent ASAC will doubtless address, although not eliminate, this important contributory factor to the land pressure problem. It is impossible to draw conclusions concerning the extent to which the land assets of vulnerable families are disposed of in response to hardships; the combination of strong kinship ties and the absence of a market for land may exclude such irreversible decisions. Mkandawire and Phiri (1987) cite evidence of the growing incidence of *kubwereka* (borrowing of land at a fee) in Central Region as a result of land pressure. Although these arrangements are usually very temporary, the charging of a fee, which is a relatively new development in the rural economy, reflects financial hardship on the part of the families lending land; it could also be interpreted as reflecting real desperation on the part of those venturing on the loan.

While adjustment may create expanded employment opportunities for the most vulnerable households, their own access to labour is likely to be little affected. The increase in the supply of ganyu labour will not be of benefit to resource-poor families unable to pay for it. The most urgent need is rather for an increase in the returns on those assets over which these families do have control, so that they may disengage from off-farm seasonal labour themselves and devote adequate time to own-holding production to ensure household food security.

Annual Survey of Agriculture   data point to some improvements in credit availability in the rural sector: between 1982/3 and 1984/5 all ADDs, except Lilongwe and Mzuzu, experienced an increase in the proportions of farmers obtaining fertilizer on credit. It is encouraging that the two ADDs with the highest proportion of small farmers have had the biggest increases (from 14 to 42% in Liwonde and from 23 to 43% in Blantyre), while the two with declining proportions were those with the highest proportions in the past. This in part reflects the protection of donor-funded credit projects from government budget cuts during adjustment and is thus not necessarily a direct result of the economic recovery programme itself.

From this evidence it would seem that the reform programmes have done little to address the severe factor constraints facing vulnerable smallholder households.

Rates of return on assets

For vulnerable households, the most important productive asset in terms of scarcity is land. And since for this group maize is the most important crop, in terms of its significance in the cropping pattern and its country-wide cultivation, it is important to examine relative price changes instituted as part of structural adjustment programmes as these give an indication of how relative rates of return on assets have been affected.

Appendix Table 4.3 shows that before the 1987/8 price increase, the price of maize, and returns to land under maize, relative to other crops, had been falling. This resulted in land reallocation from maize to groundnuts in a bid by smallholders to maintain returns on their land. The prime reason for the stagnation of maize prices was its strategic importance for food-deficit households, whom ADMARC's pricing policy has sought to protect. These price movements are, however, unlikely to have much influenced the cropping decision of vulnerable households who are noted for protecting their food base, where maize is the most important crop, in both production and marketing decisions. The rising maize prices will only mean greater difficulty in supplementing any deficits. The activities of the now licensed private traders, especially with respect to pulses, could result in further negative effects for these families if continued exportation is allowed.

In the same way, deteriorating real producer prices have reduced the returns to labour and capital invested in own-holding production. The deterioration has been partly caused by a downturn in world commodity prices and, as such, is the result of external as well as domestic policy factors. Nonetheless, the declining proportion of the world price passed on to producers by ADMARC is evidence that at least some of the deterioration has a policy origin. Surplus-producing households in more remote regions, where ADMARC has pulled out of markets following liberalization, will also be adversely affected by the lower prices offered by private traders (although net consumers may benefit). As regards returns to labour, family labour allocated to off-farm wage employment will furthermore be penalized by declining real wages.

In sum, rates of return on all productive assets have deteriorated during the adjustment period. This is reflected in declining GDP per capita and stagnant growth in the smallholder sector. Although the decline has been in part caused by external factors (declining world prices), much is directly attributable to the direct and indirect influence of the reform programmes on real producer prices and real wages. Given this, and the severe factor constraints affecting most vulnerable households, their most profitable option would appear to be to move out of agriculture altogether. But similar declining real returns in the formal wage employment sector and official discouragement of rural-urban migration limit the attractiveness of this option.

The terms and opportunities for employment

Participants in the ganyu market are drawn predominantly from rural families with small holdings or no land at all, whilst employers are typically those farmers with larger holdings. An important component of the reform programme has been increased agricultural producer prices to encourage production, particularly of exportable cash crops. Land pressure decrees that this increased production comes from yield increments rather than expansion of hectarage and, as labour is the variable input to which smallholder farmers have greatest access, increased demand for ganyu labour has resulted from the higher prices.

However, the production constraints faced by the smallest farmers – which existed prior to the introduction of the reform programme – have been so severe and widespread as to create a large pool of would-be ganyu labourers and over-supply in the market. In the absence of any systematic study of the market, it can only be assumed that increased demand has served merely to absorb excess supply and there has not been any upward movement in rates of remuneration. Indeed, for those labourers paid in maize rather than cash (the preferred form of payment for the majority coming from food-deficit households) the stagnation of maize prices in recent years will have reduced real returns to labour. Thus, although continued participation in the ganyu labour market may be expected as a result of continued land pressure, reform is unlikely to bring about any improvement in the opportunities for employment and may well reduce real returns to this type of labour.

The reform is unlikely to have reduced any of the constraints outlined earlier on vulnerable households engaging in significant self-employment in the informal sector. On the supply side, opportunities for the independent accumulation of capital from other income-generating sources, such as agriculture, have not improved, whilst the rise in interest rates will not have encouraged the uptake of bank credit – although this is now theoretically targeted away from government towards the private sector. Informal credit sources are drying up in the face of increasing pressure on rural incomes. Institutional credit from small business promotion organizations has not increased in quantity or accessibility. Furthermore, although the small- and medium-scale informal sector enterprises in which vulnerable households are likely to be involved are less heavily import-dependent than the larger-scale formal manufacturing sector, increased raw material costs resulting from devaluation and domestic inflation will raise costs of production. On the consumption side, deteriorating real rural incomes will depress markets already limited by the exceptionally low level of average per capita income in Malawi. The only means by which the reform programme might augment the terms and opportunities for self-employment for such households would be via the influence of devaluation on import-substituting domestic manufacturing: the market for imported products (in the rural sector particularly hand tools, clothing and processed foods) may decrease as domestically produced equivalents become cheaper in real terms. Thus there may be limited increased opportunities for self-employment in this sector.

From the earlier discussion of the impact of reform on estate agriculture, it may be concluded that, although the opportunities for formal agricultural employment have increased as a result of structural adjustment, real returns to labour in this sector are declining. The observed increase in estate employment must therefore be explained by the strength of push factors operating in the smallholder sector (land pressure and constrained access to inputs) rather than the attractiveness of estate employment per se. Thus for vulnerable households, moving out of own-holding production into estate employment because of the influences described above is merely to swap one poverty situation for another.

Again, retrenchment in the civil service will not influence the terms and opportunities for employment of vulnerable smallholder households as their more limited access to education largely precludes them from participating in public sector employment.

As long as the South African economy continues to grow, the mines' expressed preference for Malawian labour will ensure opportunities for external migration. The Malawi Government's policy towards migration has remained for the most part encouraging. Thus, relative returns to domestic employment and migration will be the key influence on the decision to migrate. Lack of data prevents an empirical assessment of this issue but circumstantial evidence suggests that the number of migrants has been increasing significantly in recent years, implying that migration has become a relatively more attractive employment option. Employers favour educated applicants and relocation costs are substantial, even under the assisted migration scheme; it may therefore be concluded that external migration will be a feasible option only for those vulnerable households with adequate accumulated resources.

The impact of economic recovery programmes on employment may be summarized as follows. The landless and near landless will have increased opportunities for employment as ganyu or estate wage labourers but real returns are declining; the increase in the numbers of landless resulting from population pressure and the falling real incomes of this group will thus create an increasing number of impoverished rural households. The better resourced smallholders will experience a limited increase in opportunities for self-employment in the import-substituting informal sector. They can also take advantage of expanded job opportunities in the non-agricultural formal sector and on the estates and of increased relative returns to external migration. Estate wage labourers and visiting tenants are unlikely to benefit from the increased returns to export crop production experienced by their employers and will thus benefit little from structural adjustment.

Social infrastructure and human capital

Health services in Malawi are provided by a variety of institutions; all but the Ministry of Health operate a fee-paying service. The health sector – and social services in general – have always received a low priority. The ratios of medical staff and hospital beds per head of population stand at 1:2,660 and 1:692 respectively. With an exceptionally high under-five mortality rate of 330 per 1,000 (accounting for 57% of all deaths) and the major causes of mortality and morbidity (measles, pneumonia, TB, malnutrition and malaria) all being preventable diseases, Malawi clearly has some way to go in achieving adequate levels of service provision.

There are virtually no figures available that distinguish between rural and urban health services, although it is known that about 35% of the health budget is allocated to the three central hospitals and the ratio of hospital beds per head of rural population is 2.5 times lower than the national average. Although community-based primary health care is the Ministry's basic philosophy, it is estimated that 65% increase in the number of health centres is needed to provide full coverage. Recent figures suggest that 40% of those attending under-five clinics and dispensaries have to walk between 5km and 50km to reach them (GOM, 1987).

The reform programme impacts most directly on the health service through its promotion of reductions in the budget deficit and cost-recovery in service provision. To date, the latter has not been implemented. In relation to budget reductions, the proportion of development expenditure devoted to health has actually increased, whilst recurrent expenditure has remained roughly constant. The overall budget, of course, has been pruned as a result of structural adjustment, so proportions mask an overall decline in absolute expenditure – plus an erosion of its real value by inflation. Nonetheless, the relative priority attached to the health budget has not changed over the 1980s (and cuts have been less drastic than in the education sector, for example). Absolute expenditure on urban facilities may have been maintained by allowing a deterioration in services in the rural areas but it is not possible to document this. It would appear, however, that Malawi is not making an adequate investment in its rural human capital in terms of health service provision; this acts as a severe constraint to maximizing productivity in peasant agriculture.

Education has also historically received low priority in the budget – less than 10% of development and recurrent expenditure – and in recent years nearly one-quarter of the education budget has been devoted to the development of the University of Malawi. Illiteracy rates remain high, particularly in the rural areas. Only 50% of the 8-to-13 age group is enrolled for primary education and drop-out rates are high (50% of pupils leave before completing four years, making them functionally illiterate according to government criteria). The primary sector is under-resourced and class sizes of 100 are common. In contrast, the secondary sector has excess capacity with around 5% of the 14-to-17 age group enrolled and a further 2.75% taking correspondence courses organized by the Malawi College of Distance Education.

Lack of data prevents a quantitative assessment of the impact of reform programmes in these areas, and in any case it is likely to be felt in years to come rather than during the timeframe of the present analysis. However, it is possible to present some projections. In the education sector development expenditure has been protected from budgetary cuts and the teaching force has been excluded from public sector employment cuts, although this may not be enough to maintain facilities in the face of a rapidly growing school-age population. However, recurrent expenditure has not been maintained and the reform programme includes plans for increasing school fees (currently accounting for less than 5% of total education expenditure). Thus it is likely that both the accessibility and quality of education will deteriorate.[6] Furthermore, low real earnings in private sector employment may serve to reduce the perceived returns to education and therefore the incentive to participate, as will fee increases at a time of declining real rural incomes. Therefore vulnerable households' access to and participation in education is likely to decline as a result of the reform programmes – although it is not possible to say by how much relative to other economic groups. In the short term this may lead to an increase in on-farm labour availability as children are released from the classroom. However, in the longer term the off-farm income-earning potential of the unschooled generation will be reduced and child malnutrition is likely to increase.[7]

Changes in the health sector during the reform period have followed much the same pattern. Again, both accessibility (in cost as well as physical terms) and quality of service available to smallholder families are likely to deteriorate as a result of structural adjustment, although it is not possible to estimate by how much relative to other sectors of the population. This will result in an immediate increase in the incidence of untreated wet-season illnesses (malaria, diarrhoea, etc.) which will have a detrimental impact on labour productivity. In the longer run increased child mortality and morbidity will reduce both the quantity and quality of the economically active population in years to come.

As a high proportion of smallholder families are food-deficit, correspondingly

---

[6] Primary school fees for the senior standards are already equivalent to annual per capita expenditure on education, so further cuts in the education budget would not appear to be a very equitable adjustment.

[7] There is a proven strong negative correlation between maternal education and child malnutrition (CSR, 1988a, 1988b).

the number of stunted and wasted children and the incidence of malnutrition-related illness in the rural population are also substantial. For the poorest households the adjustment programme's increased input and producer prices will have little influence, as their input use is low and risk aversion, owing to resource constraints, restricts their movement out of food production into cash crops. On the other hand, whilst the official consumer price of maize has been kept constant during the reforms, ADMARC's reduced role in maize marketing has forced an increasing number of rural consumers to obtain food supplies on the currently more expensive open market. This increased real cost of maize may therefore be expected to add to the number of food-deficit families and exacerbate the vulnerability of existing deficit households. At a time when traditional community support networks are breaking down, this chain of events is likely to cause a deterioration in rural human capital resulting from increased and more severe malnutrition.

Indeed, there is limited evidence that this is already occurring: although the incidence of seasonal malnutrition may be declining, permanent stunting – caused by inadequate food intake over a prolonged period – is clearly on the increase. Furthermore, all recent studies of malnutrition in Malawi have demonstrated that its primary cause is the inability of households to provide adequate food for their families and not merely the provision of ample but inappropriate foods or incorrect feeding practices (see CSR, 1986; Quinn, Chiligo and Gittinger, 1988).

In sum, although rural human capital is little affected at present by the reform programmes, it would appear that government retrenchment will, given the present structure of the rural economy, have a long-term detrimental impact on the quality of human capital at the disposal of vulnerable rural households. Given the importance of family labour resources to households with minimal access to other productivity-augmenting inputs, this appears to be a particularly serious development.

V. CONCLUSIONS

The set of policy measures loosely described under the heading of a reform programme would appear to have had only limited success in Malawi. It is difficult to determine objective lines of causality explaining this performance. Nonetheless, it is clear that external factors – particularly declining world commodity prices and disrupted international transport routes – have been highly significant in inhibiting the economy's return to growth. The achievements of policy and institutional reform must be viewed in the context of these deep-seated external constraints.

The nature of the early stages of the reform programme would appear likely to reduce distributional equity both directly and indirectly. Features such as increased user charges and reduced subsidies on government services may be expected directly to hinder access by low-income groups. In addition, economic reform indirectly favours better-resourced groups who are able to take greater advantage of initiatives such as increases in agricultural producer prices and improved access to bank credit. In practice, Malawi appears to have been sensitive to these equity implications in that it has moved more slowly in implementing the components of the reform programme with negative distributional effects (e.g. the suspended Fertilizer Subsidy Removal Programme).

Donors too appear to be revising their early approach to reform by including support for initiatives to alleviate the impact of some of the more deep-rooted structural constraints, such as access to land, as well as more market-based incentive structures.

For vulnerable smallholder households in particular the differential distributional impact of reform is clear. The programme has only recently started to address their access to and rates of return on agricultural assets. The failure to deal early on in the programme with the severe factor constraints under which many smallholder families operate has served to prevent the 'trickle-down' of benefits from macro policy initiatives. Thus vulnerable households remain risk-averse and unwilling to produce more remunerative cash crops. Restricted to the production of security food crops and frequently without the previously price-guaranteed supply of consumption maize from local ADMARC markets, their food security situation is deteriorating. In fact, the confusion surrounding ADMARC's functions in the post-reform domestic market – coupled with the traditionally heavy reliance of food-deficit households on the Corporation – has meant that the way in which market liberalization was implemented has made it the reform with the single most detrimental impact on vulnerable households. The only area in which they have so far benefitted from reform is in off-farm employment generation (on the estates, etc.) – although even here the advantages of increased job availability have been offset by declining real wages.

This leads to the conclusion that alternative or supplementary policy instruments need to be used to generate a more favourable adjustment impact for the most vulnerable households. In particular, more importance could have been attached to the improvement of smallholders' access to sector support services – so that they could take advantage of the benefits of the adjustment process – by redesigning credit packages and extension messages to encompass their potentials and needs. More could have been done to open up the industrial sector to private entrepreneurs by reducing the dominance of the quasi-public organizations: until recently manufacturing monopolies and restricted access to capital for private firms created significant barriers to entry. In the agricultural sector measures to improve the equality of land distribution could have increased the benefit the smallest farmers were able to derive from structural adjustment.

That a number of these support activities are now being funded is largely the result of lessons learnt during the first decade of adjustment experience. This leads to a second conclusion, that the reform programme would have benefitted from a greater emphasis on investigation of sector specifics during the early stages of the programme design: we have seen how a number of the macro perspective reforms ultimately impacted adversely on individual sectors apparently because the nature of macro-micro linkages was not identified. At the same time, the unequal pace of reform has limited the benefit to be derived from the package approach: retail price decontrol and foreign-exchange allocation revision have proceeded more slowly than the implementation of demand management measures designed to promote private sector expansion, and this decoupling has limited the ability of the manufacturing sector to respond to reform. Perhaps the most significant constraint affecting economic performance, however, stems from the problems associated with economic diversification in a low-income agricultural economy, where attempts to promote private sector expansion are often frustrated by supply-side weaknesses and by the low level of effective demand.

Although better targeting and design should improve the impact of the economic recovery programme on both the macro and micro economy in the second decade of reform, it is of vital importance to reiterate the caveat that Malawi's vulnerability to changes in the external environment has made the achievement of macroeconomic equilibrium a moving target and has consequently acted as a significant brake on successful economic restructuring.

Proceeding from this conclusion some lessons may be drawn for future donor policy from Malawi's experience. In comparison with other countries in sub-Saharan Africa Malawi began the process of economic reform from a position of only moderate destabilization. In addition, the implementation of the adjustment programme did not require a radical change in government policy. Thus implementation failures reflect government shortcomings to a much smaller degree than in other countries and the adverse influence of inappropriate package design and of external factors has been relatively much more important. For small, resource-poor, open economies such as Malawi's, therefore, adequate time and resources need to be devoted to designing country-specific interventions and allowing for their impact to work through the economy, and, most importantly, adequate attention needs to be paid to ameliorating the influence of detrimental external developments. Without these features being incorporated into the design of reform programmes, structural adjustment is unlikely to achieve the intended economic impact and may, conversely, work to the detriment of the more vulnerable sectors of the economy.

References

AES (1987) *A Production Cost Survey of Smallholder Farmers in Malawi*. Report No. 55, Lilongwe.

Bowbrick, P. (1988) *An Economic Analysis of the Impact of Private Traders on Agricultural Marketing*. Planning Division, Ministry of Agriculture, Lilongwe.

Centre for Social Research (1986) 'Nutritional problems in Malawi: Situation Analysis'. Paper presented at Symposium on Nutrition, Mangochi, Malawi, 31 July–2 August.

Centre for Social Research (1988a) *The Characteristics of Nutritionally Vulnerable Sub-groups within the Smallholder Sector of Malawi: a Report from the 1980/81 NSSA*. CSR, Zomba.

Centre for Social Research (1988b) 'The Malawi Maternal and Child Nutrition Study: interim findings from the baseline census'. Paper presented at Household Food Security and Nutrition Workshop, Zomba, 29–31 August.

Chipeta, C. (1982) *Economics of Indigenous Labour*. Vantage Press, New York.

Collier, P. (1988) *Macro-economic Policy, Employment and Living Standards in Malawi and Tanzania, 1973–84*. ILO International Employment Policies Working Paper No. 18, ILO, Geneva.

Dean, E. (1966) *The Supply Response of African Farmers: Theory and Measurement in Malawi*. North Holland, Amsterdam.

Fischer, K.M. (1988) 'Experience with NRDP in Salima ADD'. Paper presented at Symposium on Agricultural Policies for Growth and Development, Mangochi, Malawi, 31 October–4 November.

Government of Malawi (1987) *National Physical Development Plan*, Vol.I. Government Printer, Zomba.

GOM (1988) *Statement of Development Policies 1987–96*. Government Printer, Zomba.

Harrigan, J. (1988) 'Malawi: the Impact of Pricing Policy on Smallholder Agriculture 1971–88', *Development Policy Review* 6(4).

Kaluwa, B.M. and Mkwezalamba, M. (1988) *Socio-economic Impact of Malawi's Rural Centres Project: Estates Survey Results*. Report for GTZ, Lilongwe (mimeo).

Kydd, J. (1988) 'Policy Reform and Adjustment in an Economy under Siege: Malawi 1980–87', *IDS Bulletin* 19(1).

Kydd, J. (1989) 'Maize Research in Malawi: Lessons from Failure', *Journal of International Development* 1(1).

Kydd, J. and Christiansen, B. (1982) 'Structural Change in Malawi Since Independence: Consequences of a Development Strategy Based on Large-scale Agriculture', *World Development* 10(5).

Kydd, J. and Hewitt, A. (1986a) 'The Effectiveness of Structural Adjustment Lending: Initial Evidence from Malawi', *World Development* 14(3).

Kydd, J. with Hewitt, A. (1986b) 'Limits to Recovery: Malawi after six years of adjustment 1980–85', *Development and Change* 17.

Ministry of Health (1986) *National Health Plan of Malawi 1986–95*. Ministry of Health, Lilongwe.

Mkandawire, R.M. and Chipande, Graham H.R. (1988) 'Smallholder Agricultural Development in Malawi: The Case for a Targeted Approach', Paper presented at Symposium on Agricultural Policies for Growth and Development, Mangochi, 31 October–4 November.

Mkandawire, R.M and Phiri, C.D. (1987) *Malawi Land Policy Study: Assessment of Land Transfer from Smallholders to Estates*. Report for World Bank, Lilongwe, (mimeo).

Murison, S. (1987) *Malawi: Seasonal Credit for Smallholders*. UNCDF Report No. MLW/79/CO2. (mimeo).

Mwakasungura, A.K. (1986) *The Rural Economy of Malawi: a Critical Analysis*. DERAP Working Paper No. 197, Christian Michelsen Institute, Bergen.

Nankumba, J.S. (1988) 'Tenure Systems in the Estate Subsector of Malawi: The Case of Tenancy Arrangement'. Report for Winrock International, (mimeo).

NSO (1983) *National Sample Survey of Agriculture*, Vols. I–III. National Statistics Office, Zomba.

NSO (1987) *Malawi Population and Housing Census 1987 – Preliminary Report*. National Statistics Office, Zomba.

Pachai, B. (1978) *Land and Politics in Malawi*. Limestone Press, Ontario.

Peters, P.E. (1988) 'The links between production and consumption and the achievement of food security among smallholder farmers in Zomba South'. Paper presented at Household Food Security and Nutrition Workshop, Centre for Social Research, Zomba, 29–31 August.

Pryor, F. (1987) 'The political economy of poverty, equity and growth: economic development and income distribution in very poor nations: Malawi and Madagascar'. Paper presented at Conference on the Political Economy of Poverty, Equity and Growth, Fez, Morocco, April.

Quinn, V., Chiligo, M. and Gittinger, J.P. (1988) 'Household food and nutritional security in Malawi'. Paper presented at Symposium on Agricultural Policies for Growth and Development, Mangochi, 31 October–4 November.

UNDP/MTIT (1988) *Industrial Sector Study and Project Formulation Mission*. Report No. MLW/87/001. (mimeo).

Winter, C. (1984) 'SAL: boon or blow for Malawi'?, *Journal of Contemporary African Studies* 4(1/2).

World Bank (1987) *Malawi: Smallholder Agricultural Credit Project*. Report No. 6886-MAI. World Bank, Washington DC.

World Bank (1990a) *Malawi: Growth Through Poverty Reduction*. Report No. 8140-MAI. World Bank, Washington DC.

World Bank (1990b) *Project Completion Report: Malawi Smallholder Fertiliser Project (Credit 1352-MAI)*. Report No. 8534-MAI. World Bank, Washington DC.

Appendix Table 4.1. *Nominal smallholder producer prices (t/kg), 1980–90*

Year	Fertilizer	Maize	NDDF tobacco	SDDF tobacco	Sur/air tobacco	Oriental tobacco	Conf. groundnuts	Oil	Pulses	A grade cotton	B grade cotton	Sorghum	Millet	Cassava
1980/81	21	6.6	n.a.	n.a.	n.a.	n.a.	n.a.	n.a.	n.a.	28.5	22	5	2	3
1981/82	21	11.1	52.08	43.69	44.42	82.48	33.84	13.51	13.5	32.5	23	5	2	3
1982/83	26	11.1	75.64	67.13	64.09	82.48	51.85	19.42	13.5	42.0	29	5	4	3.5
1983/84	28	12.2	83.74	77.52	70.24	80.31	59.46	24.66	30.0	46.0	32	10	6	4
1984/85	31	12.2	102.03	81.50	84.60	90.87	69.28	42.01	40.0	46.0	32	12	6	4
1985/86	38	12.2	101.52	71.48	80.60	92.10	73.76	42.12	40.0	50.0	32	14	6	4
1986/87	39	12.2	105.52	71.48	66.66	117.25	73.76	48.95	40.0	55.0	32	14	6	4
1987/88	59	16.6	109.64	85.77	90.00	107.30	63.60	53.77	40.0	65.0	35	14	6	6
1988/89	27.50	24.0	164.00	124.00	138.00	106.00	75.00	63.00	44.0	77.0	37	18	8	10
1989/90	34.00	26.0	145.00	220.00	175.00	111.00	75.00	77.00	n.a.	81.0	39	n.a.	n.a.	n.a.

Source: Ministry of Agriculture Planning Division data.

Notes:

Fertilizer = C.A.N.

The average is used where different prices apply for different grades of produce.

Appendix Table 4.2. *Commodity terms of trade indices*

Crop	1981/2	1982/3	1983/4	1984/5	1985/6	1986/7	1987/8
Maize	100	91	88.11	73.41	66.46	57.91	63.34
NDDF tobacco	100	132.22.	135.38	148.91	121.15	122.71	101.28
SDDF tobacco	100	139.87	149.36	141.76	101.56	99.08	94.45
Sun/air tobacco	100	131.36	133.12	144.75	112.63	90.89	97.48
Oriental tobacco	100	91.05	81.97	83.73	69.32	86.09	62.59
Confect. groundnuts	100	139.48	140.89	136.8	131.78	115.66	79.58
Oil groundnuts	100	130.87	146.44	207.86	188.57	192.3	168.62
Pulses	100	91.05	178.29	198.01	179.2	157.23	125.52
A grade cotton	100	117.67	113.48	94.56	93.02	89.78	71.65
B grade cotton	100	120.02	116.62	97.2	87.96	77.13	67.38
Sorghum	100	91.05	160.4	160.4	169.35	148.55	118.57
Millet	100	182.12	240.22	200	181	159.22	126.82
Cassava	100	106.34	107.04	89.18	80.59	70.52	84.7

Notes:
Calculated from Ministry of Agriculture Planning Division data.
Pulses' price taken as average of all types.

Appendix Table 4.3. *Real producer prices for smallholder crops (t/kg)*

Year	CPI	Fert. price index	Maize	NDDF tobacco	SDDF tobacco	Sun/air tobacco	Oriental tobacco	Confect. groundnuts	Oil groundnuts	Pulses	A grade cotton	B grade cotton	Sorghum	Millet	Cassava
1980/81	100	100	6.6	59	59	59	64.5	33	13	13.5	23	18	5	2	3
1981/82	111.8	100	11.1	46.58	39.08	39.73	73.77	30.27	12.08	12.07	29.07	19.68	4.47	1.79	2.68
1982/83	122.8	122.8	9	61.59	54.66	52.19	67.17	42.22	15.18	10.99	34.2	23.62	4.07	3.26	2.85
1983/84	139.4	132.8	9.19	63.06	58.37	52.89	60.47	42.65	17.69	21.52	32.99	22.95	7.17	4.3	2.87
1984/85	167.3	147.1	8.4	69.36	55.4	57.51	61.77	41.41	25.11	23.9	27.49	19.13	7.17	3.58	2.39
1985/86	184.9	180.1	6.77	56.37	39.69	44.75	51.14	39.89	22.78	21.63	27.04	17.31	7.57	3.24	2.16
1986/87	210.7	184.6	6.61	57.16	38.72	36.11	63.51	35.01	23.23	18.98	26.1	15.18	6.64	2.85	1.89
1987/88	264	232.4	7.14	47.18	36.91	38.73	46.17	24.09	20.37	15.15	20.83	13.26	5.3	2.27	2.27
1988/89	353.3	131.0	6.78	46.40	35.10	29.00	30.00	21.12	17.82	12.44	21.78	10.47	5.1	2.26	2.83
1989/90	399.4	161.0	6.51	36.30	55.10	43.83	27.80	18.78	19.28	12.52	20.28	9.76	4.51	3.75	3

Notes:
Calculated from Ministry of Agriculture Planning Division data.
Maize and tobacco nominal prices deflated using fertilizer price index; all other crops using consumer price index.

Appendix Table 4.4. *Total production of smallholder crops ('000 tonnes)*

Crop	1981/2	1982/3	1983/4	1984/5	1985/6	1986/7	1987/8	1988/9
Maize	1244	1369	1398	1355	1295	1202	1420	1520
NDDF tobacco	6.5	7.6	14.7	12.5	10.9	9.6	7.7	4.6
SDDF tobacco	0.6	0.8	1.5	0.6	0.5	0.5	0.4	0.3
Sun/air tobacco	1.2	0.7	1.9	1.1	0.9	0.9	0.6	0.4
Oriental tobacco	0.6	0.2	0.3	0.1	0.1	0.1	n.a.	
Conf. groundnuts	n.a.	50.99	50.72	59.48	82.81	87.91	70.67	
Oil groundnuts	n.a.	n.a.	2.14	2.76	5.49	3.72	4.11	
Pulses	n.a.	n.a.	n.a.	n.a.	39.1	59.17	58.16	52
Cotton (all grades)	13.3	31.7	32.1	32.7	21	21.3	35.1	35.9
Sorghum	n.a.	6.83	14.27	22.04	20.76	15.64	21.78	
Millet	n.a.	1.62	8.32	10.58	9.53	8.05	8.94	
Cassava	n.a.	143.69	258.69	209.32	218.28	166.15	134.79	

Source: Ministry of Agriculture Planning Division data.

5

NIGER

JOHN DE CONINCK,
WITH KIARI LIMAN TINGUIRI

I. INTRODUCTION: THE CHOICE OF NIGER

The choice of Niger for this comparative study offers a number of advantages – arising from the geographical, ecological and socio-political specificity of an enclave in the Sahel and from its membership of the Franc Zone. Niger is a good representative of the group of countries belonging to the Sahel zone. As Raynaut (1988b: 15) has pointed out, 'It is of special value as an example because of the stability of the political institutions and the relative efficiency of the administration of the country . . . If there is one country from which one can learn the realities of Sahelien conditions, it is surely this one.'

As a member of the Union Monétaire Ouest-Africaine (UMOA), Niger has a fixed parity currency which is freely convertible with the French franc. In the context of the present study, this situation has two important implications. First, UMOA's own status means that devaluation, which elsewhere can be an important instrument in the policy of adjustment, has not been resorted to in Niger. Secondly, as a result of economic and monetary management which has perhaps been stricter in the countries of the Franc Zone than elsewhere in Africa and because of the guaranteed convertibility of the CFA franc, the necessity of adjustment, as Guillaumont (1985: 21) has observed, has 'made itself felt more belatedly not only because the imbalances . . . were initially less or slower, but also because they were borne more easily. In this respect the countries of the union seem to have been less vulnerable [than many other African countries].'

At the same time Niger also presents certain constraints which are linked, as we shall see later, to the impossibility of dissociating the effects of economic policies from the important ones of climatic hazards. Like its neighbours, whose economies are strictly constrained by climatic conditions, Niger is going through a severe crisis resulting from the significant deficit in rainfall since the beginning of the 1970s. This has led to chronically weak levels of agricultural production which jeopardize the balance of the country's food production, and a rapid intensification in the utilization of natural resources. From a situation of surplus cereal production in 1970 the country has moved into a situation of structural deficit leading to an increased dependence on food imports. The repeated droughts also illustrate the seemingly insurmountable difficulties encountered in undertaking investments which are indispensable to the improvement of productivity at a time when the increasingly vulnerable agricultural sector has to face growing needs resulting from significant demographic pressures.

There is also the further constraint of lack of microeconomic data. Any serious analysis of the effects of mesoeconomic changes on rural populations must depend on a solid base of microeconomic data. Such a base was found to be non-existent in Niger, despite the exhaustive study of the agricultural sector carried out by SEDES in 1987 (SEDES, 1987: 229). Comments are therefore often reduced to observations which it has not been possible to quantify. Thus, if the effects of the (still recent) adjustment programmes seem to have been very limited up to now, it must be borne in mind that any evaluation is constrained by the impossibility of separating these effects from the consequences of exogenous factors, especially of climate variations.

II. THE EVOLUTION OF THE ECONOMY (1979–88)

General constraints on development

Growth perspectives for Niger's economy are limited by certain well-known factors. *The extreme poverty of the country* (in 1988, GNP per capita was estimated at $346, one of the lowest in Africa) reflects the enormous natural obstacles which confront it. The narrowness of the resource base is illustrated by the following:

(a) The economy is dominated by a largely subsistence rural sector, and by the extraction of uranium. Agriculture involves between 80 and 90% of the population and represents 40–45% of GDP (for sources of GDP see Appendix Table 5.1). The serious and growing shortage of agricultural land (12% of the country's surface area) has been aggravated in recent years by recurrent drought which has accelerated a process of desertification on the small amount of land available, land which, furthermore, is generally very sandy and thus particularly vulnerable to water and wind erosion. The isohyet line of 300 mm, which corresponds approximately to the northern limit of cultivation, has shifted southwards 70–100 km during the last 15 years.

Climatic hazards and the low organic content of the soil have resulted in an extension of the cultivated areas (mostly taken by millet and sorghum) thus diminishing land reserves and fallow periods. This extension has also led to a reduction of pastoral areas, especially in regions of high forage productivity. Rural populations are therefore drifting from the land or are employing low-risk production techniques which use few inputs: in rain-fed agriculture, 98.5% of the production units operate manually.

(b) A recent population census confirms a marked demographic expansion. The population in 1988 was 7.2 million; the growth rate is 3% per annum (7% in the urban areas). The average density remains low (5.5 inhabitants/sq.km), but this masks a much higher density in the 'useful' south (20 inhabitants/sq.km) and is even greater in the valleys. This expansion supplies plentiful manpower, but of low productivity – with rudimentary production techniques and a very low level of education: primary education registration in 1982 was 23%, and the adult literacy rate in 1980 was barely 8%.

(c)   Apart from the extraction of uranium (which contributed 5.8% to GDP in 1987) and the tertiary sector, the so-called modern sector is barely developed at all. Manufacturing industry represented on average only 1.3% of GDP during the period 1982–6 and employed only 3,000 people (two-thirds of whom were in the public sector) in 1986.

Lack of autonomy and the limited impact of economic policies.   The structural dualism of a very small-scale 'modern' sector alongside a sizeable 'informal' sector which is largely insensitive to state intervention limits the scope for responses via traditional tools of economic policy. This limitation is increased in the case of Niger a) because of its membership of the Franc Zone which excludes independent recourse to certain policy instruments and restricts the use of others; in effect, Niger can neither devalue its currency nor manage an independent monetary policy. And b) because of the proximity of Nigeria, which, based on powerful historical and particularly trading links (the peoples living on either side of the 1600 km-long frontier share a cultural identity), if not always in Nigeria's favour, nevertheless frustrates, and indeed sometimes nullifies, the effects of economic measures taken in Niger.

While external factors are in part to blame for poor development performance, and despite the fact that the administration has shown itself to be relatively effective, the government's strategies have sometimes been ill-adjusted or poorly translated into projects or programmes, whether sectoral or general. This is of particular importance, having regard to the dominant role of the public sector in the economy. Public expenditure has in fact been regarded as the essential instrument for the allocation of resources and as a catalyst of growth: and it has favoured the infrastructure and construction without being able to develop a sufficient volume of viable projects in the agricultural sector.

Evolution of the economy since 1979

Table 5.1, which charts changes in GDP over the period 1960–85, reveals a growth pattern which is both limited (with a declining rate per capita) and cyclical.

The first half of the 1970s, with its disastrous droughts, witnessed a large fall in agricultural production and heavy losses of livestock, while the rural sector continued to dominate the national economy (providing 50% of GDP and 75% of export revenues). A net improvement was recorded during the second half of the decade: good rainfall and the building up of livestock herds allowed the rural sector to get off the ground again, while uranium production soared. The first years of relevance to this study mark the end of this period of rapid expansion.

The end of the boom years (1979–80).   The conjunction of growth in the agricultural sector (record production of millet in 1979 and 1980) and progress in uranium exports (80% of export revenue in 1980) indicated a promising future. According to the World Bank (1986: 3), 'although the debt stock had more than trebled and despite substantial deficits in the budget and the external current account which had begun to be evident at the end of the decade, the forecasts were optimistic and predicted sustained long-term growth'.

This boom period was also accompanied by marked changes in the economy, the most important being that the rural sector became of secondary importance and remained relatively isolated from the 'modern' economy. In 1980, it represented 43% of GDP and contributed only 20% to exports. The economy became more dependent

Table 5.1. *Annual rates of growth (Five-yearly averages)*

	Nominal rate	Actual rate	Actual/head
1960–65	8.6	6.8	4.0
1965–70	5.6	−4.5	−7.3
1970–75	14.3	0.2	−2.4
1975–80	22.9	8.8	5.9
1980–85	10.9	1.6	−0.9

Source: SEDES, 1987:44.

on the mining sector: uranium exports accounted for over 75% of the total and up to 41% of state revenues came from the uranium industry. This income, together with an increasing recourse to loans, allowed for an increase in investment which, in 1980, represented 28% of GDP and was more than two-thirds financed from domestic savings.

The 1979/80 public investment programme represented more than two-thirds of total investment. About ten new public enterprises were created, bringing their number to over 60. As a whole, these enterprises then represented 11% of GDP and 50% of employment in the modern sector. The government's current expenditure also increased rapidly, mainly due to growth in the public service where salaries and social advantages were becoming increasingly favourable. The money supply grew fast during this period (20% annual nominal growth from 1978 to 1981) and internal credit followed this development (see Appendix Table 5.2).

The crisis: 1981–4.   Just as they provided the basis for growth in 1975–80, the same agricultural and mining sectors almost simultaneously brought about the recession which Niger experienced from 1981 to 1984. GDP stagnated in 1981 and 1982, and then decreased in real terms by 3% in 1983 and 16% in 1984 (Appendix Table 5.3).

As the recession deepened, investment dwindled to 14% in 1983. The reduction in world demand for uranium resulted in a noticeable fall in its price (terms-of-trade indices deteriorated rapidly from 1980 = 100 to 63.5 in 1981 and 60.6 in 1985, also reflecting the devaluation of the CFA Franc) and then in a decrease in production (by 22% between 1981 and 1983).

The mining sector's share of GDP fell from 13% in 1980 to 8% in 1983, and budgetary receipts, which were heavily dependent on this sector, contracted rapidly. Expenditure, however, continued unchecked in the expectation that the world price of uranium would pick up: the budget deficit doubled from 1978/9 to 1979/80 and from then on the authorities called on foreign lending (usually commercial) to finance the deficits. Expenditures on maintenance were cut back and led to the deterioration of equipment and of the public services, particularly in the rural areas. Expenditure on personnel, on the other hand, grew rapidly (by 9% per annum in 1979/80–83/4). Investment now has to be financed entirely from outside.

At the same time, the foreign debt has been increasing. After the overall surpluses up to 1979, the small deficits of 1979 and 1980 gave way to a balance of payments deficit of more than CFAF 42 bn in 1982 (Table 5.2). During the period 1982–5, Niger suffered the after-effects of the drought (imports of cereals almost quintupled) and of the closing of the border with Nigeria at a time when the net supply of capital was falling off and world demand for uranium remained weak. In order to face up to emergency programme funding and to imports which were more costly following the devaluation of the CFA franc, the money supply was increased by more than 22%

Table 5.2.　*Balance of payments, 1982–86 (CFAF bn)*

	1982	1983	1984	1985	1986
Trade balance	− 57.9	− 26.0	− 6.3	− 44.3	− 11.6
Exports fob	120.5	141.2	132.8	112.6	114.6
Imports cif of which	− 178.4	− 167.2	− 139.1	− 158.9	− 126.2
Cereals	(− 9.1)	(− 12.3)	(− 11.0)	(− 41.0)	(− 8.4)
Services (net)	− 36.2	− 38.1	− 36.2	− 37.8	− 40.3
Transfers	31.8	32.9	32.0	58.4	36.4
Private	(− 16.0)	(− 17.0)	(− 14.0)	(− 14.5)	(− 15.0)
Official	(47.8)	(49.9)	(46.0)	(72.9)	(51.4)
Current balance	− 62.3	− 31.2	− 10.5	− 25.7	− 15.5
Excluding public transfers	(− 110.1)	(− 81.1)	(− 56.5)	(− 98.6)	(− 66.9)
Capital (net)	30.8	23.9	4.8	8.4	− 3.0
Public long-term (net)	17.3	21.9	11.8	11.7	6.8
Private long-term (net)	− 0.5	− 1.7	− 4.6	− 5.5	− 4.1
Short-term (net)	18.5	3.7	− 2.4	2.2	− 5.7
Errors and omissions	− 11.2	8.7	1.8	0.4	2.4
Overall balance	− 42.7	1.4	− 3.9	− 16.9	− 16.1
Financing	42.7	− 1.4	3.9	16.9	16.1
Net external flows	42.7	− 4.8	− 17.6	− 3.1	− 3.9
Central Bank of which	20.9	4.8	− 14.8	− 0.6	0.5
IMF (net)	(−.)	(12.3)	(7.4)	(8.9)	(7.4)
Commercial banks	21.8	− 9.6	− 2.8	− 2.5	− 4.4
Debt relief	−.−	3.4	21.5	20.0	20.0

Source: Data from Niger authorities.

in nominal terms. The current account recorded a deficit equal on average to 9% of GDP during the period 1980–3. Imports fell and foreign debt represented 54% of GDP by 1983. The ratio of debt servicing/exports moved from 22% in 1980 to 34% three years later.

Over the same period, agricultural production suffered a succession of bad seasons due to poor rainfall. The severe drought of 1984 caused a decrease of between 30 and 40% in foodstuff production while the number of livestock, an important export product, fell by about 40%. The sector's structural constraints aggravated these effects at the same time as the frontier with Nigeria was officially closed, affecting those areas of the country which produced the bulk of its agricultural wealth for the 40% of the population living in the frontier zone.

Growth of production was solely the result of the increase in area cultivated for food crops. Appendix Table 5.4 shows the extent of the fluctuations in yields reflecting gradual soil exhaustion and the recourse to marginal areas. The expansion was accompanied by a reduction in areas allocated to cash crops, chiefly groundnuts, which were not therefore able to fill the gap when exports of uranium dropped.

A contributory factor was the rapid growth of the public sector during the 1970s, the government using the revenues accruing from uranium to increase its control over the productive sectors of the economy. In 1985 the state held interests in 64 concerns spread over a large number of activities, although the two companies engaged in uranium extraction were two-thirds owned by foreign interests. By the early 1980s, the public enterprise sector, excluding uranium, represented around 7% of GDP, employed some 11,500 workers and supplied 21% of the value added of the modern sector.

Its performance has been mediocre, largely because of poor investment decisions, inappropriate pricing and marketing policies, excessive government intervention, a lack of financial discipline and shortage of qualified personnel. The policy of keeping producer prices high and consumer prices low resulted in operating losses in numerous undertakings, particularly the OPVN (the cereals marketing board). The lack of financial discipline in the administration and the parastatals led to a complex network of debt transfers and arrears.

Between 1979 and 1983, the annual losses of these enterprises rose from CFAF 2 to 9 bn (from 3 to 13% of public revenue). As the budgetary situation deteriorated, the banking sector (essentially the Development Bank of Niger, BDRN, and the National Bank for Agricultural Credit, CNCA) was called on to finance deficits, credit rising from CFAF 5.6 bn in 1980 to 37.6 bn in 1983, or from 11 to 35% of the national total (80% of the long-term credit in 1979 and 1981, according to a different source). Furthermore, by the end of 1983 the parastatals had accumulated nearly half the country's foreign debt. Resources allocated to the sector came to represent 17% of total government expenditure in 1981. This situation contributed to the bankruptcy of the CNCA (whose operations were suspended in 1985), to a serious liquidity problem and to reducing the access to credit for other sectors of the economy.

Efforts towards recovery.   GDP in real terms recovered in 1985 and 1986 (with a growth of 7.1% and 6.9% respectively). Nevertheless, the recovery remained relative: real GDP in 1986 reached only 92% of the average achieved between 1981 and 1983 before the 1984 drought. The recovery was primarily due to better climatic conditions: agricultural production increased by 40% in 1985 and 15% in 1986, offsetting a fall of 3% for the mining sector in 1986. Figures for 1987 and 1988 again reflected the poor rains in 1987, followed by outstanding harvests the following year.

The first effects of the stabilization programmes negotiated with the International Monetary Fund involved a radical contraction of the monetary supply from 1982/3. The budget for that year froze salaries, cut back on non-salary expenditure and investment, and imposed stricter controls on foreign borrowing. The annual increase in the government's net credit slowed down as a result (Appendix Table 5.2).

At the same time debt rescheduling agreements were reached with the Paris Club each year from 1983 to 1986 and with the London Club in 1984 and 1986. The proportion of grants to commercial loans grew as a result and the debt-service ratio was re-established at 33.3% in 1985. A first structural adjustment loan was made by the International Development Association in February 1986.

These measures – described in greater detail in section III – resulted in a contraction of imports, a reduction in the current account deficit from 9.7% of GDP in 1982 to 2.3% in 1986 (from 17.1% to 9.3% if grants are not taken into account), while the budget deficit fell from 7.1% of GDP to 3.6% during the same period chiefly thanks to a reduction in expenditure on equipment (Appendix Table 5.3). Inflation dropped from 9.8% in 1982 to 1.5% in 1986.

III. THE ECONOMIC REFORM PROGRAMME

The different economic reform programmes undertaken since 1983, elements of which frequently overlap, were backed by the IMF (with four standby agreements up to November 1986), by the World Bank (with a structural adjustment loan of US$60m. for 1986 and 1987 (first phase) and a $80m. credit for 1987 and 1988 for an adjustment programme affecting public enterprises), and finally by USAID (with an aid programme for the agricultural sector: the first phase amounting to $29m. to be disbursed between March 1985 and August 1987). Further IMF support was agreed in December 1988, amounting to SDR 50m.

The reforms contained in these programmes, whether at the macroeconomic or the sectoral level, were aimed at accelerating the growth of the economy while keeping the external and budgetary imbalances at tolerable levels. Structural problems directly responsible for the imbalances which most hampered economic growth were, according to the World Bank's analysis:

- the poor management of public resources, mainly because of the dominant role of a large and inefficient parastatal sector;
- a modern private sector constrained by lack of raw materials and with development hampered by a system of incentives encouraging investment per se and not the economic viability of projects;
- a weak resource base, rapid demographic growth in an isolated economy in which agriculture, always at the mercy of climatic hazards, remained the principal sector, and agricultural policies which failed to encourage appropriate production through adequate price incentives;
- the inefficient use of human resources.

General objectives

The general objectives of the reforms concern three areas which present the most damaging inefficiencies:

Budgetary stringency. The IMF stabilization programmes were aimed at reducing internal demand through improvement of the tax structure, limiting the growth of government current expenditure, reducing and restructuring capital expenditure, reducing arrears in internal payments to the state, improving the financial returns of parastatals, limiting external borrowing, and, lastly, curbing the expansion of domestic credit. The World Bank's structural adjustment programme (SAP) aimed to encourage growth through a more effective use and allocation of resources (restructuring of current expenditure, reorganization of the parastatals, emphasis on the productive sectors and the development of human resources, and improvement in expenditure planning).

Reform of the parastatal sector. The SAP and the World's Bank adjustment programme for the public enterprise sector (PASEP) were aimed at a reduction of the sector's role (through privatization and incentive policies for the private sector) and at greater efficiency in those parastatals remaining under state control (via a revision of the legal and institutional framework, and the easing of restrictions on prices and trade).

The rural sector.   The USAID and SAP programmes were aimed at increasing agricultural productivity by means of a reorientation of rural investment, a revision of the cereals policy, the phasing out of input subsidies plus other measures for recovering costs, revision of the system of agricultural credit, the lifting of administrative and fiscal restraints hindering exports and, lastly, the reorganization of agricultural research.

A series of *complementary studies* aimed to supply the necessary data to complete reforms undertaken in certain areas (for example in education and health) and extend them to other sectors of the economy.

Management of public resources

To limit the dominant role of the public sector and improve its efficiency, the SAP, in particular, put forward the following measures:

(a) A *restructuring of recurrent expenditure* by increasing the share of expenditure on the existing infrastructure, with expenditure on materials and services rising from 2% for the period 1982/3–83/4 to 10% for 1986/7–87/8. To compensate, growth of expenditure on personnel is restricted to the rate of inflation by stabilizing certain categories of staff, while direct subsidies are reduced through cost recovery measures and improved efficiency. (Table 5.3).

Table 5.3.   *Public budget, 1982/3–1987/8*

| | | | | | CFAF bn | | |
| | | | | | Programme | | Growth |
	1982/3	1983/4	1984/5	1985/6	1986/7	1987/8	1985–88
Revenue	68.8	70.1	68.0	72.6	76.0	83.6	7.1%
Tax receipts	62.6	61.1	60.7	65.3	68.0	75.6	7.6%
Non-tax receipts	6.2	8.9	7.3	7.3	8.0	8.0	
Expenditure	55.4	65.2	71.4	71.1	80.8	82.8	5.0%
Personnel costs	22.2	23.1	25.1	26.9	28.8	30.8	7.1%
Non-personnel costs	11.4	12.8	11.8	12.4	13.6	15.0	8.3%
Interest on debt	9.2	13.6	17.1	16.2	22.6	21.3	
Other	12.6	15.7	17.5	16.6	15.8	15.7	
Current surplus	13.4	4.8	–3.4	1.5	–4.8	0.8	

Source: SAP.

(b) *The establishment of a sliding three-year investment programme,* set at CFAF 275.5 bn for 1985/6–87/8, with annual totals rising from 9.7% to 11% of GDP in favour of the productive sectors and the rehabilitation of the existing economic and social infrastructure.

(c) *Better mobilization of fiscal resources.*   The fiscal system was modified with the introduction of VAT in January 1986, the revision of taxation on petroleum products and the restriction of customs duties exemptions. The investment code is being revised and a series of studies aimed at the reform of industrial and commercial policies for the next phase of the SAP is being undertaken.

(d) *Expansion of measures for the recovery of public service costs* to complete the steps taken in 1985-6 in the health, education and water-supply sectors (improved application of hospital charges, recovery of costs relating to urban school supplies, functioning and maintenance of irrigation systems, water supplies for both rural and urban populations, and a reduction in students' grants).

(e) *Better management of the foreign debt.*   The authorities' prudent policy, avoiding resort to commercial borrowing during the period 1985/6–87/8, is to be continued with an appeal for further aid and concessional loans. The government is committed to contracting no new loans at a higher interest rate than 6% and with less than 12 years maturity.

These measures are to be accompanied by *institutional improvements*. The analysis and follow-up capabilities of the Ministries of Finance and Planning are to be improved and an office of organization and method is to be attached to the office of the Prime Minister to co-ordinate efforts to build up managerial capacity in the civil service and the public enterprises.

Reform of the parastatal and private sectors

The principal measures taken were as follows:

(a) *Incentive policy.*   A gradual liberalization of prices and trade was started in 1985. The list of products and services subject to price controls was reduced from 27 to 7 (petroleum products, salt, water, electricity, bread, flour and transport) and, with the exception of petroleum products, all monopolies and quasi-monopolies on importation and marketing for both state-controlled and private enterprises were lifted. To the extent that the marketing policy (including agricultural products) initially implemented was based on often exclusive state intervention, this marked a fundamental reversal of policy. In 1985 also, tax regulations applicable to parastatals were brought into line with those of the private sector through the withdrawal of exemptions. The prices of local industrial products, previously controlled, were freed (except for annual increases over 7%) and tariff regulations on imports were simplied and the number of affected items reduced from 200 to 64 in 1986. By 1987, only 39 (pharmaceutical and educational supplies and essential basic products) were still subject to this legislation. These reforms were completed by the liberalization of private companies' registration procedures and further tariff dismantling introduced in May 1987.

(b) *Legal and institutional framework.*   A ministry to supervise parastatals was set up in August 1984, thus replacing the previous dual supervision (by the relevant technical ministry and the Ministry of Finance), in order to strengthen follow-up and evaluation. In 1985, new legislation was passed, to give the parastatals greater autonomy and allow them to concentrate on their financial and economic results.

(c) *Restructuring.*   Following studies undertaken in 1983–4, the government decided to keep 25 enterprises in the public sector and to privatize 23 (totally or partially), while the activities of 4 others (among them the CNCA) were suspended. Three enterprises were integrated within the Ministry of Animal Resources in December 1985. A programme for reducing government participation was worked out in 1985, involving 9 enterprises including SONARA (the groundnuts marketing board) and RINI (the rice marketing board). The priority restructuring programme, the objective of PASEP, dealt with 10 enterprises, representing 95% of the sector's financial losses and 45% of its production in 1982-3. These included the BDRN (representing 80% of the economy's credit and 50% of the assets of the banking system) where a programme of capital formation and debt recovery (CFAF 22.65 bn was repaid by the end of 1984) was instituted. These measures were accompanied by a programme of repayment by the state by 1990 of the sector's considerable financial arrears, at a total cost of CFAF 61 bn largely financed by the Bank and the Caisse Centrale de Co-opération Economique (CCCE).

The rural sector

Within the framework of the SAP and the USAID programme, the following measures were undertaken in the rural sector:

(a) Reorientation of the investment programme   in favour of small rural development initiatives mobilizing local resources and relying on the devolution of responsibility to village groups. It is hoped that 'each investment should be able to create the resources necessary to cover its operation and maintenance costs and thus its ability to survive without recourse to external financing' (World Bank, 1986: 82). This strategy implies the re-examination of current projects case by case, possibly leading to their reorientation or cancellation.

In areas of rain-fed cultivation, development policy should strengthen the productive base by means of small-scale irrigation and soil improvement, by emphasizing an integrated approach to production (agro-sylvo-pastoralism) and the comparative advantages of different agricultural products in each geo-climatic zone, and by developing national monitoring and evaluation services.

In the irrigated zones, priority is given to the rehabilitation of existing schemes and the need to encourage co-operatives to shoulder full responsibility for their operation and maintenance.

In the pastoral zone the policy is to encourage the participation of herders in the protection of their environment; state support should be limited to the provision of a qualified extension service.

(b) Revision of cereals policy.   From 1983-4 the government reduced the role of the OPVN by freeing the marketing of cereals. By then the OPVN's import monopoly had been abolished and a system of tendering for its purchases and sales introduced, to encourage the participation of the private sector and co-operatives in cereals marketing. The number of OPVN sales outlets was reduced at the same time.

This policy was continued in 1985-6. The OPVN now holds no more than a security stock whose ceiling is fixed at 80,000 tonnes, the stabilization stocks having been eliminated, and OPVN purchases and sales cut down to the renewal of one-third of this stock each year. At least 80% of these operations (50% in the USAID programme) must be carried out through invitations to tender. Finally, official producer prices for millet and sorghum have been abolished. Imports remain free from price control and, in the event of the national market becoming saturated, exports are also freed. Only the 'remote areas' (essentially the pastoral areas) still benefit from the OPVN's retail sales and only 'emergencies' allow the security stock to be renewed by more than one-third annually.

Prices of other agricultural products have also been liberalized: those for ground-nuts and cow peas are 'indicative', while those for rice and cotton are 'floor' prices. Cow peas and livestock exports are to be stimulated through the removal of fiscal and administrative barriers, and the marketing monopolies held by SONARA and RINI have been abolished (that on the marketing of cow peas by SONARA since October 1984).

(c) Removal of subsidies and cost recovery.   Subsidies for the purchase of agri-cultural equipment were abolished from 1985, thus reducing costs to the state and encouraging competition from artisan blacksmiths. Fertilizer grants have gradually been reduced to a ceiling of 15% of the supply price from 1988. An increased role for the private sector in the production and marketing of agricultural inputs is envisaged within the framework of the USAID programme, aimed, among other things, at produc-tion from agricultural workshops which are better adapted to local needs.

In the livestock sector, vaccines and medicines (apart from vaccines used to combat serious endemic diseases) are to be subject to cost recovery, with the total privatiza-tion of VETOPHAR (the veterinary service pharmacy) by the end of 1987.

(d) Restructuring of agricultural credit.   The operations of the National Bank for Agricultural Credit (CNCA) were suspended early on essentially as a result of its low rate of debt recovery – from the parastatals amongst others – though its continuation for certain projects was assured by donors supplying the appropriate funds. The deci-sion to liquidate the CNCA came in 1986, based on an evaluation according to which 'the low level of demand for credit in the rural areas does not justify the existence of a specialized institution' (World Bank, 1987: 22). A new system of agricultural credit was scheduled to start in 1988-9.

(e) Increased role for co-operatives.   The USAID programme puts particular emphasis on encouraging the co-operative movement to play an intermediary role in the supply and marketing of cereals and in supplying farmers with inputs. It envisages, among other things, the expansion of cereal banks (handling at least 6,000 tonnes by the end of 1988) in order to reduce OPVN expenses and stabilize prices, and institu-tional support for co-operatives including turning the agricultural inputs supply agency (CA) into a co-operative (CCA).

(f) Reform of agricultural research by directing it towards a limited number of prac-tical subjects 'capable of responding to the most urgent problems facing the peasant' and, through INRAN in particular, focusing research on the improvement of rain-fed cultivation and analysing individual projects to 'evaluate their consistency with the research capacities and budgetary endowment of INRAN'.

Other sectors

Health.   To reduce the imbalances between curative and preventative medicine, ser-vices in rural and urban areas, and expenditures on personnel and materials, several measures are proposed in the framework of the SAP, including:

- the priority assignment of paramedical personnel to basic health units, with more extensive training programmes and the application of staff training quotas;
- limiting hospital investment to rehabilitation or improvement of existing services, with priority being given to health cover in rural areas;

- limiting the importation of medicines, with priority for the purchase of basic drugs;
- improvement in financial administration, with strict application of hospital charges and the introduction of charges for local health care.

Education.   To balance current trends with the country's long-term training needs, priority has been given to checking the fall in primary schooling by the training of assistant teachers, the adaptation of syllabuses to the population's real needs, and the expansion of capacity by cutting building costs (via increased use of local materials) and by stimulating the setting up of primary schools in the private sector.

Simultaneously, a slowing down in the expansion of secondary and higher education is planned (via reduction of scholarships, and intake in accordance with the country's needs).

Cost recovery measures are also included, such as involving beneficiaries in the construction and upkeep of classes and making parents responsible for the purchase of school supplies in the department, commune and district centres, the latter representing a saving of CFAF 64 m. in 1984–5.

Water supply.   To ease the main problems faced by the sector (investment and maintenance costs greater than the financial capacity of the state; deterioration of installations in rural areas; limited management capacity; preference of villagers for expensive technology – wells rather than boreholes), the reorientation will entail, amongst other things:

- for urban supplies, institutional reorganization accompanied by full cost recovery from the beneficiaries;
- for rural supplies, priority to be given to the rehabilitation of existing installations, and the emphasis of investment programmes placed on actual demand as expressed by village communities, and on their agreeing to contribute financially to the investment and maintenance;
- for pastoral supplies, the handing over of existing installations to groups of pastoralists who will undertake their maintenance.

Energy.   To counter the existing imbalance between supply and demand for firewood (which represents 80% of energy consumption) and so to protect the vegetation cover while limiting imports and supporting the growth of national production, measures are planned to encourage conservation, to promote new technologies (promotion of improved cooking stoves) and to encourage the private sector particularly with regard to planting and marketing forest products.

Roads.   Emphasis is put on the rehabilitation and maintenance of the existing network and the continuation of current projects. New initiatives are limited to a minimum programme of expansion of secondary roads and rural tracks.

Other areas

The first phase of the SAP planned several studies to prepare for the extension of the reforms in a later phase. These comprise: reform of the public service; extension of cost recovery measures; reform of the financial sector; reform of industrial and commercial policies; land reform; reforms in the forestry, livestock and transport sectors.

Expected effects

Macroeconomic impact.   Modest results are expected from this programme. The growth rate of GDP, for instance, should be no higher than to allow for the stabilization of per capita income (2.9% from 1991), assuming that production is not affected by severe droughts (Appendix Table 5.5). This figure compares favourably with the fall of 1% per annum over the period 1960–1985, excluding the uranium boom years.

This growth will be due primarily to the increased effectiveness of investment 'to the extent that its level will not be raised because of persistent financial or material constraints'. In the same way public investments will reach 9–10% of GDP 'given that the choice of viable projects in the agricultural sector will initially be limited through the lack of appropriate technical approaches'.

The budget deficit will reach a ceiling of 2% of GDP (a level described as tolerable). Thanks to a recovery in agricultural and livestock exports (which reduce, albeit marginally, the country's dependence on uranium), and a reduction in cereal imports, the current account deficit will also be brought down to 2% of GDP. 'The increased efficiency of the modern sector will be reflected one day or another (sic) in the expansion of import-substituting activities and small-scale export industries' (World Bank, 1987: 31). Expenditure on servicing foreign debt is forecast to level out but 'significant contributions of gross capital in the form of aid and highly concessionary loans will continue to be necessary to help Niger discharge the very large sums that it still has to repay' (*ibid.*).

The World Bank identifies four main risks associated with the SAP:

- the danger of delayed and/or partial execution, notably as a consequence of public reaction to such measures as recovery of costs;
- insufficient reaction (especially from the private sector) to the proposed incentive measures;
- uncertainty about developing the basic resources of the economy, namely the rural sector, given the lack of technically and economically viable policies that could ensure the long-term development of the sector;
- unfavourable exogenous factors (climatic conditions, economic circumstances such as a further fall in uranium exports).

Social impact.   Thanks to the restructuring of public expenditure and the sustained contributions from foreign sources made possible by the SAP, the World Bank expects the SAP to lead to a progressive though modest improvement in the standard of living. The social costs, which basically have already been suffered since the collapse of the uranium market, are low, according to the Bank, because the structure of expenditure programmes has been modified so that a larger proportion of the population benefits from them. And the short-term costs are of less importance than the long-term advantages which flow from increased economic efficiency.

Cost recovery measures (covering curative medicine, middle and higher education, the supply of subsidized products) will chiefly affect the urban population and the economies thus realized will enable the financing of basic services (primary schools, preventative medicine) in the rural areas. This also applies to the investment programmes.

As to pricing policies, according to the Bank, it is 'still too early to evaluate the effect of the reforms, the current level of prices being still strongly influenced by other factors' (*ibid.*: 31). Nevertheless, it is probable that growth in cereal production in the medium term will translate into 'a permanent decrease in consumer prices of food cereals, but considerable fluctuations in these prices must be expected because of climatic hazards' (World Bank, 1986: 40), whereas the prices of certain other essential products will stabilize because of increasing competition. This competition will nevertheless be limited to the intervention of a few traders, thus risking the concentration of economic power in a small number of hands rather than giving rise to an entrepreneurial class.

Moreover, the Bank notes that the removal of official subsidized prices for millet and sorghum risks lowering the prices (and therefore the incentives) for production. Nevertheless, these effects will not be very widespread in so far as the purchases formerly made by the OPVN constituted only a small fraction of national production.

Lastly, redundancies in the parastatal sector will be partly compensated by redundancy payments, grants of land in irrigated areas and the absorption of personnel by the private sector.

Measures affecting the tertiary education sector have proved politically perhaps the most difficult for the authorities. In February 1990 riots in many towns followed a reduction in student scholarships and the ending of a system guaranteeing government employment for all graduates, precisely at a time when opportunities in the contracting 'modern' sector of the economy were continuing to dwindle.

IV.   SMALLHOLDERS AND THE RURAL POOR

A blocked agriculture

Subsistence agriculture remains the norm, despite the gradual changes that have been taking place. According to some official estimates only between 10% and 20% of cereal production is marketed and only 5–8% of trading in the rural areas is monetarized. The rural economy is characterized by:

(a)   family-owned smallholdings. Existing studies point to a very small percentage of large land-owners: 70% of holdings are less than 5 ha and are cultivated by 2.4 to 3 people. The average size is 4.67 ha (or 6 ha, depending on the source) for an average family of 5.7 people.

(b)   apart from the developed irrigated areas (which represent only 13,000 ha), very limited use of inputs apart from labour and land. Agricultural work depends on tools made by local blacksmiths and woodcutters (hoe, daba, hilère, and axe). Although the plough was introduced in the 1950s, its use has remained very limited and has even been abandoned in some areas. In the same way, fertilizers, already very little used (outside the irrigated areas), are used even less as a result of declining rainfall.

(c)   soil regeneration through the practice of leaving land to lie fallow. In dry cultivation just as on irrigated plots, there is usually mixed cropping of food crops – often linked with a leguminous crop, most frequently millet/cow peas, sorghum/cow peas, and millet/sorghum. The Ministry of Rural Development estimates that 90% of the cultivated land is used for growing cereals.

(d)   a growing integration between livestock production and agriculture. These two activities have for a long time followed distinct lifestyles, agriculture being practised by settled peoples and livestock-keeping by nomads in pastoral areas with very low rainfall. Interaction is increasing with use of natural resources, population movements and exchange of work, financial links, etc. Three main forms of livestock production are practised: nomadic, transhumant and sedentary. Cattle fattening is expanding in the South using millet stalks, wheat bran, maize, cow pea leaves, and supplementary feeds such as cotton seeds.

Environmental degradation.   The agricultural sector is far from static (see SEDES, 1987). As a consequence of climatic hazards and demographic pressure, the determining factor has been the rapid extension of land under cultivation (at a greater rate than the increase in population). The ratio of leguminous crops to cereals has remained stable, cow peas making up for the decline in groundnuts. The irrigated areas, although increasing in absolute terms, have not seen their relative share growing, unlike sorghum which has recorded a significant increase.

The extension of the cultivated area has entailed a rapid reduction in fallow time. In the department of Maradi, where the situation is most serious, there is practically continuous cultivation, and the same is likely to be true of Dosso and Tahoua within 10 years. There is, however, a much closer correlation of yields with rainfall. Recorded yields have either stagnated or fallen back (Appendix Table 5.4), with the exception of rice. In addition, lack of rainfall has led to soil depletion.

Rainfall plays just as decisive a role in livestock production. Its reduction has led directly to a reduction of foraging possibilities while the extension of cultivated land has removed the best pasture land and thus jeopardized herd productivity. This shrinkage has led to over-grazing (which is also furthered by borehole drilling) thus reducing the potential for forage and augmenting the harmful effects of erosion. As a consequence of climatic hazards, the proportion of small ruminants, which are more prolific than bovines, is growing in relation to the total number of livestock (which, as noted above, had still in 1985 not yet reached its 1960 numbers).

The 1987 SEDES report (p. 93) thus concludes that demography, the rainfall deficit, the mechanical effects of wind and rain are 'so many key variables which can in no way be controlled, and the system . . . can only end up in deadlock: deterioration of the soil, reduction of agricultural and pastoral production, deepening of the deficit in foodstuffs'.

Social framework.   These physical changes tend to accelerate burgeoning social differentiation and economic inequality, often the result of hereditary social status (with respect to access to land, for example) or of extra-agricultural activities (trade, migration in the dry season) rather than a capacity to generate surplus and capital. There are few rich farmers, and the 'rich' and the less 'rich' practise agriculture more because they come from a rural background than, with few exceptions, because it is a means of accumulation.

This unprofitable agricultural sector consequently attracts little investment, despite the priority often given to social obligations, and must be put into context with the risk coefficient of the activity. Inequalities inevitably increase in areas where conditions are either particularly favourable because of greater availability of water (river valleys) or of proximity to urban centres (market gardening) or marked by impoverishment and/or shortage of land (the Maradi valley, for example). In these areas, one can observe competition for land, and divisions signalled by the use of modern inputs or hired labour.

The impact of capital accumulation in land or livestock by traders and salaried employees in the modern sector is another factor whose scale is not easy to gauge. At the other extreme is the manpower prepared to hire out its labour, whose numbers are growing as a result of climatic and economic crises, and which creates new situations, exemplified by migration on a national or international scale. An agricultural census in 1980 showed that 6% of the male rural population were wage-earners and another 12% had extra-agricultural activities. 90% of the villages now send migrants abroad in the dry season and SEDES observes that 'once destined for investment in cattle, the remittances from emigration serve today to buy millet to bridge the hungry gap'.

These embryonic or current changes, however, must not overshadow the persistence of older divisions linked to cultural and social values, the most pronounced of which is the non-status of rural women as producers who can aspire to autonomy and control of their holding.

Characteristics of smallholder systems

Three case studies are put forward here using existing data concerning the departments of Maradi, Diffa and Niamey. The development of the livestock sector is then also briefly described.

Situated 600 km to the east of Niamey, the *Department of Maradi* makes an important contribution to national agricultural production (with 140,000 holdings cultivating 707,000 ha in 1980), though its physical setting is rapidly deteriorating, particularly in the southern districts. The cultivation system is of the Sahelian type based on rain-fed cultivation of millet, sorghum and cow peas. Livestock is also important, especially small ruminants. The great droughts of 1972–3 and 1983–4 have led to a considerable fall in groundnut production, the gap being filled by cow peas, where there is an expanding market. The droughts have also led to a growth in the export of labour, especially to Nigeria, and to extensive sales of animals.

Since 1977 the department has benefitted from an important rural development project concentrated in the four southern districts. A study of 8 control villages intensively affected by the project (Raynaut, 1988a) examined the widening of inequalities between holdings, apparent at the level of control over land, ownership of cattle, use of inputs and the flow of labour. Some of its main findings are as follows:

- pressure on available farmland is leading to disputes and increasingly unequal distribution;
- the majority of households own sheep and goats (89% and 70% respectively), but only 38% own cattle. Among the latter, between 3% and 6% of households own half the stock;
- only 21% had animal traction equipment, ownership patterns being closely linked to control of sufficient land to warrant the investment;
- the wage-earning class is playing an increasingly important role in rural differentiation. Overall one-third of households were net sellers of household labour and one-third were net users.

The Department of Diffa, in the extreme east of the country, has a relatively small population; the area under cultivation reached only 61,000 ha in 1979–80 and land ownership problems are much less acute than in Maradi. The average size of holding is 2.1 ha but crops grown on the flood plains (Lake Tchad and the valley of the Komadougou) and in small irrigated plots are becoming increasingly important. The department is of special interest in that it was the subject of one of the rare studies of household income and expenditure conducted in Niger during the past few years. Undertaken by the Ministry of Rural Development in 1983–4 (a period of severe drought), it covered 36 holdings in 9 villages (in the Komadougou, lake and basin areas). The principal results of this study (which excludes all estimates of non-monetarized exchanges) are as follows:

– The average income per smallholding was CFAF 455,111 (roughly 60% from the sale of agricultural produce and livestock, essentially market produce, and 39% from craft activities). Wage income was very little developed; while gifts represented more than a fifth of total income. The small proportion from sales of cereals was probably more marked because of the department's food deficit in 1984. Cattle losses during the drought will have had a similar effect.

– The food deficit is also reflected in the large proportion spent on the purchase of cereals (39% of total expenditure). There were purchases of animals as some farmers exploited the price variations in different markets and substituted sheep for cattle during the drought. Overall, agricultural and food products absorbed nearly 75% of total expenditure. Lastly, in the three areas studied, outgoings were greater than receipts, reflecting the very difficult position in Diffa in 1984.

Another source of household income data is given by IFAD (1987: 69) in the context of small-scale irrigation in the Komadougou valley:

Per holding	With small pump CFAF	With shadouf CFAF
(i) net agricultural revenue less labour costs and own-consumption	383,251	203,878
(ii) net revenue in cash	260,072	82,601

The Department of Niamey made up about a quarter of the cultivated area of the country in 1985. Rain-fed cultivation is constrained by particularly poor soils and yields are lower than in the other departments on the southern fringe of the country. Irrigated cultivation is important in the river valley (25,000 ha).

As in Maradi, the area under millet has expanded as far as possible into areas of marginal productivity, with reduced manuring of the fields to avoid 'burning'. At the same time new possibilities have been opened up by the extension of irrigated cultivation (mainly for rice, partly as a cash crop enabling purchases of millet to make up the deficit in production from rain-fed plots which is largely destined for domestic consumption). Opportunities for out-of-season crops are extensively taken up and, as in Maradi, emigration plays an increasingly important role in the household economy (with income now used for the purchase of cereals rather than – as previously – for the capitalization of production units).

There are no data on income and expenditure per holding in the rain-fed areas. A recent study carried out in some irrigated areas by ONAHA in the river valley shows a net income per holding (including income from rain-fed plots as well as off-farm activities) of CFAF 168,112 for the winter season 1987/8, non-agricultural income being only 5% on average of the total. IFAD estimates the incomes of farmers working on small irrigated areas in the river zone as follows (in CFAF):

Per holding	Small pumps	Calabash	Arboriculture irrigated by calabash
Net revenue (CFAF)	520,602	431,646	429,982
Net revenue in cash	270,731	189,931	192,632

At the national level, according to the Ministry of Agriculture, a traditional agricultural holding should produce an average net agricultural income of CFAF

26,000 per head. A 1985 study noted that 60% of the households surveyed benefitted from non-agricultural income (more than or equal to agricultural income in 35% of cases).

The pastoral and agro-pastoral sector.   The loss of stock in 1973 and 1984 started up a process of decapitalization which confirms the impression that herders are, without doubt, the segment of the population most vulnerable to the events of the last two decades. Droughts particularly affected the 'pure' livestock-breeders in the pastoral areas, who currently make up far less than half the population of this zone. Their income is almost totally dependent on their livestock in different ways:

- sale of animals in the markets in the south of the country, to brokers on the spot or by participating directly in their export;
- sale of by-products (milk, skins, crafts);
- barter, primarily to obtain cereals;
- the caravan trade, an important source of income for some groups of families.

According to a study on cost recovery (African Asian Office, 1987, 1988) and on the basis of 'intuitive rather than mathematical' estimates due to lack of precise recent data, the income of the nomadic livestock-breeder is potentially higher than that of the farmer in the settled areas (few purchased inputs and high profitability of livestock in times of good rains). Several factors, however, militate against this: environmental deterioration, irregularity of the rains, increase in cultivation, imperfect legal frame-work, distant markets. It is estimated that the great majority of livestock-breeders no longer possess the herds thought necessary for independent pastoral production and the droughts have forced many families who lost most or all of their animals, and who wished to remain in the pastoral economy, to go into the employ of rich land-owners or else to seek seasonal employment in the south. A market for factors of pro-duction is, in fact, developing with the appearance of investors (sometimes strangers to the area) who buy up animals at a low price, resort to paid labour and buy pastoral watering points. This trend threatens even further the fragility of the system and the viability of the traditional family units of production which thus become even more vulnerable to future droughts.

This largely explains the recent growth of mixed pastoral systems which can be combined with rain-fed cultivation and within which agricultural activities can repre-sent up to half the income for the holdings concerned. These vary from a situation in which the farming investment is very low (broadcast sowing, no weeding, return of population at harvest time) to one of regular work on the land while the herds, sometimes in the charge of hired workers, independently pursue their quest for pastures. In this case, livestock fulfils a new function as a factor of agricultural pro-duction, in addition to that of investment and as a source of liquidity in anticipation of unusual expenditure.

Conclusion

This section has indicated the extent to which recent socio-economic data at the household level are lacking. In fact, no complete study exists on rural households which could be considered representative of a particular area of the country, taking into account the radical changes that Niger has gone through during the last decade. What is more, household budgets calculated in the context of development projects make it possible only to define the profitability of this or that form of cultivation or system of production. The share of non-agricultural income, whose growing importance is widely acknowledged, generally does not figure in such exercises and no time-series are available. Consequently, it is impossible to quantify, even approximately, the effects of the economic reform programmes on the rural population. Nevertheless, a tentative qualitative assessment is put forward in the next section.

V. THE IMPACT OF THE REFORMS

The evolution of state intervention in rural areas

At Independence, the government stated its principal development objective as improvement in the standard of living of the rural population. In particular, food self-sufficiency was aimed at via price incentives, rural credit, research, support for and training of producers and area-specific measures (large regional projects in the rain-fed areas, irrigated developments and, more recently, microprojects; livestock projects). The method was a 'top-down' approach towards a passive peasantry: 'development' often involved only the diffusion of new techniques such as animal traction or the use of fertilizers.

The Interim Consolidation Programme (1984–5) and the latest Five-Year Plan (1987–91) stressed a new approach whose main elements included:

* an emphasis on popular participation;
* reducing the role of state organizations, and reducing public expenditure;
* improvement of the terms of trade in favour of agriculture;
* in the livestock sub-sector a new priority for traditional producers; and
* natural resource conservation.

Table 5.4 shows the evolution of investment in the rural sector as a whole – with increased absolute and relative levels of expenditure planned from the time of the uranium boom, but capacity failing to respond.

The main institutions.   State interventions and their accompanying measures have necessitated the establishment of an impressive institutional apparatus, the main components of which are:

* administrative structures from the national level to that of 10,000 villages;
* a hierarchy of village councils and committees at the canton, district and departmental levels, with a national council for development at its apex;
* a co-operative structure based on some 10,000 groups, with unions at local, sub-regional, regional and national levels;
* three key technical ministries with responsibilities respectively for water and the environment, agriculture, and livestock; and
* parastatal bodies including those for crop marketing (OPVN, SONARA and RINI) and technical bodies (CNCA, ONAHA, OFEDES and VETOPHAR) (see below).

The technical content.   Smallholders in the rain-fed areas have been little affected by formal extension services, working either directly with the farmers, or through the Centres of Technical Proficiency (CPT). The effectiveness of these services is limited by the lack of viable extension messages and by the small numbers of staff (one agent

Table 5.4.   *Evolution of public investment in the rural sector*

Period	Av. annual costs CFAFm. current 1985		Av. annual costs CFAFm. constant		Costs of primary sector (% of GDP)	
	Planned	Actual	Planned	Actual	Planned	Actual
1960–63	1.115	0.965	9.812	8.492	3.1	2.7
1965–68	2.665	1.415	18.575	9.862	5.3	2.8
1976–78	17.003	7.983	37.917	17.802	11.3	5.3
1979–83	22.066	13.902	30.672	19.324	10.9	5.5
1984–85	29.900	ND	31.015	–	10.1	–
1987–91	(57.400)	–	(48.970)	–	–	–

Source: SEDES, 1987:54.

per 2,400 households). Regional development projects are able, to a certain extent, to make up for the limited means of the extension services but even so the impact is modest. Often fewer than 3% of holdings, according to SEDES, use the entire recommended package (fertilizers, selected seeds, animal traction) in these areas.

Irrigated cultivation has benefitted from more effective support. In 1987 irrigation represented nearly a third of current financing in the primary sector. Irrigated areas have increased rapidly: from 835 ha in 1965 to 4,675 ha in 1975 and 12,900 ha in 1985 and they have continued to absorb the majority of inputs (animal-drawn implements and fertilizers) used. These areas are mainly devoted to rice cultivation and are characterized by very high capital costs, while maintenance costs exceed the taxes paid by the farmers. These developments allow average yields of 7 to 8 tonnes of paddy per hectare over two annual cycles but the high costs preclude any hopes of profitability.

Livestock policy.   State intervention has not generally achieved the expected results. During the 1960s and 1970s, in particular, the creation from scratch of a modern production, processing and marketing sub-sector which should have become the driving force for the development of the sector as a whole, did not meet expectations, despite the relatively sizeable resources devoted to it.

Neither have efforts directed towards pastoral water-supply met their targets. In 1975, OFEDES (the office for underground water) listed 375 modern watering-points out of the 2000 planned and was already facing financing problems which jeopardized their maintenance. Towards the end of the 1970s, water-supply was down-graded chiefly as a result of ecological considerations and because of the new approaches after 1982 which insisted on the participation of herders in the management of the public watering-points.

The workshop on livestock strategies held at Niamey in 1986, following the drought of 1984/5, appealed for the reform of legislation applicable to pastoral development and focused attention on the improvement of traditional livestock production. In this context pastoral associations were to become a key element in ensuring the continuity of development activities (such as credit, supply of cereals, marketing and management of pastures).

Factor markets

Credit.   Agricultural credit was initially promoted for groundnut cultivation, then the principal export product, to enable producers to buy seed, pesticides and other inputs. Managed initially by UNCC, the national co-operative union, it became the responsibility of the CNCA after 1967. But the bank did not have much freedom of action, granting credit to producers chosen by UNCC which was recovering debt in the name of CNCA.

The latter thus had no direct link with its borrowers and its role as 'wholesaler' gave it no opportunity to develop 'shop-floor' experience. Moreover, credit handed over by the bank was destined essentially for the promotion of new inputs. The very low volume passing through the CNCA was subject to heavy overheads (up to 35% of the amounts lent). The size of its outstanding debt (up to 80% following loans to other parastatals rather than to rural producers) led, as noted earlier, to the suspension of its activities in 1985. It should also be noted that the credit component of the various regional projects played a very small part in the investment programmes (and was oriented towards improving immediate productivity, rather than towards establishing a system of rural credit which would be viable in the long term).

While the banking infrastructure was already extremely limited (one branch per 226,000 inhabitants), the banks reduced their operations still further during the recession. Consequently, a 1987 study (Ohio State University, 1987: 1) could conclude that:

> The absence of an institutional system of financial intermediation in rural Niger is obvious. All that exists at the present moment is a very expensive system for delivery of inputs. This system of truncated credit does not play the role of an intermediary between depositors and savers on the one hand, and borrowers on the other. Primary banking functions are still at an under-developed stage. . . . Indigenous mechanisms of loans and saving are the only ones to play a rudimentary but nevertheless useful role of intermediation in the flow of investments.

No less than 86% of the households surveyed for this study had recourse to informal loans and two-thirds had lent to other villagers during the preceding year; 70% borrowed cereals and 48% cash. The average value of these loans was CFAF 30,000 and the loans amounted to nearly 90% of the cash transactions entered into by these households.

To the network of traders (retail or wholesale) who lent to villagers 20% of the sample) must be added the practice of mutual credit and savings groups and the activities of *gardes-monnaies* or money-holders. A random sample of 56 mutual credit and savings groups in 22 villages in 1986 revealed for an average total life cycle the 'impressive' figure of a circulation of CFAF 27m. in liquid cash (*ibid.*: 6). As for money-holders, a sample of 56 of these (78% of whom also gave loans) showed that average total deposits fluctuated between CFAF 13m. and 30m. according to the season.

To the extent that a large part of the institutional credit allocated to the rural sector had been allotted to the purchase of agricultural inputs and that these were used by only a small minority of farmers, the effects of the suspension of these credits have also been minor (although the impact has been felt in certain projects). This observation is confirmed by a summary of the changes in the rural population's access to inputs.

Inputs.   Only very few farmers outside the irrigated areas use inputs purchased through the formal procurement system. Agricultural equipment for animal traction is used by only a small minority. From SEDES estimates, based on 700,000 production units, only 7,500 to 10,000 traction units are in use for cultivation.

In general, the same is true of holdings using fertilizer (mainly used for out-of-season cultivation and on irrigated areas, while their use for rain-fed crops is declining). About 1.5% of farmers use fertilizer from official government sources. The officially recorded consumption of fertilizer rose to a peak of 3,900 tonnes in 1984/5, before falling to 2,200 tonnes in 1986/7. These are very small amounts for the country as a whole. The decline in consumption has no doubt been made up by free provision on the part of donors who now provide 90% of fertilizer used but also – a very important factor – by the lower prices of fertilizer imported from Nigeria, with the devaluation of the Naira.

Table 5.5. *Movement in sale prices of fertilizer (CFAF per tonne)*

	1982	1983	1984	1985	1986
Urea price					
– official	50,000	50,000	60,000	60,000	65,000
– parallel	35,500	33,200	40,000	38,000	36,800
Simple superphosphate price					
– official	35,000	40,000	45,000	45,000	50,000
– parallel	24,000	22,750	29,000	39,600	25,800

Source: Agricultural Statistics, Annual Report 1986

We can therefore summarize the impact of the reform measures according to our typology of smallholder producers as follows:

(a) For rain-fed cultivation with 'high' rainfall (hence where farmers have decided to use fertilizer, i.e., essentially in the southern fringes of the departments of Dosso, Maradi and Zinder) virtually all the fertilizer used comes from Nigeria. There is therefore no perceptible effect of the withdrawal of subsidies. We note the emergence of co-operative fertilizer banks in Maradi (in 80 villages in 1987).

(b) For rain-fed cultivation with 'low' rainfall (hence in the zones furthest from the Nigerian frontier) the increase in the cost of fertilizer ought in principle to have had a negative effect. Given the low consumption, this was in fact very marginal. Moreover, the area in which unofficially imported fertilizer is competitive has moved northward.

(c) On the large irrigated schemes the impact is greater. These in fact absorb more than half the fertilizer officially imported. Any negative effect must, however, be seen in the light of the part played by fertilizer costs in the total cost of production (estimated at 8% in the areas devoted to rice cultivation) and the small number of farmers in these areas (estimated by Elliott Berg Associates, 1983 at 15,000).

(d) Small irrigated areas and out-of-season crops have not generally depended on officially imported fertilizer but get supplies from Nigeria on the parallel market; the withdrawal of subsidies has therefore had no impact.

(e) The withdrawal of subsidies on agricultural equipment will in general have had no effect since it has been purely theoretical. Clients for this equipment are essentially to be found, according to SEDES, among units of production in the large irrigated areas. In any event, we have seen that the price structure remains generally unfavourable to such investments.

Product markets

The marketing system is characterized by a dual structure: on the one hand, exchanges between producers and traders in the private sector (rural buyers, retailers, wholesalers) and on the other hand, exchanges between producers and the official network (co-operatives, OPVN, SONARA, RINI). It is based mainly on the marketing of millet, sorghum, cow peas, rice (including considerable imports of the latter) and, to a lesser extent in the last few years, groundnuts.

According to various estimates, only around 10–20% of cereal production is likely to be marketed, depending on the year. These figures are a rough estimate in view of the difficulties of accounting for the considerable amount of trade which takes place at village level as well as international trade which eludes all control.

As noted earlier, rainfall variability results in significant fluctuations in cereal production (apart from the irrigated areas), and these, in turn, give rise to considerable inter-annual variations in the volume marketed. According to Elliott Berg Associates (1983: 1), a fall of 6.6% in cereal production leads to a fall of 50% in the quantity marketed. It is therefore not surprising that cereal prices show extreme year-to-year changes: arithmetical average of CFAF 119 per kilo of millet; minimum 50 Fr./kg; maximum 179 Fr/kg; standard deviation: 41. Over a longer period (1970–86) and at constant prices, an analysis carried out by the Ministry of Agriculture (1987) also shows important variations. The variations in Niamey were: arithmetical average CFAF 32.5 per kilo; minimum: 18.4; maximum: 65.6; standard deviation: 8.6; variation coefficient: 0.264.

To these inter-annual price fluctuations must be added considerable seasonal price movements which, according to Ministry of Agriculture figures in the last few years, could entail a trebling of millet prices in the course of a few weeks. These are, however, very unpredictable and price rises before harvests or at times of low production, for example, cannot be guaranteed. The unpredictability is probably explained by the movement of private stocks, and the impact of imports (official or otherwise) and of food aid.

The cereal market is also characterized by the great diversity of the participants. Intra-community transactions at the village level (often in the form of gifts and loans) are very important, greater than the volume sold to traders. Moreover, ' . . . the sale of cereals is no longer a simple transfer of surplus. It is part of the whole economic policy of the household, which sells animals, cereals, mats and other articles and also exports the labour of its young people depending on its needs' (Elliott Berg Associates, 1983: 1).

Competition between intermediaries at the level of small-scale transactions is very strong, as the barriers to entry are low and consequently the profit margins small. The majority of traders are part-time (according to Berg Associates, there are about 25,000) and undertake transactions which are both casual and limited in volume.

There are, however, a smaller number of wholesalers who have at their disposal a network of agents and considerable funds. These networks often straddle the frontier with Nigeria and control significant movements of cereals. Storage capacity is important (up to 2,500 tonnes and more) and is most frequently hired (as is transport). Competition may be imperfect at this level and accusations of collusion and speculation are frequently made, although the evidence for this is somewhat limited.

Marketing and the public sector

The OPVN. This agency was created in 1970 primarily to short-circuit the activities of traders who were thought to be inefficient and to be exploiting producers and consumers. Its original objectives were: to organize the marketing of basic foodstuffs (millet, sorghum, rice, cow peas, maize), to draw up annual estimates of food resources and needs, to set up annual storage, import and export programmes and to establish regular stocks in order to stabilize producer and consumer prices, and lastly to assure inter-regional balances (particularly in setting up food aid programmes).

From the 1983/4 campaign, however, operating difficulties caused the number of OPVN purchasing centres to be cut back from 418 to 67, mainly affecting areas of low production. Sales points were similarly reduced (from more than 200 in 1982–3 to 79 in 1983–4) and were concentrated in areas of heavy cereal deficit and in urban areas. Consumers bought either direct from the OPVN, or through an approved agent at a ceiling price fixed annually. The office's stock-keeping policy centred on two stocks (for security and for price stabilization) planned at 100,000 and 50,000 tonnes respectively.

Though some of the OPVN's aims were achieved (the establishment of stocks, the management of food aid), its pricing policy was largely unsuccessful. *At the producer level*

- its prices were on average only 78% of the free market prices for millet according to Berg Associates;
- the lack of accurate data made it impossible for it to target its interventions;
- its weak finances caused these to be unpredictable, a factor which was exacerbated by purchase prices being announced at the time of harvest rather than before sowing;
- farmers were frequently dissatisfied with the poor performance of OPVN's licensed agents, often the co-operatives;
- its interventions tended to favour larger producers in the surplus areas and large traders, some of whom sometimes sold OPVN grain from Nigeria.

An analysis of the evolution of the official and free prices offered to producers leads to the following observations (Appendix Table 5.6):

- the deflated prices shown in SEDES (1987) indicate a rapid fall in farmers' purchasing power during the 1960s, a slight recovery after the 1972 drought (but still lower in real terms) followed by a new fall in the terms of trade. The 1981–4 drought set recovery going again but the 1985 index was no higher than in 1974;
- the official prices for cash crops fell more rapidly than cereal prices, which explains in part the decline of cash crops during the period;
- free market prices, on the other hand, maintained producers' purchasing power better. They displayed greater inter-year fluctuations than official prices so that, in some years, there was an advantage in using the official market and in others in selling on the free market.

At the consumer level. The interventions of the OPVN only partially achieved their goal of reducing price fluctuations. According to Berg Associates' calculations, price variations, both inter-annual and seasonal, were in fact larger during the period of the office's significant intervention (1976–83) than during the preceding four years. SEDES calculations, however, comparing the periods 1961–70 and 1971–83, indicate that the policy of intervention did have a limited effect on seasonal fluctuations but the benefits were not in proportion to the costs.

As regards sales, the OPVN came up against the same obstacles as for its purchases. Its prices were always lower than the prices prevailing in the open market and the small quantities marketed often allowed certain privileged buyers to benefit considerably, especially in the urban areas.

The pricing policy followed by the OPVN as well as its high operating costs are reflected in the size of its deficits, which have grown very rapidly (CFAF 11 bn or one-third of the debt of the parastatal sector in 1983).

Impact of the reforms.   The failure of OPVN's pricing policy led to a programme of reform, the essential components of which have been:

• abolition of its monopoly (1985) and marketing of millet and sorghum opened to co-operatives and the private sector;
• reduced intervention in the management of a security stock of 80,000 tonnes renewable at the rate of one-third annually (1986/7);
• liberalization of prices from 1985/6 (except for rice);
• purchases by the OPVN (up to 80%) through calls for tenders (1985/6);
• reduction in the number of purchasing and selling points (1983).

An analysis of the impact of these measures is constrained by their recent nature and the influence of fluctuations in rainfall on patterns of agricultural production (Appendix Table 5.4).

Retail prices in Niamey for millet and sorghum fell from 156 and 182 CFAF/kg in 1984 and 1985 to 73 and 65 CFAF/kg in 1986 and 1987. The abolition of OPVN's monopoly as well as the lifting of certain restrictions has meant that it is easier for anyone to market cereals. Have the markets become more efficient as a result? Comparing the margins on the markets of Zinder and Niamey between 1982/5 and 1985/8, a study carried out by the University of Michigan (1988) records a small fall, which, however, is not statistically significant.

OPVN's interventions in the markets (43,600 tonnes) did not raise prices to the indicative price of 100 CFAF/kg for millet for the 1985/6 season. Its purchases for the following year were 16,500 tonnes and prices continued to fall. Clearly, during this period, fluctuations in production, frontier trade and food aid were the factors determining price movements.

The OPVN's system of calling for tenders has favoured the larger traders (though often under the cover of regional co-operative unions). The system of controls has not allowed the development of competition (despite a ceiling of 150 tonnes per transaction decreed by the office for the 1986/7 season). In addition, purchases were generally late and poorly advertised: consequently producers did not benefit from them. Prices were regularly higher than the market price (and well above those at the start of the season), putting large profits at the disposal of some big traders able to meet the conditions imposed on these transactions.

To sum up, the effects of the reforms have been marginal (though impossible to quantify with any degree of precision) to the extent that the impact of the OPVN in the rural areas was itself marginal before they came into effect. The efficiency of the market has probably improved to a certain extent but these gains have been offset by the increased power of the most important private operators. As to the budgetary effects, they have to be seen against the fact that OPVN transactions during the past few years have been largely financed by foreign aid.

The aim of *SONARA*, set up in 1962, was to promote groundnut production through price incentives to producers, to ensure supplies to the local oil mills and to develop exports. In addition, it was entrusted with the monopoly for cow pea marketing from 1975 (withdrawn from the OPVN) mainly for export.

As noted earlier, SONARA's pricing policy ended in failure. Production regularly decreased from 1972/3 and exports were suspended from 1973. Production no longer meets the needs of SICONIGER (a recently privatized oil mill), SONARA's sole customer, and the Board only marketed between 5 and 10% of production from 1975 to 1985. In addition to SONARA's very large margins, the problems described with regard to the OPVN were replicated so far as groundnut marketing is concerned: belated purchasing campaigns, unfavourable prices for producers, impact minimized by numerous intermediaries and considerable penetration by groundnuts of Nigerian origin. According to Grégoire, for instance, the Maradi traders bought their supplies in Nigeria during the 1986/7 season at a cost of CFAF 7,000 per sack while the selling price to SONARA was CFAF 14,000 (Amselle and Grégoire, 1988). Prevailing prices were well above world prices and SONARA had difficulties in disposing of its stock. As a result, its purchasing operations were suspended in 1987.

As regards cow peas, despite SONARA's legal marketing monopoly, the Board's share remained small (an average of 9% of production from 1973 to 1986). This partly reflects the fact that prices on the open market were higher than official prices (by 80% on average from 1976 to 1982) and producers therefore sold their surplus through private traders. Removing the monopoly from SONARA in 1984 consequently only made official what was already a fact.

Established in 1967, *RINI* buys paddy from the large irrigated schemes through the intermediary of co-operatives and on the basis of official prices. It holds the monopoly for large-scale processing, the remainder being consumed domestically or sold through the private sector and milled by hand. Machine-treated rice, in its turn, is sold at an official price.

Local rice production is not sufficient, however. National consumption is covered to a large extent by imports (120,000 tonnes in 1985, 69,000 tonnes in 1986) at a price considerably lower than the cost price of the rice passing through RINI (see Table 5.6), despite the rise in yields from the big rice-growing schemes since 1982 (up to 4,700 kg per ha in certain areas by 1987 (ONAHA, 1988: 33)) which has meant a rapid increase in national production from 40,000 tonnes in 1981 to 81,000 tonnes in 1987/8 (see Appendix Table 5.4).

The difference between the RINI selling price and that of imported rice has made it necessary to protect national production: a tax was introduced in 1984 and collection quotas of local produce by importers were applied from 1986 (25% quota,

Table 5.6. *Price of rice (CFAF/tonne)*

	1983/4	1984/5	1985/6
Cost price (Rice 32 RINI)	204,658	229,172	205,470
Price imported rice (Retail average)	142,500	162,500	123,500
RINI selling price (retail)	165,000	180,000	145,000

Source: Ministry of Agriculture.

reduced to 20% in 1987). The economic reform programmes have not questioned the principle of tariff protection for rice (even though restrictions on the quantities imported and the number of importers were lifted in 1987) or of a floor price for producers. These protective measures have not, however, led to the expected results, either because they have not been strictly applied, or because of fraud (re-importation of rice from Nigeria after importation to Niger 'in transit') and RINI has experienced constant difficulties in selling its product. These difficulties have compromised its cash flow and led to frequent delays in payments to co-operatives. The delays explain the attraction of sales outside RINI while the hulling units function below their capacity (out of the 22,800 tonnes produced by the co-operatives for the winter season of 1987, RINI only bought 7,500 tonnes), and why unsold stocks accumulate.

Livestock marketing.   From the 1960s, livestock marketing has been considered inefficient, badly controlled, and unfavourable to consumers. The setting up of a 'modern' livestock sector had among its objectives to guarantee price stability to the consumer, to increase the quantity of livestock sold and to develop exports. Cattle-fattening ranches, refrigerated abattoirs, markets, feed factories, tanneries and dairies managed by a series of public bodies (SONERAN, SCPN, SONITAN, OLANI) were designed to attain these objectives.

Like the marketing of agricultural produce, these investments proved unsatisfactory: the sales of SONERAN (the marketing board), for example, at the start of the 1970s represented only 2–3% of national marketed volume (and this in Niamey only), while the breakthrough in exports did not materialize. Consequently, fluctuations in price were not reduced by this type of intervention and continue to reflect the importance of factors beyond government control: droughts and the rate of exchange of the Naira.

Control over the export of livestock by private operators (through customs duties, health regulations, and prohibition of exports since the drought of 1984) has also been completely ineffective: up to 90% of exports are undertaken on the parallel market. The abandonment of these controls advocated in the economic reforms has therefore not altered the situation significantly.

Marketing of imported consumer goods.   The economic reform measures with respect to imported consumer goods have been primarily concerned with liberalizing prices and marketing systems. Until 1985 a parastatal body, COPRONIGER, held the monopoly of a wide range of consumer imports including tea, sugar, matches, sea salt, wheat flour, etc. It was also responsible for their distribution through agents or its own sales points. The closure of the latter and the withdrawal of the monopoly in 1985 allowed the private sector to compete officially: well before then, however, a considerable quantity of manufactured products were coming in unofficially from Nigeria, allowing traders in the frontier areas to recycle the Nairas arising from the export of agricultural products from Niger.

The prices and availability of consumer goods have been affected in recent years by the loosening of administrative controls (by 1987 only bread and motor fuel were still subject to direct price controls) and by reductions in import restrictions. However, data on recent developments in the price levels of consumer goods do not allow conclusions to be drawn as to the effect of the reform measures. This is because price levels have reflected, during this period, the devaluation of the Naira as well as the fall in price of certain products (sugar, for example) on international markets. It is nevertheless probable that price liberalization will have had a positive effect for consumers: increased competition on the part of private traders seems to be developing and their costs are certainly lower than those of COPRONIGER.

Supporting sectors

Rural development services.   Information collected by SEDES (1987: 289) highlights the fact that the recurrent expenditure allocated to rural development decreased as a proportion of the recurrent budget as a whole from 1977 (only the rural engineering section, devoted mainly to large irrigation schemes, has increased). A growing share of these resources is allocated to salary costs, reaching 71% in 1985. Personnel as a whole rose from 2,290 in 1981 to 3,711 in 1985, a growth of 6% per annum.

This collapse was especially serious for services in the livestock sector: there was a reduction in the recurrent budget in real terms of 44% between 1960 and 1984, the funds for equipment dropping by 60%. To the extent that the SAP will actually increase the resources at the disposal of the rural development services, two questions remain as to increased effectiveness:

* to what extent could such an increase, even if it were considerable, have any real effect in view of the very limited existing effectiveness of the services?
* would any increase be accompanied by a fundamental recasting of the technical content of these interventions and of the methodological approach?

Cost recovery and livestock.   Certain parastatals in the livestock sub-sector have been subjected to a decision to privatize, namely the factory for animal feed (UAB), the pharmacy responsible for importing and distributing veterinary products (VETOPHAR), the milk board (OLANI) and the company for animal resources (SONERAN, responsible for marketing operations). Some concern has been expressed, however, that the conditions for effective competition may not exist. Replacing public monopolies with private monopolies may not lead to the desired improvement in services.

The study on cost recovery undertaken under the SAP fully recognizes the limits of pastoralists' capacity to contribute to the full recovery of costs of services. This is aggravated by the instability and 'disorganization' of livestock systems following the repeated droughts. Consequently, the study finds that only intensive production systems in the settled areas lend themselves to such recovery and this only if some targeted subsidies are continued.

The macroeconomic budgetary effects of such cost-recovery measures are modest and should be compared with the probable effects of the measures. Vaccination campaigns in Niger have met with considerable success and compare favourably with other countries in the region; in 1985, for example, 70% of cattle were vaccinated against epidemics and pleuropneumonia. The study quoted above foresees that this rate of cover might not be reached again for 4 years after the introduction of cost-recovery measures.

Water supply.   In 1986, Niger had 11,055 watering points (double the number in 1980) supplying 47% of the requirements of the rural population (calculated on the basis of one watering point per 250 inhabitants). Of this total, 17% were pastoral watering points and 61% were other wells. Since 1980, virtually all new watering points have been for village supplies. Attempts to introduce a cost-recovery system in the water-supply sector go back to 1983/4 when the OFEDES (office for underground water) was given responsibility for new installations and major upkeep, while the minor maintenance work was to be taken care of by the beneficiaries, organized by a village management committee which was supposed to raise a working capital of CFAF 50,000 per year and per water point. Further, from 1984, each water-supply programme was to include a section for 'supporting action' so as to create an auspicious climate for taking over the maintenance unit at village level.

In spite of some positive local experiences, this system has not led to the expected results: at the end of 1986, for example, 48% of pumps in the department of Niamey had broken down and 70% of the wells in the department of Dosso were sanding up. In addition to insufficient resources to ensure upkeep (badly trained or under-used village craftsmen, for example) and the lack of a well-structured distribution network for spare parts, one important reason seems to be that water-supply installations are seen by the majority of the population as belonging to the state (or to a project), rather than being part of the village patrimony.

The study on cost recovery recommends, therefore, that the existing infrastructure be repaired and the management of the recovered funds improved before any new measures are undertaken. The effective takeover of recurrent costs by the beneficiaries, on the basis of CFAF 60,000 per installation, would have led, according to the estimates in the study, to a total of CFAF 662 m. recovered in 1986 for the country as a whole. It should also be noted that the functioning and upkeep of the large irrigation systems have been the subject of taxes which rose, according to calculations on several schemes, by 29% in the dry season between 1985 and 1987 (ONAHA, 1988: 18).

Social services

Health.   The general level of health remains poor and is constantly jeopardized by the chronic shortfalls in agricultural production. The importance of primary health care has been emphasized since 1965, but the system did not really get under way until the end of the 1970s. It is based on village health teams (ESV) made up of first-aiders and midwives, with rural dispensaries and medical posts run by nurses. In 1985/6, there were 239 dispensaries (i.e. 1 per 28,000 inhabitants). The number of villages and camps equipped with ESV has grown from 2,283 in 1980 to 3,955 in 1986 and the number of teams has gone up from 6,560 to 13,451 during the same period. It is estimated that half the population live within a 10 km radius of a dispensary or medical post.

Despite this progress, serious gaps persist, linked in part to the lack of resources: in 1987, the budget of the Ministry of Health and Social Affairs rose to CFAF 5.5 bn (or 5.3% of the national total). In the last few years these sums have suffered a decline in real terms. The main repercussions of this constraint are felt at the operational level. General shortages of both supplies and equipment do not inspire popular confidence. On the other hand, expenditure on personnel represents more than half the budget.

The resources allocated to curative medicine in the towns seem disproportionate. The study on cost recovery notes, for example, that hospitals receive 50% of the funds for personnel for 350,000 hospital admissions, while the outlying medical posts deal with a total of 10 million consultations annually.

A 1987 Ministry of Health enquiry indicated that the use of health services was high when these were accessible and that treatment was nearly always given free, but the majority of medicines had to be bought. The three major problems faced by clients were difficulties of access, inadequacy of medical supplies and inactivity of many ESVs.

The first reform proposals, aimed at involving beneficiaries in the costs of health care, through for instance paying a higher proportion of the cost of drugs and contributing to the cost of salaries and buildings, date from 1983. While not advocating any new cost-recovery measures because of a lack of data enabling an assessment of the contributive capacity of the population, the study on cost recovery examined the impact of a more exhaustive application of measures, such as those recommended by the SAP. Their overall financial effects would be significant but these benefits would have to be set against the expected effects: drop in consultations, spread of diseases, etc., especially for the under-privileged rural population.

Some improvements can, however, be expected from a 'health project' supported by the World Bank within the framework of the SAP. This started at the end of 1986 and is aimed at improving the efficiency of the sector (investment planning and recovery of costs, development of policy as regards nutrition, protection against infectious diseases, mother and child health, family planning and support for training).

Education is a favoured sector, benefitting from 21% of the national recurrent budget. Imbalances noted in the context of the SAP are evident; 40% of the budget is allocated to the primary sector representing 84% of the school population, while 20% is allocated to higher education representing only 1% of students. Further, the funds set aside for adult literacy teaching are negligible (CFAF 36m. in 1987).

Overall achievements are disappointing, however. The rate of school attendance at the primary level barely reached 20% in 1980/81; primary schools are in poor condition and generally have little or no equipment (the success rate for the certificate at the end of primary studies dropped from 43% in 1976 to 23% in 1984); secondary and tertiary teaching does not seem to meet the needs of the country for qualified personnel.

A number of cost-recovery measures have already been taken by the authorities. However, the study on cost recovery concludes that 'the introduction of new school charges (especially in the rural areas) would reduce school attendance and thus the rate of classroom occupancy which is already lower than the average for the country' (African Asian Office, 1987: 88). It therefore proposes that educational supplies should continue to be distributed free and that this distribution should be expanded through cost-recovery measures affecting primary schools in the urban areas, thus increasing the resources placed at the disposal of rural schools.

Conclusion

To sum up, an unhappy picture has emerged of the relative ineffectiveness of state involvement in the rural areas of Niger. Against the background of a stagnant or declining sector, a costly structure is in place which, with a few exceptions, has not been able to provide producers or consumers with the services they need in order to contribute to economic recovery. Instead, they have been obliged to rely on their own resources or on an informal sector which has, in many instances, considerable shortcomings.

The weakness of the link between the rural populations and a formal public sector, which has been the focus of the economic recovery programmes, leads to the inevitable conclusion that the rural populations have so far been little affected.

VI. CONCLUSIONS

The preceding discussion has shown that the dominant influences on the evolution of the economic status of smallholders and the rural poor in Niger over the past 25 years have been climatic, ecological and demographic factors and the proximity of the Nigerian economy. Furthermore, over recent years this section of the population has been poorly served by, and has relied little on, the formal public services in the agricultural sector. There are some exceptions: the irrigated areas, certain area-specific development projects, and the livestock vaccination services. But there are few policy instruments which, in the short run at least, can have a major effect on the great majority of the rural poor.

The general conclusion must therefore be that these groups have not so far been greatly affected, adversely or beneficially, by the reform programmes that have been implemented. To summarize the reasoning underlying this conclusion:

(a) The bulk of output sold by the rural smallholders is traded on the open market rather than through the parastatal agencies. Prices received are influenced principally by conditions of supply and demand (with a strong influence from Nigeria) rather than through official price policy whose implementation has anyway been halting. The Niger Government is not in a position to use major instruments such as currency realignment and monetary policies, which can influence open market prices.

(b) The great majority of rural households use informal credit systems rather than borrowing through the formal sector. The linkages which might transmit the effects of changes in formal capital markets to the informal system are little understood, and are likely to be weak.

(c) Few smallholder producers use fertilizer or other inputs purchased through the formal system, although some do buy them on the open market via Nigeria. Reductions in subsidies, which have anyway been more apparent than real, will therefore have had little influence on them.

(d) The opportunities for rural households to earn non-agricultural incomes are strongly linked to the economies of Niger's southern neighbours through extensive seasonal and longer-term migration.

The principal issue arising is that of cost recovery in those cases – principally vaccination and social services – where significant numbers of low-income rural people do use the service. Here it is important to ensure that any damage to the rural interest is not out of proportion to the budgetary benefits.

(a) Efforts to recover costs must be seen in a context where data regarding the capacity of the rural population to contribute are either fragmentary and out-of-date, or completely absent. The cost-recovery study notes: 'reliable and complete statistical data along with recent systematic censuses are lacking at practically all levels of the collection system but particularly as regards costs of goods and services and the capacity of beneficiaries to contribute' (African Asian Office, 1988: 2).

(b) Such a situation does not permit one to measure the effects of the measures adopted or in preparation. It is clear, however, that the cost-recovery measures already introduced represent, for the rural population as a whole, burdens which are not negligible. In the health sector alone, for example, one can roughly estimate the contribution of the rural population at about CFAF 4.5 bn (ESV

salaries and consumption of 50% of the medicines sold through private channels).
Even admitting that the cost-recovery system for village water supplies works in
only 50% of cases, the contributions would amount to CFAF 331m. For these
categories of cost alone, and on the basis of 800,000 households, the annual contribution per household would be CFAF 6,250. This sum should be seen in the light
of the very partial estimates of income in the rural milieu presented above, and
suggests that in the face of extra costs the room for manoeuvre for the great
majority of rural households is very narrow.

(c)   To introduce extra cost-recovery measures, as is proposed in the recent study for
the Ministry of Planning (African Asian Office, 1988: 2), would represent extra
burdens for the population as a whole varying between CFAF 1.1 and 1.4 bn for the
health, education and livestock sectors. According to the figures put forward, this
would represent a national average of CFAF 1,875 p.a. (10,000 in the urban areas),
taking account of the exclusion of under-privileged households.

(d)   The budgetary effect of such measures seems very limited. The additional
measures mentioned in the preceding paragraph compared with total state
expenditures would result in a saving of only 0.8%.

(e)   The effects of such measures on the smallholder population would probably be
mitigated to a certain extent. On the one hand, contributors who are not con-
vinced of the need for the goods or services offered may not take them up (for
example, herders after the introduction of cost recovery for vaccination campaigns), and households not currently enjoying exemption from charges will be
excluded, especially in view of the fluctuations in their income from year to year
and season to season. The fact that they have not been, or have been incompletely,
prepared in advance, that the necessary accompanying measures have not been
fully planned, and that the contributions are not directly linked to, and do not
result in, an improvement in the quality of the goods and services provided are
so many factors which obstruct the progress of such measures.

On the other hand, these effects are compensated by:

• the low level of cover previously attained by several of the services concerned (less
than half the rural population have access to 'modern' water points, a rate of
primary schooling at 20% and declining – from 28% in 1983, etc.) and the poor
quality of the benefits (incompetent ESV teams, pumps out of order, out-of-date
infrastructure, etc.);
• the existence within some projects of directly subsidized services;
• exemptions contemplated or already granted (in the health sector) for the under-
privileged;
• measures contemplated or already taken (education sector) to favour the rural
population.

The view that the reforms have so far had a limited impact on the rural population
does not lead to the conclusion that they should not be undertaken nor that attempts
to improve the services available to low-income rural groups should be abandoned. On
the contrary, it is clear that improvements to the objectives and performance of the
public sector are a requirement if economic prospects, and specifically those of low-
income rural groups, in Niger are to improve.

Achieving agricultural growth, or even halting ecological decline, calls for sustained efforts to deal with the basic causes of the blockage in agriculture discussed
in section IV. There is no short cut, nor any ready solution that has been overlooked.

Favourable policy measures and efficient administration, however necessary they may be, will not deal with the underlying weakness in the productive base. This must be addressed by developing the low-cost technology that is relevant for the majority of producers, by human resource development, by maintenance of the infrastructure, and by the encouragement of locally-based enterprise, be it the small-scale private sector or community actions to provide the services and resources that are needed.

References

Africa Asian Office (1987, 1988) *Etude sur le recouvrement des coûts*. 2 vols. Africa Asian Bureau Gesellschaft für Entwicklungsplannung, Köln.

Amselle, J.L. and Grégoire, E. (1988) *Politiques nationales et réseaux marchands transnationaux. Les cas du Mali et du Niger – Nord Nigéria*, Institut de Recherches et d'Applications de Méthodes de Développement, Institut National de Recherches Agronomiques, Université Nationale de Benin.

Elliott Berg Associates (1983) *Etude conjointe du programme de commercialization de céréales au Niger*, Rapport Principal, unpublished report.

Guillaumont, P. (1985) *Croissance et Ajustement*, Economica, Paris.

IFAD (1987) *Niger: Programme Spécial National, rapport d'évaluation*, Texte Principal. Rome December.

Ministère de l'Agriculture et de l'Environnement (1987) *Analyse de l'évolution à moyen terme des cours céréaliers au Niger et de leur variabilité par rapport aux niveaux de production*, November.

Ministère de l'Agriculture et de l'Environnement (1986, 1987) *Annual Reports of Agricultural Statistics*.

Ministère de la Santé, Projet Université de Tulane (1987) *Enquête nationale sur l'utilization des services de santé*, September.

Office national des aménagements hydro-agricoles (1988) *Rapport de suivi de l'impact socio-économique des aménagements hydro-agricoles dans la vallée du fleuve Niger*, T. Loutte, April.

Ohio State University (1987) *Rural Finance in Niger: a Critical Evaluation and Recommendations for Reform*, final report, February.

Raynaut, C. (1988a) *Le développement rural de la région au village. Projet de développement rural de Maradi*. GRID, Bordeaux.

Raynaut, C. (1988b) 'La crise de l'agriculture au Niger', *Development and Cooperation* (3).

Société d'études pour le développement économique et social (1987) 'Etude du secteur agricole du Niger, Bilan-diagnostic, Phase I SEDES, Paris', September.

University of Michigan Technical Assistance Team (1988) *Agriculture Sector Development Grant, Interim Economic Assessment*, ASDG, July.

World Bank (1986) *Rapport et recommandations du Président de l'AID aux administrateurs sur une proposition de crédit de développement de 18.3 millions de DTS et sur une proposition de crédit du fonds d'aide à l'Afrique de 36.6 millions de DTS à la République du Niger pour un programme d'ajustement structurel*. World Bank, Washington DC, January.

World Bank (1987) *Rapport et recommandations du Président de l'AID aux administrateurs sur l'octroi éventuel d'un crédit du fonds d'aide à l'Afrique de 15.4 millions de DTS à la République du Niger pour un programme d'ajustement du secteur des entreprises publiques*, World Bank, Washington DC, June.

Appendix Table 5.1. *Indicators of national income, 1978–85*

				Year				
	1978	1979	1980	1981	1982	1983	1984	1985
				GDP (CFAF bn)				
Rural sector	166.1	188.7	228.1	269.3	299.5	311.5	268.2	332.1
Agriculture	87.3	96.5	120.8	154.0	156.6	159.7	153.1	207.5
Livestock	61.4	72.2	89.0	104.1	120.8	128.0	92.7	100.0
Forestry & fisheries	17.4	20.0	18.4	20.2	22.1	23.8	22.4	24.6
Mines	37.0	63.1	67.4	52.0	49.8	55.5	53.6	59.3
Industry & energy	16.4	19.4	22.2	27.0	32.4	36.9	35.7	38.5
Construction & public works	17.1	24.6	32.1	26.6	24.8	23.9	19.2	23.7
Commerce, transport & services	84.1	103.2	125.5	147.6	159.1	169.0	161.9	171.6
Government	22.8	25.1	33.8	39.6	45.8	49.8	52.8	54.9
GDP at factor cost	343.5	424.1	509.1	562.1	611.4	646.6	591.4	680.1
Import Taxes & Duties	15.6	19.1	27.1	27.8	31.3	28.0	24.0	25.0
GDP at market prices	359.1	443.2	536.2	589.9	642.7	674.6	615.4	705.1
GDP at constant 1976 prices	268.2	307.6	323.9	327.0	321.4	313.0	262.7	280.1
Implicit GDP deflator (1970 = 100)	133.9	144.1	164.0	182.1	199.9	215.5	234.3	251.3
Annual Growth Rate %								
Real GDP	7.2	14.7	6.3	-0.9	-0.8	-2.6	-16.1	6.6
Real GDP/capita	4.5	11.1	3.6	-3.7	-3.5	-5.3	-18.9	3.8
GDP deflator	16.0	7.6	13.8	11.0	9.8	7.8	8.7	7.5

Source: IMF, *International Financial Statistics.*

Appendix Table 5.2. *Monetary profile, 1978-85*

	1978	1979	1980	1981	1982	1983	1984	1985
A. Monetary total (CFAF bn) mid-year points								
Monetary total	54.20	64.51	77.93	94.07	82.98	82.69	101.02	107.99
Cash and current account	46.30	57.27	64.59	74.75	70.93	66.55	78.41	80.48
Quasi money	7.80	7.24	13.34	19.32	12.05	16.14	22.62	27.51
Net foreign assets	20.00	18.69	8.72	18.64	-24.00	-18.59	-0.95	1.85
Long-term foreign borrowing	1.38	3.50	9.45	16.55	20.03	28.12	28.01	25.74
Domestic credit	42.36	57.45	82.31	98.97	126.70	130.81	120.20	114.79
Net government borrowing	-11.88	-18.36	-7.49	-2.98	16.34	17.86	22.01	26.37
Net private borrowing[a]	54.24	75.82	89.80	101.95	110.36	112.95	96.19	88.42
Other (net)	6.78	8.14	3.65	6.99	-0.31	1.41	-9.79	-18.05
B. Annual change (%)								
Monetary total		19.02	20.80	20.71	-11.79	-0.35	22.18	6.90
Cash and current account		23.45	12.78	15.73	-5.11	-6.18	17.82	2.64
Quasi money		-7.18	84.25	44.87	-37.63	33.94	40.15	21.62
Net foreign assets		-6.55	-53.34	113.76	-228.76	22.54	94.89	194.74
Long-term foreign borrowing		153.62	170.00	75.13	21.03	40.39	-0.39	-4.53
Domestic credit		36.65	43.25	20.24	28.02	3.24	-8.11	-4.50
Net government borrowing		-54.55	40.80	60.21	648.32	9.30	23.24	19.61
Net private borrowing		39.79	18.57	13.40	8.25	2.36	-13.07	-9.96
Others (net)		20.06	-55.16	91.51	-104.43	554.84	-794.33	-84.68

a: includes other financial institutions.
Source: IMF, *International Financial Statistics.*

Appendix Table 5.3. *Key macroeconomic indicators, 1982–91*

Indicators	1982	1983	1984	1985	1986	1987	1988	1989	1990	1991
	Actual				*Est.*			*Projected*		
GDP growth	-0.8	-2.6	-16.1	7.1	6.9	2.7	2.1	2.2	2.3	2.4
GDP growth/capita	-3.6	-6.4	-18.9	4.3	4.1	-0.1	-0.7	-0.6	-0.5	-0.4
Growth of consumption/capita	-12.9	7.6	-10.6	-6.4	2.2	-1.9	-1.4	-1.2	-1.0	-1.0
Debt-service (US$m.)	193.3	132.5	133.9	142.0	174.1	207.6	216.9	197.0	192.2	190.3
Debt service/GDP	9.9	7.5	9.5	9.0	7.9	7.8	7.6	6.3	5.7	6.2
Gross investment/GDP	26.9	11.4	-1.4	13.7	10.3	10.5	11.6	11.3	11.4	11.8
Domestic saving/GDP	16.4	6.6	-4.4	4.9	6.7	7.1	7.1	7.5	8.0	8.6
Public investment/GDP	16.0	9.8	8.7	7.5	8.3	8.4	8.7	8.9	9.0	9.1
Private investment/GDP	10.9	1.6	-10.1	6.2	2.0	2.1	2.3	2.4	2.4	2.7
Public revenues/GDP	11.3	10.2	11.4	10.0	9.9	9.9	9.8	10.0	9.9	9.9
Public expend./GDP[a]	18.4	16.8	16.6	14.7	13.4	13.6	12.4	11.7	11.1	10.8
Budget deficit/GDP	7.1	6.6	5.2	4.7	3.6	3.7	2.6	1.7	1.2	6.9
Growth of export volume	-20.1	9.7	-7.9	-12.9	5.7	-0.9	1.3	1.4	1.4	1.5
Exports/GDP	21.3	22.6	23.4	17.5	16.4	15.4	15.8	15.3	15.1	15.2
Growth of import volume	6.2	-6.1	-16.2	14.2	-12.0	2.8	5.0	1.2	1.8	2.0
Imports/GDP	31.7	27.9	26.4	26.3	20.2	19.2	19.4	18.8	18.2	18.4
Current account balance (US$m)	-189.6	-18.9	-24.0	-57.2	-44.3	-66.7	-65.0	-58.0	-46.2	-56.1
Current account balance/GDP	-9.7	-4.6	-1.7	-3.6	-2.6	-2.1	-2.3	-1.9	-1.4	-1.5

a: excluding grants.
Source: Estimates and projections from policy framework documents.

Appendix Table 5.4. *Production, area and yield of main crops, 1963–86*

Year	Millet Prod.	Millet Area	Millet Yield	Sorghum Prod.	Sorghum Area	Sorghum Yield	Rice Prod.	Rice Area	Rice Yield	Niebe Prod.	Niebe Area	Niebe Yield
1960	717	1692	424	220	440	500	7	8	875	46	375	123
1961	781	1640	476	276	454	607	9	8	1043	45	405	112
1962	933	1844	506	316	464	680	11	9	1228	57	454	126
1963	977	1868	523	353	485	727	10	9	1072	63	484	131
1964	1013	1777	570	315	453	696	11	9	1260	66	493	134
1965	789	1810	436	266	465	571	12	9	1340	48	432	111
60/65 average	**868**	**1772**	**489**	**291**	**460**	**630**	**10**	**9**	**1136**	**34**	**441**	**123**
1966	842	1743	483	277	546	508	20	9	2218	67	608	111
1967	1002	1865	537	342	530	645	34	12	2829	77	690	112
1968	733	1895	387	215	556	386	38	15	2553	75	745	100
1969	1095	2272	482	2990	596	486	40	16	2521	83	968	66
1970	871	2310	377	226	593	381	36	16	2259	84	980	86
66/70 average	**909**	**2017**	**453**	**270**	**564**	**481**	**34**	**14**	**2476**	**77**	**798**	**99**
1971	959	2356	407	267	579	461	27	17	1596	72	1000	72
1972	927	2370	391	200	581	344	31	17	1850	144	921	156
1973	626	2007	312	126	448	282	44	17	2605	92	832	111
1974	1104	2230	495	221	548	404	31	15	2037	132	919	144
1975	557	1623	343	253	791	320	29	17	1705	218	829	260
71/75 average	**834**	**2117**	**390**	**214**	**589**	**362**	**32**	**17**	**1959**	**132**	**902**	**149**
1976	1810	2527	403	287	616	466	29	22	1320	216	837	258
1977	1129	2728	414	342	732	467	27	33	1155	207	726	285
1978	1124	2747	409	371	796	466	31	25	1245	271	952	285
1979	1256	2922	430	351	717	489	25	20	1225	304	944	322
1980	1346	3072	444	368	768	479	32	21	1500	266	1105	241

	Production	Area	Yield	Production	Area	Yield	Production	Area	Yield	Production	Area	Yield
76/80 average	**1178**	**2799**	**420**	**344**	**726**	**473**	**29**	**22**	**1289**	**253**	**913**	**278**
1981	1314	3037	433	321	982	327	40	22	1850	275	1216	226
1982	1292	3084	419	355	1131	314	42	21	2000	272	1372	198
1983	13135	3135	419	362	1114	325	46	23	2025	260	1550	168
1984	779	3031	257	240	1091	219	49	19	2527	192	1503	128
1985	1449	3163	458	329	1141	288	56	20	2803	115	1556	74
81/85 average	**1229**	**3090**	**398**	**321**	**1092**	**294**	**47**	**21**	**2238**	**223**	**1441**	**155**
1986	1383	3239	427	360	1109	325	75	27	2730	293	1590	184
1987	996			366			81			209		
1988	1766			560						300		
1989	1734 (millet and sorghum)											

Notes: Production in thousand tons; area in thousand hectares; yield in kg/ha.

Sources: Berg and SEDES Reports; Ministry of Agriculture.

Appendix Table 5.5.   Scenarios with and without structural adjustment

Indicator	Average for the period			
	With structural adjustment		Without structural adjustment	
	1987–1990	1991–1995	1987–1990	1991–1995
Growth of GDP (annual %age)	2.3	2.9	1.3	1.1
Share of GDP (%)				
Investment	11	12	10	8
Public investment	9	10	7	6
Recurrent public expend.	6	7	7	5
Budget deficit	2	2	3	1
External debt	51	40	54	41
Growth of exports (annual %age)	0.8	4.1	0.8	1.2
Growth of imports (annual %age)	2.7	3.2	1.0	0.6
Debt service/exports	44	25	47	34

Source: SAP.

Appendix Table 5.6.　*Index of product prices*

I. Official prices (base 1960 = 100)

	1960	1965	1970	1973	1975	1980	1981	1982	1983	1984	1985
Millet	100	100	120	250	250	200	700	800	800	1,000	800
Sorghum	100	77	77	154	154	346	462	538	538	769	616
Rice	100	75	108	150	175	275	360	425	425	425	500
Niebe	100	42	50	125	167	187	229	354	375	375	500
Groundnut	100	92	88	117	229	313	354	417	417	417	417
Cotton	100	100	94	94	152	200	253	387	387	387	387
GDP deflator	100	109	150	219	347	633	665	714	771	838	900
CPI	(100)	109	132	169	190	377	469	518	505	548	542
Average index used	100	109	156	194	269	505	577	616	638	693	721
Ratio 1:2 × 100											
Millet	100	93	83	129	93	79	121	130	125	144	111
Sorghum }a	100	71	49	79	57	69	30	87	94	111	35
Rice	100	69	69	77	65	54	61	69	67	61	39
Niebe	100	39	32	64	62	37	40	57	59	54	69
Groundnut }b	100	85	56	60	85	62	51	68	65	60	58
Cotton	100	93	50	48	56	40	45	63	61	56	54
Average	100	75	58	76	71	57	68	79	77	81	74
of which											
Group a	100	78	67	95	72	67	87	95	92	105	88
Group b	100	72	49	57	70	47	49	63	62	57	60
Ratio a/b	1	1.08	1.37	1.67	1.03	1.43	1.78	1.51	1.48	1.84	1.47

Appendix Table 5.6. (cont.)

II. Estimated free market prices (base 1960 = 100)

	1960	1970	1973	1975	1980	1981	1982	1983	1984	1985
Millet	100	173	275	277	276	1,111	784	755	1,266	606
Sorghum	100	173	275	217	561	711	566	633	1,098	560
Rice	100	127	197	201	331	412	397	390	472	500
Niebe	100	56	212	211	519	388	571	635	577	666
Groundnut	100	28	117	229	(366)	(414)	(488)	(488)	(388)	(488)
Cotton	100	94	94	152	200	255	387	387	387	387
Average deflator	100	156	194	269	505	577	616	638	693	721
Ratio 1:2 × 100										
Millet	100	111	142	103	155	193	127	115	183	34
Sorghum ⎫ a	100	60	56	81	115	123	92	99	158	78
Rice ⎭	100	35	102	75	66	71	64	51	68	69
Niebe	100	36	109	78	103	67	93	100	83	92
Groundnut ⎬ b	100	56	60	95	72	72	79	76	70	68
Cotton	100	50	48	57	40	45	63	61	56	56
Average	200	69	91	90	92	95	86	86	103	74
Average a	100	69	91	80	92	95	86	86	103	74
Average b	100	51	72	73	72	61	78	79	70	71
Ratio a/b	1	1.69	1.53	1.18	1.56	2.11	1.21	1.18	1.94	1.08

Source: SEDES, 1987:327.

CONCLUSIONS

Beyond Adjustment

ALEX DUNCAN
& JOHN HOWELL

In the Introduction we examined what are generally held to be the most important factors which link the incomes and welfare of small farmers and the rural poor to the wider economy. Of particular significance were the general conditions of the economy itself, the structure of product markets and institutions, the quality of transport and physical infrastructure, and the supply of agricultural services. All these factors have been influenced, in different ways, during the period of structural adjustment and the five country chapters have shown how the effect of this has been felt.

Two types of conclusion can be drawn. First, we can assess the evidence of the impact of economic reform programmes on rural households and derive overall conclusions; second, we can attempt to draw implications from these conclusions for agricultural development in sub-Saharan Africa, particularly for policies to enhance the production and incomes of poorer farming households. But first we must look at the extent to which the programmes have been implemented rather than simply agreed and pronounced.

IMPLEMENTATION

The implementation of structural adjustment and stabilization measures in economic recovery programmes has been uneven and has also been a learning process for governments. During the early 1980s, the instruments and objectives of reform programmes were refined, and there has been a later shift towards sectoral adjustment programmes. However, the difference between agricultural sectors among countries shows clearly that there can be no single formula for reform which can be applicable across Africa.

There are problems of differing degrees in all the economies reviewed in this book which current reforms cannot alleviate, at least in the short term, and which will limit the effects of internal reforms. First, there is the lack of progress in diversification and the continuing reliance for export earnings on a small range of primary commodities with poor prospects on the world markets. Second, there is the pressure of population, in some countries at least, on a limited land base, and ecological and resource constraints which constrict the range of options that offer growth potential. Third, there is a continuing absence of technological innovations which are feasible and financially sound for smallholders. Fourth, there are weak links between agriculture and other sectors, and fifth, there is a persistent shortage of skilled personnel.

These are issues of long-standing concern in low-income countries, although they may have moved into the background in the crisis of the 1980s. The severity varies between countries, and suggests caution in expecting too much too soon from policy reform.

The record of implementation of recovery programmes also varies between countries and according to the type of measures adopted; but it has often been slower than anticipated. Two factors appear to explain this variability. First, there is administrative complexity: institutional reform of marketing parastatals has proved particularly halting in several countries. Secondly, reform has been most marked and its effects most lasting where government policy is in favour of the change it represents. In contrast, there are instances where reform is viewed as externally imposed, without the close and full involvement of the government concerned.

The evidence of these country chapters shows a need for more comprehensive analyses prior to implementation. Such analyses were not always done in the early stages of recovery programmes, partly because of the pressure of events. Although the record is now improved, there are still instances where measures have been taken which in retrospect should have been approached differently, and where a fuller analysis might have helped clarify important issues. The lack of detailed knowledge of the rural economy is often the most important obstacle to the design and implementation of economic recovery.

THE IMPACT ON RURAL HOUSEHOLDS

For some advocates of structural adjustment it is the longer-term aspects of economic recovery programmes which may have the most important impact on poorer rural groups. In this book, however, we are concerned with shorter-term effects. Such effects may be drawn from an examination of the three major aspects of these programmes – supply responses and rates of return on production, access to capital and credit, and employment opportunities. These are considered in turn and in terms of the aggregate effect on rural households.

Supply responses and rates of return

The effects of recovery programmes on the rates of return to household production are manifested primarily through the markets for the products of rural households. There are two aspects to this: changes in the relative prices of products, and the institutional changes that affect the quality, cost or coverage of the marketing services provided by governments.

It is a general objective of adjustment in all countries to raise producer prices and profits in the productive sectors, especially those generating exports. Changes in the ratios of the prices of main commodities are a valuable indicator of the implementation of adjustment measures, although care must be taken to allow for external factors such as climate and changes in the relative world market prices.

In Kenya, Ghana and Malawi, the price shifts desired under adjustment programmes clearly took place. In Kenya, up to 1982, the domestic price of export commodities fell relative to imports as a result of unfavourable international terms of trade and continuing restrictive import quotas, while the price of non-tradables declined because of depressed demand as incomes fell. From 1983, however, the price of exports increased relative to imports following trade liberalization, but the price of non-tradables also rose as a result of a more expansionary monetary policy. In Ghana the pattern is similar, showing a relative rise in the price of export commodities compared with imports following adjustment in 1983, although the persistence of import restrictions limited this shift. The price of imports also rose relative to non-tradables. Similarly, in Malawi relative price changes favoured export commodities.

In Madagascar and Niger, the trends are less evident. In Madagascar, liberalization of trade appears to have increased the availability of imports, which suggests that prices may have fallen. The price of exports, however, appears to have improved only from about 1986, some years after the adjustment process might be said to have begun. The effects of adjustment on prices in Niger are muted by the fixed currency and the influence of market conditions in Nigeria, although tariff reforms are likely to have led to a relative fall in the price of imports.

Taken together, these changes have resulted in improvements in the terms of trade for agriculture, although their impact on different rural groups, in different countries, varies according to the patterns of production and consumption. In Kenya, the improvement in the terms of trade for agriculture has benefitted smallholders who produce the great majority of export products. By the late 1980s, both government and World Bank analyses indicated that the price distortions that had been a major concern in the earlier part of the decade had largely been resolved, and the desired shift in incentive structures towards tradable commodities achieved.

The record of price changes in Ghana, however, demonstrates a major dilemma for the design of adjustment programmes. An early result of policy changes was a sharp improvement in the price of exportables, notably cocoa, with a marked increase in the quantities marketed. Yet this increase almost certainly contributed to the fall in world price levels, as Ghana is a substantial producer for a market with price-inelastic demand. Ghana's export earnings did not, therefore, recover as had been expected, and they may have fallen over time as a result of the recovery in production. Ghana is unusual in that, unlike most African countries, it is a major contributor to the world market. But the dilemma has become a general one as export-promoting measures are taken in many countries relying on the same limited range of primary commodity exports.

Nonetheless, where improvements in the terms of trade for the agricultural sector have occurred, conditions have been created which potentially benefit producers, the majority of whom are smallholders. The country studies show that the extent to which these groups have in fact benefitted depends on whether they produce export crops, and on policy or institutional factors which determine whether taxation or market inefficiencies negate the increased profitability of these commodities. Smallholders in Malawi, for instance, have been subject to shortcomings in official pricing and marketing structures, and in the bias of public institutions and policy towards estate agriculture, which means that they have benefitted comparatively little from improved terms of trade for the sector.

In all countries producers of non-tradable crops consumed locally have also benefited much less from price changes. These groups include farmers in the more marginal areas producing millet and sorghum, who are numerically large in most of the countries under review. While there are considerable differences between the countries in this respect, the majority of smallholders in most countries are unlikely to have benefitted directly, in the short term at least, from increases in the price of tradable commodities.

There are potentially two principal effects of changes in commodity prices on pastoralists, although in neither case are they substantial. In the first place, the food they purchase in both Niger and Kenya consists primarily of non-tradable items – sorghum, millet and to a lesser extent maize – which are little affected directly by reform measures but whose relative prices are likely, if anything, to fall. In the second place, the prices of livestock – which for both countries represents an export commodity – would be raised. However, in both countries, any effect of policy measures is attenuated, in Niger especially, by the extensive informal export trade and the limited nature of the reforms to date, and in Kenya by the long-term decline in the quantities of livestock exported. Overall, the impact of the reforms on pastoralists is negligible when compared with the wider influences, such as increased frequency of droughts, on their economic well-being.

Liberalizing domestic marketing systems for food crops has been a feature of the reform programmes in all five countries, but the extent and detail of the changes vary considerably. The effect of the changes depends largely on the role of the parastatal marketing agencies before the reforms, and here there are great differences among the countries.

In both Kenya and Malawi, local trading has been largely in private hands, but large-scale marketing of staple grains has been undertaken by the main parastatal agency, although this is changing in both countries. Attempts are also under way to find means of ensuring national food security while reducing the agency's trading activities and budgetary losses. In both cases, this has proved to be more complex than expected, at least by the donor agencies involved.

In Madagascar, the extensive state involvement in food marketing prior to 1983 was reduced drastically for rice, and more gradually for other crops. Competition is now free on the internal markets for all crops except sugarcane. The quality of the now largely private sector services available to producers is also poor, although not necessarily worse than the systems they replaced.

In Niger and Ghana the prior role of the parastatal agencies was much more limited, the proportion of nationally marketed food-crop production which they handled being less than 5%. The nominal reduction in their roles has therefore had limited effects on the services available to rural households, both as producers and as consumers.

In Malawi, where ADMARC has played an active role in the marketing system, the cutback in the number of its trading points appears to have reduced the quality of service to producers and consumers in the more isolated areas. In Kenya also, major changes have included a two-thirds reduction in the number of buying points of the parastatal marketing agency. In this case, however, a more active network is in place in much of the country to respond to the change, suggesting that the quality of the service to producers may not have declined. There have also been some improvements in the timeliness of payments to producers.

In all countries, two factors have strongly influenced the impact of reforms in marketing institutions. The first is the extent of the rural infrastructure. Where the rural road network is poor, it is difficult to maintain any reliable and low-cost service, whether public or private, to farmers and consumers. This is demonstrated particularly in Ghana (at least up to 1983) and in southern Madagascar. The second is the level of development of the private sector, where the countries under review show a large variation in the extent to which the private sector is able to offer competitive services to farmers and consumers.

Access to resources

Given the undeveloped nature of land markets in most of the five countries, the main channels through which recovery programmes are able to influence rural households' access to resources are the capital and credit markets and the input delivery systems.

The main direct effect of adjustment on *capital markets* is felt in the formal system. There are two aspects of this: the cost of borrowing and the quantity of money available. Except in Niger, higher nominal interest rates have resulted from adjustment. The record of real interest rates, measured as the difference between nominal rates and the rate of inflation, is more variable. In most cases they have risen over the period. In Ghana, interest rates were positive in real terms only for a short period, but became negative again in 1987. In Kenya, real interest rates have generally been positive since the reforms. This was also the case in Malawi up to 1986, although rates were again negative in 1987 as a result of accelerating inflation.

Interest rates are one dimension of the changes in capital markets. If farmers are prepared to pay much higher rates on the informal market, this suggests that the availability of credit may be more important than its price. Reforms have had diverse effects on the quantities available. In Ghana, as a result of renewed external support, formal credit for agriculture, much of it going to smallholders, rose by 100% between 1983 and 1987. In Niger and Madagascar, by contrast, credit available through formal lending institutions fell because of the unwillingness on the part of finance ministries and donors to provide funds in the face of poor performance by the lending institutions. However, there are cases of credit projects (e.g. in Kenya with the Agricultural Finance Corporation, and in Madagascar from 1986) which seek to improve lending institutions' performance and to direct a higher proportion towards small producers.

In Madagascar, from the late 1970s, state-owned lending institutions became unviable because of very low repayment rates. Total agricultural credit was cut back and by 1983 was in nominal terms only 16% of 1977 levels, with only about 2% of farmers, many of them larger-scale, receiving credit. However, during the last two years of the structural adjustment programme the total amount of formal credit available increased. Real interest rates, which were still negative as late as 1986, were later set closer to market levels. There is the intention to establish a more effective service for smallholders, although it is still too early to assess whether this has in fact taken place.

Recovery programmes have thus had a mixed impact on formal capital markets. However, even where changes have occurred, the direct effect on rural households has been minimal since, as the country chapters show, only a small minority have been borrowing or saving formally. The indirect impact on households through the informal system may be greater, but knowledge of the interaction between the formal and informal systems and of the impact of adjustment on the latter is negligible. It is to be expected, however, that if there are substantial rises in the cost of capital on the formal markets, potential borrowers would resort to the informal markets, raising interest rates there also.

The main impact of the reforms on *access to supplies* in several countries relates to the pricing and distribution of fertilizer. Even here, however, the impact of changes on smallholders is diminished by the fact that there is very low fertilizer consumption among the poorer categories of smallholders. In Ghana, the domestic distribution has been improved by the recovery of the transport system since 1983, but there has been a decrease in the amount of fertilizer imported as compared with the years before adjustment. In Madagascar and Kenya, the opposite is true with significant amounts under aid programmes.

Adjustment has involved attempts to remove subsidies on fertilizer. In Kenya, a 20% increase in price in 1987 brought domestic prices in line with world prices; in Madagascar, the rice/fertilizer price index fell from 100 to 71 between 1978 and 1988; in Malawi, a Fertilizer Subsidy Removal Programme was implemented from 1985 to 1988 but subsequently suspended; and in Niger, modest budgetary savings were made by reducing subsidies from 1985. Where price increases were significant, there is evidence of reduced use, as in Malawi and Niger.

In reforming input supply systems, several countries are attempting to substitute private sector for public sector distribution. This has been actively pursued in Ghana, Malawi, Madagascar and Kenya, and some progress has been achieved. In Madagascar, the country chapter finds that some twenty private companies are involved in supplying fertilizer, while in Ghana a programme of phased transfer to private distributors has only recently begun. In Kenya, significant progress was made in the late 1980s in opening new distribution channels, but no significant increase in fertilizer use has resulted as yet.

The country chapters indicate that privatization is no panacea for the problems of input supplies, since it is by no means clear that private suppliers will in fact enter the trade, or that there will be effective competition in the short term. The main impediments are the high costs of transporting fertilizer, a bulky commodity, and the low level of development of private trade in some countries, particularly in isolated areas. There is clearly a risk that freer distribution may not improve access to inputs among rural households, especially those isolated from the main distribution networks.

Employment opportunities

The effect of adjustment on employment opportunities depends on the extent to which economic growth generates a demand for labour. The Ghana country chapter concludes that the macroeconomic effect of the adjustment programme on employment has been positive. The demand for labour in cocoa-producing areas was manifested by labour shortages and rising wage rates, but there may have been a ripple effect elsewhere. The increased demand for labour benefitted those who were net sellers of family labour, often lower-income groups, but it had little impact on those producing non-traded crops, for instance in the north, where production is mostly for subsistence.

In Kenya, macroeconomic reforms have contributed to resumed growth, which was much stronger during the second half of the decade than in 1980-84. This, together with the policy-induced shift in the terms of trade towards agriculture, undoubtedly promoted the demand for labour. Any such effects have not, however, been strong enough to outweigh the continuing growth in the labour force which results from population increase. Wage rates stagnated or even fell from 1979 to 1987, while during the same period much of the 47% growth in formal employment was in the public sector rather than in agricultural production. Thus even under the most favourable circumstances, growth in real incomes is not assured.

Madagascar's continuing macroeconomic stagnation, which limited growth in formal employment to only 5% between 1983 and 1987, accounts for an apparent decline in real terms in earnings. The decline has been much sharper in the urban sector than among the producers of major crops. While data on actual earnings are sparse, the ratio of revenues from one hectare of rice to the annual minimum urban wage rose from 74 in 1984 to 85 in 1987, while that for coffee rose from 55 to 101 over the same period.

The Malawi chapter shows that the increased profitability and production of some crops, notably tobacco and groundnuts, had led to increased demand for labour. However, as the supply of labour from the poorest rural groups has increased, wage rates have remained depressed. Thus while the opportunities for formal employment on the estates have increased as a result of adjustment, real returns for workers are declining.

In Niger, the impact of adjustment on growth and on rural employment has so far been very limited. Some specific measures of adjustment programmes may have more direct, but limited, employment effects – for instance, retrenchment in the public service. The magnitude of these direct effects on the groups studied, through redundancy or urban-rural transfers, has, however, been small in all countries – with the possible exception of Ghana where several thousand Cocoa Board labourers lost their jobs. Even in this case, however, the country chapter concluded that the redundancies had not significantly expanded the rural labour supply.

On balance, this evidence suggests that adjustment has in some countries – Kenya, Ghana and perhaps Malawi – at least created the conditions for greater labour absorption in some sectors and that this has expanded the base for general employment, improving the conditions of workers' access to the labour market. In several countries, including at least Madagascar and Malawi, this takes place against continuing economic stagnation and growth in the labour force, and therefore real incomes are still declining. In countries where policy change has increased the demand for labour, the rural households which might benefit from such an effect (notably lower-income groups and the landless and near landless) are those who are net sellers of family labour to the expanding sectors. However, the beneficial effects on households of expanded employment are still negligible. This is partly because the recovery is recent and halting, but also because the linkages between sectors and sub-sectors are often weak.

The net effect on households

The balance of evidence from the country chapters is that where adjustment measures have been significantly implemented, their impact on most groups of smallholder households has been positive, if limited. First, a significant number of producers has been directly affected where reforms have improved prices for tradable commodities, thus increasing incomes from production. These groups include smallholders of cocoa in Ghana, of coffee and tea in Kenya, and of tobacco in Malawi.

Second, in these cases, the demand for labour has increased, improving the terms and conditions of employment for those selling their family labour. This trend is counteracted, however, by continuing increases in the supply of labour. The net effect may therefore be stagnating, or even declining, real earnings.

Third, access to agricultural inputs has improved in some instances – fertilizer in Madagascar, consumer goods and agricultural inputs (although not fertilizer) in Ghana, a range of imported items in Kenya. This is as a result of reforms, together with enhanced balance-of-payments support from donors. The same influences have improved the supply of consumer goods which are needed to underpin incentives for producers.

Fourth, there is evidence from Madagascar and Ghana that spending on rural infrastructure has increased since the recovery programmes began, though maintenance may have suffered during the early stabilization phase.

On the negative side, it is evident that some important groups in rural areas have not as yet benefitted directly even in countries where recovery programmes have been substantially implemented, and some may even have been adversely affected by particular reforms. Above all, those producing very small or periodic surpluses of tradable crops are little affected as producers by changes in relative output prices. Many of them, however, are net buyers, and will be adversely affected by higher prices. All the country chapters identify substantial groups in this category, especially those with the lowest incomes. In addition, those producing surpluses of commodities which are not tradable on world markets are disadvantaged in relative if not absolute terms by price shifts favouring exportable crops.

It is also evident that the weak links that exist between some rural groups and their wider national economy diminish any potential impact of policy reforms. Poor transport systems or lack of competition in private trade mean that the higher prices may not reach isolated rural areas. Ghana, large parts of Madagascar, and some areas of Malawi exhibit this feature. Dislocation of labour markets also limits the wider impact of growth in one particular area or subsector. An example of this is the cocoa sector in Ghana whose growth has had limited impact outside the specific cocoa zone, for instance in the north where much of the deepest rural poverty is to be found. Similarly, there are also cases in which households are now more poorly served than previously by rural services. Their decline cannot necessarily be ascribed to the effect of reforms since, in many cases, services in the rural areas were of limited use even before the recovery programmes.

Finally, the ability of households to respond to new production opportunities is frequently limited by a lack of resources or services. The details of what is lacking vary from case to case, but they generally include research and extension services which do not meet the farmers' needs and the absence of credit services. It is clear, therefore, that however significant the impact of structural adjustment on some important groups of smallholder producers, many of whom are on low incomes, there remain large groups of farmers, stock-keepers and labourers who have yet to benefit.

IMPLICATIONS FOR POLICY

The crisis of the early 1980s made some policy change unavoidable and there is no doubt that some form of economic recovery programme was necessary in all the countries under review. In important respects, public policies had contributed to economic decline, and their distributional implications were unfavourable to agriculture. Taking all five countries together, the present economic crisis, which has at its centre the failure to sustain growth in agricultural production and incomes, has led to a worsening of the welfare of many rural groups. Several years of economic stagnation or decline have also demonstrated the difficulty of enhancing the production and incomes of the rural poor.

The aims of the recovery programmes in all the countries under review have included reducing or eliminating policies that were detrimental to agriculture. The country chapters show that such changes in policy can be consistent with the needs of many smallholders and the rural poor generally. Especially where incentives are improved, these policy changes could facilitate more effective interventions on behalf of such groups in the future.

A central aim of economic recovery programmes should therefore be to achieve a sustained improvement in the incentives and resources for smallholders. However, in designing such programmes, explicit attention needs to be paid to creating opportunities for participation of the rural population as a means to achieve both equity and growth. Priority needs to be given to policies that do the most to stimulate demand for labour, especially unskilled labour, and will therefore generate incomes for the many low-income groups whose assets, other than family labour, are negligible. Family labour is virtually the only asset of an increasing number of people in the more densely populated countries. Adjustment measures which increase the returns to land and capital will not benefit such people. Employment-generation programmes and policies are needed which encourage linkages between agriculture and other sectors with the aim of stimulating agriculture's use of inputs produced in the domestic economy, as well as the local processing of agricultural produce through on-farm micro-enterprises.

Targeted interventions are needed to complement broader-based policy reforms and these, above all, should be designed to increase the supply response of agricultural producers. Many measures, beyond price incentives, are need to relieve constraints or to ensure that smallholder farmers and others have access to the productive assets they need. In all countries with recovery programmes, new relationships between public and private sectors (in production, processing or distribution) are being considered or created and there is a clear tendency to promote private sector operation. However, where a continued role for the public sector is warranted – especially in providing rural infrastructure, health and education services and in assuring national food security – sustained measures are required to ensure the operation of these functions.

In this book the importance of smallholders and the rural poor to the performance of the wider economy has been highlighted. However, more effort could be made to capitalize on the existing links between agricultural producers and other sectors, and between rural consumers and the sectors which produce the goods and services they require. Improving these linkages will help to strengthen the role of smallholders in the wider recovery of the economies in question.

Meanwhile, there continue to be resource, institutional and infrastructural constraints for the agricultural sector in all the countries examined, which will require longer-term measures if sustainable growth is to be achieved. These constraints could be overcome by a variety of interventions. For example, greater support could be provided to the informal sectors that supply many of the services, such as farm equipment and repairs, local transport and processing, and storage and handling of planting materials, used by smallholder farmers. This would enhance the income-earning opportunities available to the suppliers and thus improve the quality of the services they offer and in turn stimulate smallholders' productive performance.

In addition, there is a need to develop rural financial markets as a whole and there should be less emphasis on the provision of formal credit alone. Policies need to promote the operations of financial markets as a whole and fuller use needs to be made of the various financial intermediaries including banks, credit unions and credit groups. In all countries, a better understanding of the links between the different aspects of capital markets is required for this situation to develop.

Similarly, a weakness in technological capability is apparent in the failure of the research and extension services to develop viable recommendations for smallholder farmers and to keep them informed of current findings. The disappointing past performance of many efforts, including those with external technical support, to improve the capacity of agricultural research in sub-Saharan Africa, suggests that there is no ready solution. Structural adjustment should not be allowed to undermine spending on research; but in addition, continued efforts will be needed to address the institutional and skill shortcomings that affect research systems.

Lastly, demand for fertilizer and other inputs is increasing with the growing pressure on cultivable land. Governments and donors need to build into the design of recovery programmes the steps necessary to ensure that adequate supply systems are in place and that the inputs themselves are provided. As a consequence of this, there is urgent need in many of the countries for improved transport systems, especially in the more isolated areas.

If these policy items were incorporated into current reform programmes, small-holders and the rural poor might then experience more of the benefits which accrue to the agricultural sector as a whole from their operation. However, in the countries studied, priority has been given to encouraging the output of the export-crop sector. Large numbers of poorer farmers do not produce export crops, either because their land is not suitable or because they have limited access to necessary inputs such as fertilizer and improved seed.

Furthermore, many rural households, especially the poorer ones, are net buyers of agricultural products and may not benefit from higher overall crop prices. Whether or not all smallholders and the rural poor will benefit from agricultural sector growth will depend on the design of the policy reforms and the specific measures adopted, and the type of complementary investments made in the sector.

A common feature of these measures is that they are basic to improving the supply responsiveness of smallholder farmers to price incentives. They are of value to farmers whether producing tradable or non-tradable commodities, and are fundamental to the health of the agricultural sector. Providing these services will call for sustained effort to improve the performance of public sector agencies; but they will also need more use of alternatives from the private sector and from among farmers' organizations.

The experience to date with structural adjustment indicates that there is nothing in these programmes that is inherently incompatible with the interests of poorer smallholders or the rural poor generally, but much depends on the specific features of the design and implementation of the programmes. If, however, the aim of sustaining a broadly based growth of production and incomes is to be achieved, the price changes that are at the heart of adjustment programmes need to be accompanied by improvements in the framework of institutions and public investments needed by farmers if they are to be able to take advantage of the opportunities created.

The economic crisis of the 1980s caused these issues to be pushed into the background. The priority attention that was paid in the early period of structural adjustment to price changes and to controlling public expenditures now needs to be complemented by greater attention to these longer-term issues. Provided that they can be satisfactorily addressed, the economic policy reforms of the 1980s may come to be seen as the first stage in bringing about the recovery of smallholder agriculture in sub-Saharan Africa.

Index

DATE DUE

HIGHSMITH #45230

Printed In USA